VIOLENCE, CONSPIRACIES, AND NEW RELIGIONS

Violence, Conspiracies, and New Religions

A Tribute to James R. Lewis

Edited by
Margo Kitts

SHEFFIELD UK   BRISTOL CT

Published by Equinox Publishing Ltd.
UK: Office 415, The Workstation, 15 Paternoster Row, Sheffield, South Yorkshire, S1 2BX
USA: ISD, 70 Enterprise Drive, Bristol, CT 06010

www.equinoxpub.com

© Margo Kitts and contributors 2024.

All rights reserved. No part of this publication may be reproduced or transmitted in any form or by any means, electronic or mechanical, including photocopying, recording or any information storage or retrieval system, without prior permission in writing from the publishers.

British Library Cataloguing-in-Publication Data

A catalogue record for this book is available from the British Library.

ISBN-13	9781800505063	(hardback)
	9781800505070	(paperback)
	9781800505087	(epdf)
	9781800506176	(ePub)

Library of Congress Cataloging-in-Publication Data

Names: Kitts, Margo, 1952– editor.
Title: Violence, conspiracies, and new religions : a tribute to James R. Lewis / edited by Margo Kitts.
Description: Sheffield, England ; Bristol : Equinox Publishing Ltd, 2024. | Includes bibliographical references and index. | Summary: "Stimulated by the vast scholarly output of James Lewis, experts opine on violence, conspiracies, and new religious movements"-- Provided by publisher.
Identifiers: LCCN 2024025115 (print) | LCCN 2024025116 (ebook) | ISBN 9781800505063 (hardback) | ISBN 9781800505070 (paperback) | ISBN 9781800505087 (epdf) | ISBN 9781800506176 (epub)
Subjects: LCSH: Cults. | Sects. | Conspiracy theories. | Violence—Religious aspects.
Classification: LCC BP603 .V54 2024 (print) | LCC BP603 (ebook) | DDC 209—dc23/eng/20240701
LC record available at https://lccn.loc.gov/2024025115
LC ebook record available at https://lccn.loc.gov/2024025116

Edited and Typeset by Queenston Publishing, Hamilton Canada.

James Roger Lewis
(November 3, 1949–October 11, 2022)

Contents

1. Violence, Conspiracies, and New Religions: 1
   A Tribute to James R. Lewis
   Margo Kitts

I. Religion and Violence

2. Researching Religious Terrorism   17
   Mark Juergensmeyer

3. Conspiracy Theories Across Borders   27
   Michael Barkun

4. Lost Cause: The Rise and Fall of a Symbolic Crusade Movement   43
   David G. Bromley

5. By the Cleansing Flames of Fire: Qur'an Burnings,   59
   Racialized Religion and Politized Nostalgia in Sweden
   Mattias Gardell

II. New Religious Movements

6. James R. Lewis and Jonestown Studies   85
   Rebecca Moore

7. The Charisma of David Koresh   99
   Catherine Wessinger

III. Media and the Law

8. Invented Religions and the Law: Jediism and the Church of the   129
   Flying Spaghetti Monster
   Carole M. Cusack

9. Director's Cu(l)ts, Reel Researchers: Exploring Sects in the Movies 149
Stefano Bigliardi, Abdelmojib Chouhbi, Mohamed Amine Ghafil, Amine Nakari, Danya Tazi Mokha and Salma Zahidi

10. The Complicated Relationship between Xie Jiao and Cult in the PRC 181
Zhang Xinzhang and Xu Weiwei

Index 195

1

VIOLENCE, CONSPIRACIES, AND NEW RELIGIONS: A TRIBUTE TO JAMES R. LEWIS

MARGO KITTS

Introduction

This volume is a tribute to the work of James R. Lewis, who passed away on October 11, 2022 from complications following a brain injury. For those of us who knew him, Jim charmed us with his wry humor and generous spirit, but he was also a prodigious scholar. He was the author or co-editor of 50 books as well as author or co-author of 128 articles and reference book entries. This is not to mention his 14 book reviews. He created and edited seven book series and four journals, among them Cambridge Elements of Religion and Violence (with Margo Kitts) and Cambridge Elements of New Religious Movements (with Rebecca Moore), the Journal of Religion and Violence (with Margo Kitts), and the Alternative Spirituality and Religion Review. He co-founded important associations in the field of New Religious Movements (NRMs), such as Alternative Spirituality And New Age Studies (ASANAS) and the International Society for the Study of New Religions. Given all these accomplishments, his death was a tragedy for the field, but also a tremendous disappointment for those of us who worked with him over the years. This volume is an attempt to keep his legacy alive.

Jim Lewis began his scholarly life in philosophy. He graduated in philosophy summa cum laude from Appalachian State University (1981) and went on to earn a master's degree in religious studies from University of North Carolina at Chapel Hill (1987) and a PhD in religious studies from the University of Wales, Lampeter (2003). From graduate school, he took a position as assistant professor at the University of Wisconsin, Milwaukee (2003–2008), then as an honorary senior research professor at the University of Wales (2009–2012), then various positions at the University of Tromsø (2010–2019), with a number of posts as visiting scholar/professor along the way. When retirement pressures faced him in Norway he took a position at Wuhan University, where he was a professor of philosophy and creator of the Wuhan Journal of Cultic Studies.

James Lewis's scholarly interests spanned the gamut, from religion and terrorism to doomsday prophecies to Nordic neo-shamanism to Sikh dharma, but he was most passionate about new religious movements. He staunchly repudiated simple aspersions of "brainwashing" for members of new religious movements, as well as exaggerations of a leader's charisma to explain mass casualty events. Instead he argued, for instance in 2019, against "monolithic inferences" in grappling with the motivations of individual members of Aum Shinrikyo, to counter the group's reputation after the deadly release of sarin gas on a Tokyo subway in 1995. His interviews with the splinter group Hikari no Wa attested to a more complex narrative as well as to a pervasive ignorance of the catastrophic millennial vision held by Aum leader Shoko Asahara. As for charisma, he denied that charismatic leadership alone was enough to explain, for instance, the willingness to exit this world for the "Next Level" by 39 members of Heaven's Gate in 1997. Instead it was important to understand the extent to which the group was immersed in the New Age subculture of the 1970s and 1980s and the thinking we now associate with UFOlogy (2003). Given the vast literature on reincarnation and life after death popular in those decades, death in that subculture apparently did not have the same metaphysical finality as it has for most of us. Prophets of new religious groups such as Heaven's Gate, as do prophets of any tradition, build their ideas on preexisting strata of thinking, which, however counterintuitive to those of us on the outside, tend to resonate with people already questioning the status quo, as did members of Heaven's Gate.

Yet, while sympathetic to the aspirations of new religious movements, James Lewis was not indifferent to conceivable manipulations by unscrupulous NRM leaders who advocated self-harm or worse on the part of followers. Instead he endeavored to highlight such manipulations and their unfortunate consequences (2018, 2019), thereby drawing the wrath of champions of, for instance, Falun Gong. James Lewis also acknowledged that the cultic stereotypes of brainwashed followers and megalomaniac leaders, while for the most part farfetched, might be worth contemplating in the face of the astonishing scale of some mass deaths (2014a and 2014b, and see Moore intra). However, given that the bulk of our understanding of such incidents is drawn from movement apostates, a wide-eyed skepticism about proclaimed motives, he would argue, should be maintained.

Contents

Contributors to this volume echo that wide-eyed skepticism. They are stellar scholars with expertise in subjects as far apart as contemporary terrorism to the Chinese concept of *Xie Jiao*, covering a range of topics in between. The first set of chapters addresses religion and various forms of violence. The second addresses new religious movements. The third addresses media and law pertaining to invented religions or "superstition," as the Communist Party in China identifies *Xie Jiao*. The sets overlap.

Religion and violence

First we have a chapter by Mark Juergensmeyer, a well-known expert in studies of religious terrorism. The chapter lays out the methodology he has perfected over years of interviewing religious activists committed to perpetrating acts of terroristic violence. "Epistemic worldview analysis" is the approach he has crafted, along with Mona Kanwal Sheikh, to penetrate the imaginations of persons pledged to terroristic aspirations, persons who might seem intimidating to those of us unexposed to this world of violent extremism. Many of these interviews were conducted in jail cells or secret hide-outs; yet interviewees to various degrees were open to discussing their goals frankly with "Mr. Mark" (Juergensmeyer 2020, 2022). Epistemic world view analysis combines amiable, personalized conversation with studies of a subject's writings and transcribed interviews, as well as of the textual and historical contexts that have influenced the interviewee. The point is to try to enter into a mindset different from one's own, while bracketing all truth claims. For instance, many of us are astonished that anticipation of a triumphant endtimes battle would drive religious violence, and readily reject such an anticipation as preposterous. Yet to grasp the mentalities of those who espouse such worldviews, one must take into consideration the psychological appeal of a war seen as cosmic, the urgent compulsion to confront the approaching struggle with a corresponding degree of moral righteousness, and the thrill in anticipation of some kind of impending spiritual redemption (Juergensmeyer 2020, 69). The emotionality that can drive religious terrorism is studied too by a few other scholars, such as Thomas Hegghammer (2017), who has attempted to capture the emotionality of ISIS members given to collective and apparently contagious weeping while reading scripture. As Jim Lewis has acknowledged, simply dismissing alternative truth claims as wrong or attributing them to "brainwashing" by charismatic prophets, is unlikely to lead to the kind of understanding necessary for mitigating acts of violence (2003, 125–126; 2017, 1–5; 2019, 44–54).

Then we have a chapter by conspiracy and millennial theory expert Michael Barkun, here focusing on transnational conspiracy theories. Whereas early conspiracy theories revolved around the Catholic Church, the Masonic movement, or the Jews, these were superseded after World War II by schemes fixated on reputed international cabals, among them the United Nations, the Bilderberg conferences, the Trilateral Commission and the World Economic Forum at Davos, collectively sometimes pegged "the New World Order." Unlike religious fantasies attached to millennial schemes—already separated from secular fantasies by the end of the eighteenth century (Barkun 2013, 15–38)—New World Order supporters saw threats to sovereign states as due to the machinations of a secret elite striving to disenfranchise individuals and to concentrate power in a totalitarian global system (Barkun 2013, 39–64). The three increasingly international conspiracy theories traced here are the Sovereign Citizens Movement, the followers of Anders Breivik, and the QAnon movement. Sovereign Citizens, as the name suggests, believe they are not bound by government controls. On the one hand, the movement is simply anarchist, but on the other, it is also quite varied in expression, ranging from those who resist covid regulations to those who refuse to pay taxes on the principle that the common law legal system established by the founders was replaced by a suspicious corporate one as early as the civil war. The movement has taken root not only in the U.S., but also in Australia. Next, Anders Breivik, who massacred 77 people in Norway in 2011, had no followers when he committed his crimes, but his white supremacist manifesto subsequently encouraged lone wolf imitators to espouse elements of the White Genocide Manifesto, originally penned by David Lane in 1988. Its motto, "We must secure the existence of our people and a future for white children," was endorsed also by Australian Brenton Tarrant, who credited Breivik for his attack on two mosques in New Zealand; he massacred 51 people. Lastly, QAnon, a reputedly anonymous collective of conspiracy theorists, also endorses the deep state hypothesis, but via elliptic proclamations anticipates an imminent upheaval when Donald Trump will be brought back into power by "the storm," when a great awakening will be initiated wherein the U.S. will be "made great again" and the rest of the world will follow suit. Despite its U.S. roots, the movement has spread as far as Europe and Japan. Of course, conspiracy theory was a subject of interest to James Lewis as well, as we see in his studies, with Asbjørn Dyrendal and Leif Edward Ottesen Kennair, of the correlation of paranormal beliefs with conspiracy theory among neopagans (2017).

Next, in "Lost Cause: The Rise and Fall of a Symbolic Crusade Movement," sociologist of religion David Bromley analyzes the way failing religious groups adapt to suppression by dominant social forces, after contesting those forces and concluding that peaceful coexistence with them is intolerable. His focus is the Lost Cause Movement which followed the Civil War. The Lost Cause Movement may be understood as an alternative civil religion for defeated Southerners. It offered them a cultural identity which combined Christian rhetoric and symbology with Confederate rhetoric and symbology. Even before the end of the Civil War, religious fervor ran high, stoked on both sides by missionaries who led revivals which sought conversions among troops. After the Civil War, this fervor in the South was adapted to what was seen as an insufferable situation. The secessionist states faced not only military defeat and political submission, but massive loss of life (roughly 2 percent of the U.S. population overall), a radically disrupted economy (having lost its agricultural plantation system and captive labor force), collapsed infrastructure (bridges, roads, harbors, rail) as well as a slight on southern culture. The Lost Cause ideology was a way of transforming military defeat into moral victory: losing warriors were seen as having fought heroically against more numerous northerners, who themselves had failed to grasp the true benevolence of slavery and the southern mission of Christianizing servants. At the same time, according to Lost Cause mythology, the attempt at succession was not truly about slavery at all, but a way of defending a righteous order against northern tyranny. With the advent of reconstruction, a refashioned social power base was established in the South, buttressed by narrative accounts of the virtues of the Southern way of life and an aspiration to sacralize it, all of which was remarkably successful in building up confederate identity into this century (Bromley 2022).

Fourth, Mattias Gardell takes on the relationship between bibliocaust and holocaust. Beginning with the 20,000 condemned books burned during the National Socialist campaign with the ostensible purpose of cleansing society of "Jewish intellectualism" (Goebbels 1933). Gardell traces the bibliocaustic aspirations from literary targets—such as the works of Karl Marx, Sigmund Freud, Heinrich Mann, Karl Kautsky, Bertolt Brecht, Franz Kafka, Erich Maria Remarque, Emil Ludwig, Heinrich Heine, Erich Kästner, Albert Einstein—to more explicitly religious ones, such as the Hebrew Bible and Torah scrolls, desecrated by fire and other means during the 1938 Kristallnacht. Although Hitler youth were often chosen to perpetuate these desecrations, Jewish adults were compelled to participate as well, for example by tearing the Torah to pieces and dressing in shredded Torah scrolls. The poet Henrich Heine, whose books were among those burned by the National Socialists, pointed out in 1923 that "[w]here they burn books, they will ultimately burn people too," but Heine was not referring to the anti-Jewish pogroms of WWII. Instead he referred to the 1499 Qur'an burnings in Granada after the Reconquista, when Catholic Spain, under Isabel I and Ferdinand II, expelled Jews as "races of defiled blood" (Hering Torres *et al.* 2012), followed by Muslims, whose Qur'ans were burned under orders by Cardinal Cisneros. The relationship between exterminating religious books and religious people is evident in contemporary Sweden in the case of Rasmus Paludan, who has endeavored to launch a Reconquista to cleanse northern European society of Muslims. He promotes this via his livestreamed Qur'an burnings and racialist insults hurled at non-white citizens, as he did on Palm Sunday 2019, when he promoted Qur'an burnings in at least forty-five locations one month after Brenton Tarrant livestreamed his massacre of Muslims at Christchurch in New Zealand. In Sweden the racist spectacle was especially stark, as after the cold war Sweden enjoyed a reputation as one of the most liberal societies in Europe, but this reputation has diminished in the last few decades, amidst a surging radical nationalist discourse. While critics have picked up on Paludan's declared proclivity for sex with children, supporters delight in his notoriety and shrill cries for "the right to blasphemy." According to the Swedish foreign ministry, "expressions of racism, xenophobia and related intolerance have no place in Sweden," but Qur'an burnings continue, to much international consternation.

New religious movements

First Rebecca Moore combines three trajectories of Lewis's thought to take stock of Peoples Temple and Jonestown studies. These three are: the mental and physical health of movement champions who lead followers to violent outcomes; rejection of "monolithic inferences" (Lewis 2019, 44–54) about followers of new religious movements; and relatedly, the need to differentiate features of new religious groups and to reject the temptation to squeeze them all into ideal types. On the pathology of the leader, she notes the disproportionate attention of traditional analysts to personality issues, such as charisma and even to disorders such as derangement, madness, and the absolute control that cult leaders exercise over reputedly childlike followers, by means of, for instance, a "suicidal mystique" (Hassan 2020:35). This fixation on mentally deranged leaders and their childlike followers corresponds to the deprogramming trends of the 1970s. This was replaced in later decades by studies of ideology, such as catastrophic millennial expectations and a felt need to flee totalitarian and oppressive governmental systems. Other analysts have approached the eruption of violence among new religious groups from the perspective of the group's social isolation and internal totalitarianism. Jim Lewis, however, argued that "suicide cults" comprised a special category of new religious movements, and were to be distinguished from millennial movements whose demises were due to more disputable causes. On leadership issues in Jonestown, it is clear that Jim Jones was in failing health by the final months before the mass deaths, and similarly, the leaders of Heavens Gate and Solar Temple believed they were terminally ill. It is fair to say that the failing health of leaders might be combined with other factors as predictors of violence in new religious movements. On monolithic inferences, based on conversations with Aum Shinrikyo survivors, Jim Lewis made what may seem an obvious point for those openminded enough to appreciate it, which was that ordinary Aum members were not within the inner circle who made the decision to unleash sarin gas on a Tokyo subway in 1995 and apparently did not anticipate it. Likewise, despite discussions of personal martyrdom among Peoples Temple adherents in Jonestown, their willingness to fight and even to die may be seen as part of a larger people's liberation advocacy prevalent in the 1960s and 1970s, not due to simple manipulation by a leader. Thus, Steven Hassan's "suicidal mystique" is not precisely on point to explain the deaths of 900 people in Jonestown. Actual culpability regarding the final suicides and murders remains up in the air, as rumors of suicidal planning in the Jonestown case derive primarily from apostates. Decades of comparative new religions studies have shown us that new religions are configured differently depending on their circumstances, and therefore elude rigid stereotyping. Conflating Jonestown with other groups is "inaccurate, misleading, and dangerous" (Lewis 1994b: xv). (See also Moore 2022.)

On a related theme, Catherine Wessinger, who has published extensively on millennial movements of various types (e.g., 2000, 2016), contributes a chapter on "The Charisma of David Koresh" of the Branch Davidians. The saga of the Branch Davidians at Waco, Texas, has riveted scholars of new religious movements since at least April 19, 1993, when an armed encounter launched by FBI and ATF agents against Branch Davidians led to an inferno which consumed the Waco camp and 76 Branch Davidian worshippers (Lewis 1994), two unborn fetuses, as well as four ATF agents. On the matter of personal charisma, biblical prophecies infused the group's understanding of its leader Vernon Howell, most notably after his life-transforming pilgrimage to Israel in 1985. This is when he anointed himself David Koresh, the Cyrus messiah who would soon defeat present-day Babylon and create God's kingdom on earth. By all accounts, Koresh was a mesmerizing orator, particularly when expounding on the Book of Revelation and his role therein as the seventh angel. This was not his only proclaimed biblical persona. Followers adulated Koresh as the "Christ for the Last Days," as the Son of God, as the Word of God, as the rider on a white horse whose name was secret, and as the "Lamb slain" (Rev. 5: 6) who alone could open the Seven Seals on the book held by the Lord on the throne. Followers anticipated a violent encounter in which Koresh's followers would be martyred as a "wave sheaf" (Lev. 23: 10–14), as first fruits in the Lord's harvest of souls through the machinations of a two-horned "lamblike beast" (Rev. 13: 11–17), which is to say the United States. The charismatic authority of David Koresh was essential to what Wessinger has termed catastrophic millennial imagination, as seen in the apparent commitment of at least some members to withstand assault by powerful adversaries, and also in their reported anticipation of Koresh's resurrection as the rider on the white horse who would lead an army of resurrected martyrs in transformed bodies (Rev. 6: 2; 19: 11; 9: 15–18) to set up a Davidic kingdom on earth (as in Zech 14) (Wessinger 2018, 80). Wessinger traces the development of Koresh's character from his troubled childhood to his youthful enthrallment with the teachings of the Seventh-Day Adventists, to what he saw as his daily struggles with Satan, to his multiple love affairs and marriages, to his rooting within the Branch Davidian community as the final prophet of God. As this final prophet he granted himself extraordinary privileges, such as procreation with 12-year-old girls and all female members of the group, with the implicit consent of the male members. Rather than simply relegating the deaths of 76 Branch Davidians to brainwashing by a clever fraudster, Wessinger endeavors to grasp what it was that catapulted Koresh into a position of extraordinary authority over the lives of the Branch Davidians of Waco.

Invented religions and "superstitions"

In "Invented Religions and the Law: The Significance of Colanders, Hoods, and Pirate Costumes for Members of Jediism and the Church of the Flying Spaghetti Monster," Carole M. Cusack researches the legal standing of Pastafarians, Jediism, and others who advocate license to wear ritual garb on a par with Sikhs and Jews, who wear turbans and yarmulkes, respectively. The debate became inflamed in 2018, with the lawsuit by Dutch law student Mienke de Wilde in the highest court of the Netherlands. She argued that, on the principle that hijabs, chadors, and all the rest are allowable religious dress, she should, as a member of the Church of the Flying Spaghetti Monster, have the right to wear a colander—as in the pasta strainer—on her head in official documents, such as her driver's license. The argument was that it was discriminatory to concede to those who wear traditional religious costume but not to those who don the dress codes of hypothetical or invented religions. The chapter examines a number of legal pronouncements for and against invented religions across societies, and points out that contemporary understandings of religion in liberal societies are rooted less in ancient and static truth claims—which we tend to associate with fundamentalism—than in the loser, shared experiences and identities of everyday life, including in pop culture. Thus, "fictional religions ... explicitly reject traditional means of establishing spiritual or historical lineage, and openly announce their fictional status." Second, "invented religions understand fictions, the ludic, and play as legitimate sources of ultimate meaning." With this ludic dimension of religion in mind, Cusack focuses on "third millennium invented religions" such as Jediism (based on the Star Wars films) and the Church of the Flying Spaghetti Monster (created to contest the Christian-based movement of Intelligent Design). While these are in part religious parodies, they are also committed to making political points within the sub-cultures of popular society. With twenty-first century life being "provisional, flexible, consumerist, and the only constant is change," the boundary between legitimate and illegitimate religion is porous, to say the least, and these offer excellent test cases for legal definitions of religion. As for the moral argument, it is advocated that, whereas illiberal societies may censure deviant costuming, and even administer lethal penalties against those perceived as apostates because of violations of a dress code, participants in liberal societies in the twenty first century should enjoy freedom from costuming constraints.

Next, in "Director's Cu(l)ts and Reel Researchers: The Investigation of Sects in the Movies," Stefano Bigliardi, along with his students Abdelmojib Chouhbi, Mohamed Amine Ghafil, Amine Nakari, Danya Tazi Mokha, and Salma Zahidi, surveyed and analyzed the plots, dialogues and cinematic features of twenty-two movies which represented fictional new religious movements and their investigators. Among other foci, the group explored how culture, ethnicity, and gender were exploited to fit the films into the genre of horror. All the films are interesting, but the range may be suggested by the first and last.

First is Mark Robson's *The Seventh Victim* (1943), in which missing student Jacqueline Gibson is discovered to have been absorbed into a Satanic group, the fictional Palladists,[1] and is about to be executed for violating the group's secrecy rules. She is found by her sister and three men, two of whom are self-appointed experts on Satanic cults. The experts enter into dialogue with the group's members, at least one of whom, Mrs. Swift, is profoundly uncomfortable with the violence the group is about to perpetrate on Jacqueline. Despite the group's commitment to nonviolence, it has followed a mysterious scripture mandating death for the previous six apostates before Jacqueline. The filmscript shows the members debating

---

1 The Palladists are based on a hoax perpetrated by Léo Taxil (1854–1907).

the founder's intentions in a humane and relatable way, but this debate was cut from the cinematic production, seemingly in an effort to restrict the perceived depth of the Palladists and to identify the film with the genre of horror. The Palladists try various methods of killing Jacquelyn, who, the film suggests in an oblique way, kills herself. The last film is Ari Aster's *Midsommar* (2019), in which protagonist Dani and some college friends visit Pelle, a Swedish friend from Hårga, a sun worshipping community with libertine practices and pantheistic philosophies. The community claims that these are handed down through oracles delivered by seers intentionally inbred and therefore reputedly "unclouded by normal cognition" and "closer to the source." Inspired by Nordic myths and Swedish folklore, the film attempts to capture a blend of esoteric spirituality, fertility celebration, and most sensationally, psychedelic experience. Unlike the Brazilian Santo Daime, an actual NRM which utilizes ayahuasca to transport members to higher consciousness, the community of Hårga is portrayed as using psychedelic drugs to manipulate and control members. Two of Dani's friends, Josh and Christian, become suspicious of certain practices, such as urging elders to commit ritual suicide, while Dani, who has just lost her entire family in a fire, finds herself absorbed into Hårga as her new family. Chosen to be May Queen, Dani supervises the human sacrifice of her friend Christian, who is burned alive with eight others to purge the community of its evil. Although initially horrified, finally she smiles, suggesting her surrender to her new family dynamics. This film too partakes of the horror genre. As we can see by just these two films, the depth they ascribe to new religious movements varies, as do their stereotypes of NRM acolytes and new recruits. Professor Bigliardi and his students hope that filmmakers interested in NRMs hereafter will avoid what Jim Lewis called monolithic inferences (2019) and follow the research of religion scholars on the subject.

Finally, Zang Xinzhang and Xu Weiwei discuss the sensitive subject of *Xie Jiao*—so-called "evil cults"—as understood in the formal literature of the People's Republic of China (hereinafter PRC). In 2017 the PRC defined *Xie Jiao* as:

> [i]llegal organizations that are set up by using religions, Qigong, or other things as a camouflage [in order to] deify their leading members, and confuse and deceive people, [to] recruit and control their members, and endanger society by fabricating and spreading superstitious heresies. [These shall be] determined as "cult organizations" as prescribed in Article 300 of the Criminal Law.

The definition distinguishes the culpability of individual members of such groups from that of the leaders who intend to deceive them. It is not precisely the teachings of *Xie Jiao* that are targeted, but the hidden manipulations that are attached to them, including disturbance of the social order and monetary extractions by unscrupulous leaders. Investigation of *Xie Jiao* is carried out by public security organs responsible for prohibiting criminal activities, which attests to the protectionist orientation. In the case of Falun Gong practitioners, it is understood that, despite most practitioners' sincere desires to practice qigong and to prolong life, Li Hongzhi's leadership openly led to the destruction of human life. On the one hand, it is difficult to prosecute beliefs, even beliefs that are openly homophobic, anti-miscegenist, and anti-feminist (Zhang and Lewis 2020). Nor is it straightforward to contest Li Hongzhi's claims of incredible psychic powers, such as to be able to become invisible, to penetrate panes of glass, to be clairvoyant, to levitate, to see inside followers with his third eye, to know the true growth and apocalyptic decline of myriad civilizations, and, perhaps most strikingly, to understand the infiltration of human societies as well as human bodies by space aliens, who abduct humans to be pets on alien home planets (Farley 2014). While absurdities themselves presumably are challenging to litigate, the self-immolations of seven Falun Gong members in Tiananmen square on January 23, 2001 leave a more tangible trace, as does subsequent encouragement by Li Hongzhi that imprisoned Falun Gong members endure public martyrdom in order to promote the reputation of the group and to speed up the current period of catastrophe which will culminate when contemporary society will degenerate and finally be purged. This is hardly the first apocalyptic religious movement in Chinese history (on which see, e.g., ter Haar 2023, 428–442), a truth which might attune the ears of western readers to enduring Chinese sensibilities.

In sum, the chapters in this volume expound on some ideas mined from the work of James R. Lewis. Of course, given his immense scholarly output, his thinking cannot be captured in a single volume, but these chapters do underscore the stimulating range of his thinking. It is hoped that the volume will be useful to those interested in violence, conspiracies, and new religious movements for decades to come.

About the author

Margo Kitts is Professor and Coordinator of religious studies and east-west classical studies at Hawai'i Pacific University in Honolulu. She has authored 50 chapters/articles and edited or authored twelve books on religion and violence and/or ancient studies. Most recent of her books are *Cambridge Companion to Religion and War* (Cambridge 2023); *Sacrifice: Themes, Theories, and Controversies* (Cambridge 2022); *Elements of Ritual and Violence* (Cambridge 2018), and *Martyrdom, Self-Sacrifice, and Self-Immolation: Religious Perspectives on Suicide* (Ed. Oxford 2018). For updates see https://mkitts.netlify.app/.

References

Barkun, Michael. 2013. *A Culture of Conspiracy: Apocalyptic Visions in Contemporary America*. Berkeley: University of California Press.

Bromley, David G. 2022. "Lost Cause; Movement Timeline" https://wrldrels.org/2022/07/05/lost-cause/

Dyrendal, Asbjørn, Leif Edward Ottesen Kennair and James R. Lewis. 2017. "The Role of Conspiracy Mentality and Paranormal Beliefs in Predicting Conspiracy Beliefs among Neopagans." *International Journal for the Study of New Religions* 8(1): 73–97. https://doi.org/10.1558/ijsnr.36716

Farley, Helen. 2014. "Falun Gong: A Narrative of Impending Apocalypse, Shape-Shifting Aliens, and Relentless Persecution." In *Controversial New Religions*. edited by James R. Lewis and J. A. Petersen, 241–254. Oxford: Oxford University Press. https://doi.org/10.1093/acprof:osobl/9780199315314.003.0014

Hegghammer, Thomas. Ed. 2017. *Jihadi Culture. The Art and Social Practices of Militant Islamists*. Cambridge: Cambridge University Press. https://doi.org/10.1017/9781139086141

Juergensmeyer, Mark. 2020. *God at War: A Meditation on Religion and Warfare*. Oxford: Oxford University Press. https://doi.org/10.1093/oso/9780190079178.001.0001

———. 2022. *When God Stops Fighting. How Religious Violence Ends*. Berkeley: University of California Press.

Lewis, James R. 2003. "Legitimating Suicide: Heaven's Gate and New Age ideology." In *UFO Religions*, edited by C. Partridge, 103–128. London: Taylor & Francis Group.

———. 2014a. "The Mt. Carmel Holocaust: Suicide or Execution? " In *Suicide Cults*, edited by James R. Lewis and Carole M. Cusack, 233–250. London: Routledge.

———. 2014b. "The Earth School: The Movement of Spiritual Inner Awareness." In *Controversial New Religions*, 2nd Edition, edited by James R. Lewis and Jesper Aagaard Petersen, 131–143. Oxford: Oxford University Press.

———. 2018. "A Burning Faith in the Master: Interpreting the 1.23 Incident." *Journal of Religion and Violence* 6(2): 172–190. https://doi.org/10.5840/jrv201811957

———. 2019. "Monolithic Inferences: Misinterpreting AUM Shinrikyo." *Journal of Religion and Violence* 7(1): 44–54. https://doi.org/10.5840/jrv201941763

Lewis, James R., ed. 1994. *From the Ashes: Making Sense of Waco*. Rowman & Littlefield.

Moore, Rebecca. 2022. *Peoples Temple and Jonestown in the Twenty-First Century*. Cambridge: Cambridge University Press. https://doi.org/10.1017/9781009032025

Ter Haar, Barend. 2023. "The Demonological Framework of the Heavenly Kingdom of Great Peace." In *Cambridge Companion to Religion and War*, edited by Margo Kitts, 428–442. Cambridge: Cambridge University Press. https://doi.org/10.1017/9781108884075.028

Wessinger, Catherine. 2000. *How the Millennium Comes Violently: From Jonestown to Heaven's Gate*. New York: Seven Bridges Press.

———. 2018. "Collective Martyrdom and Religious Suicide: The Branch Davidians and Heaven's Gate." In *Martyrdom, Self-Sacrifice, and Self-Immolation: Religious Perspectives on Suicide*, edited by Margo Kitts, 54–84. Oxford: Oxford University Press.

Zhang, Xinzhang and James R. Lewis. 2020. "The Gods Hate Fags: Falun Gong's Reactionary Social Teachings." *Journal of Religion and Violence* 6(2): 281–297. https://doi.org/10.5840/jrv202121679

I

Religion and Violence

2

RESEARCHING RELIGIOUS TERRORISM

MARK JUERGENSMEYER

> This chapter explores a common problem of those who research the topic of religion-related terrorism: how to enter into the mindset of religious activists, especially those committed to violent interactions. This is the challenge for anyone trying to make sense of people and groups that are different than themselves, a problem for textual and historical scholars as well as those applying contemporary social and anthropological approaches. This chapter advocates a form of epistemic worldview analysis that adopts an approach involving informative conversations. These emphasize relational knowledge—attempts to engage with a subject either directly or through textual analysis that brackets the investigator's assumptions and allows the subject to frame the information from his or her own worldview.

Do religious terrorists engage in terrorism for religious reasons? That depends, in part, on what one means by religion, and what one counts as a motivating influence. As consistently argued in the essays in the volume edited by James R. Lewis, The Cambridge Companion to Religion and Terrorism, the term "religious terrorism" does not mean that religion causes terrorism (Lewis). It simply means that there is some association between the two. This runs counter to many popular beliefs that there is something inherently lethal about religiosity. There is a common assumption among many observers that religious beliefs—and specifically tenets of religious scripture—motivate activists to undertake acts of violence. Whether it's the teachings of the Qur'an or the incendiary verses of the Hebrew Bible (the Old Testament), religious ideas and beliefs are often thought to be the problem. My own interviews, however, indicate that very few religiously-related activists frame their motivations in scriptural or theological terms. Most are woefully ignorant about the textual and intellectual aspects of their traditions. Instead, they talk about the defense of their community and their faith in general, and the threat of certain groups, including secular politicians, in particular. Religious beliefs and traditions are a part of their worldview, but only a part of it, even though it may be the vocabulary through which other social and political issues are enunciated. But in order to discover this perspective of religion-related activists, one has to see the world as they see it.

This is the problem that I have encountered in the study of religious terrorism: entering into the mindset of religious activists, especially those with views that are quite different from our own. This is the challenge for anyone who is trying to make sense of the religious-related violence that seems to be epidemic at the turn of the 21st century. One can explain the rise of ISIS, Jewish extremism, or the outbreak of Christian Islamophobia by external factors, examining the political and social factors that lie behind them. Or one can set them within the contexts of broad historical trends and relate them to similar phenomena at other times and places. Yet as useful as these scholarly pursuits might be, these analyses seldom explain what role religion plays, and it does not help us understand the passion and commitment with which the activists are dedicated to their cause. For this we have to go inside the mindset of the activists themselves.

But how can this be done? This is the challenge for anyone trying to make sense of people and groups that are different than themselves. It is a problem for textual and historical scholars as well as those applying contemporary social and anthropological approaches. And it is the question that I have had to face in a series of interviews with radical religious activists in a variety of religious traditions and locales over the last twenty years. In my own case, the interviews involved leaders of the Palestinian Hamas movement in Gaza, an activist in prison who was associated with the al Qaeda- related 1993 bombing of the World Trade Center, a Lutheran pastor convicted of bombing abortion clinics on the East Coast of the United States, Catholic and Protestant leaders during the "troubles" in Northern Ireland, Sikh separatists in India, Muslim insurgents in Iraq, and Buddhist activists in Sri Lanka, Myanmar, and Japan (Juergensmeyer 2017).

Despite the diversity of these cases, there were some common threads that tied together these activists from varied cultures and regions. All of them had supported or participated in public acts of aggression or violence, including acts that we would regard as terrorism. None of them regarded themselves as terrorists, however. Mahmud Abouhalima, the jihadi activist associated with the 1993 World Trade Center bombing, whom I interviewed in the Lompoc Federal Penitentiary in California, made a clear conceptual difference between terrorists—by which he meant people who simply wanted to kill indiscriminately—and soldiers who were fighting a defensive war. The latter described himself and his actions, and the same can be said of all of the other militants with whom I spoke. They all regarded themselves as soldiers in a grand battle, a cosmic war between right and wrong, truth and evil. That moral element of their vision is where religion came in: all of them were fighting for social or political reasons but they framed their efforts in religious terms. Though religion was only part of their stories, it was an important part, and it was the way in which many of them characterized their struggle.

Finally they all had in common one other thing: they wanted to talk with me. In all cases I had contacted them in advance and they had willingly—in many cases eagerly—agreed to the interviews, knowing that I would use the material in the books I was writing. Abouhalima insisted that my interviews with him be tape recorded to ensure accuracy. A similar concern was expressed by a Buddhist monk in Myanmar, Ashin Wirathu, whom *Time* magazine had labelled "the face of Buddhist terror" for his role in allegedly advocating violence against Muslims in his country (Juergensmeyer 2015). Wirathu insisted on seeing the transcript of my interview before he would agree to my using it publicly. In fact, in all cases I sent transcripts or extensive notes of the interviews to the persons with whom I spoke. I wanted to make sure that I had accurately recorded their words and appropriately interpreted their meanings. This was a potentially dangerous approach, since any of them could deny that they had said such things and prohibit me from using the interview material. Fortunately none did, though the member of the Japanese movement, Aum Shinrikyo, whom I had interviewed in Tokyo was afraid that members of the movement would find him and punish him for what he had said. Though many leaders of the movement were in jail after their use of sarin gas to create a terrorist attack on the Tokyo subways, others were re-establishing the movement under a new name, Aleph. For that reason, I used a pseudonym for his name and obscured any information that might lead to his identity. Everyone else was agreeable to my using their interviews as I had recorded or made notes of them, and Abouhalima followed up the interviews with a number of letters to me adding additional information and ideas, some of which I used in the book.

But all of this is preliminary to what I actually did when I interviewed them. How did I go about these meetings, and what were the salient methodological principles? My approach was based on established patterns of social and anthropological inquiry, adapted to the challenges of confronting world views quite different from my own. In general, I followed a distinctive approach that had several formative characteristics that in a general way replicated the guidelines that the Danish political scientist,

Mona Sheikh, and I have formulated in a jointly-authored essay and co-edited book on how to do what we have termed epistemic worldview analysis (Juergensmeyer and Sheikh 2013, 2019). These principles can apply to a variety of scholarly endeavors, including those where the subjects cannot easily be interviewed, including studies that are based on the analysis of a subject's writings and transcribed interviews, as well as textual and historical analyses. They apply to any attempt to enter into a mindset different from one's own, though in the case of religious extremists the challenge is particularly daunting.

Informative encounters

The first task is to try to enter into the mindset of the subjects through direct engagement. Interviews provide that opportunity, of course, but so do analyses of the subjects' writings and transcribed interviews, and first-person narratives about them. Historical studies can bring to life figures who are centuries old in vivid detail. In my case, however, I was able to actually encounter my subjects through interviews. Then the issue was how to conduct these in a way that was most effective.

The problem with many scholarly interviews is that they follow a script of questions that are predetermined and that therefore limit the scope of what can be discovered. Even the best advice in the literature on doing interviews for qualitative research is goal-oriented, and suggests that the interviewer have specific subjects to pursue (Brinkman and Kvale, Maanen, Weiss 2014). Since my motive was to get inside the mindset of the activists, I had to abandon the comforting script of questions, and engage in a more open-ended encounter. Hence most of my interviews appeared to be conversations. When I was in a mosque in Baghdad, talking with one of the leaders of the Association of Muslim Clergy of al Anbar province in Iraq, it may have seemed like we were just chatting. To the casual observer, and most likely from the point of view of the subjects with whom I was speaking, there was nothing directive about the conversation. It was not random, however, since I had in mind areas of inquiry (though not specific topics) that I wanted to discuss. But I never posed questions in a didactic way.

These conversations were efforts at getting information through direct contact with the subjects, but they were not scientific surveys. At one point in my academic career I thought that that was indeed what social scientists were supposed to do. As a beginning graduate student doing field work in village India, I was determined to conduct a survey analysis among the lower caste workers of a Punjab village. To be properly scientific I devised a 60-question interview. It floundered with question #1 and totally collapsed with question #2. The first question was simple enough—"what is your name?" Yet among the lower caste members of North Indian villages they often had different names for different occasions: caste names, occupation names, religious names, and village names. The second question was "what is your religion?" This term, easy to understand in the West, could not be directly translated in Panjabi, Hindi, or any other Indian language. The idea of one word that corresponds to a whole range of religious activity and identity didn't exist. There was *dharma* for religious law, *qaum* for a religious community or nation, *mazhab* for religious beliefs, and *panth* for a religious fellowship (Juergensmeyer 1982, 1-7). Just what, the villagers wanted to know, did I have I mind?

The problem with social surveys is that they assume that we know what to ask before we ask the question. Instead, I began to experiment in an interactive approach, what Mona Sheikh and I have called "informative encounters." These encounters were conversational in that they were not directive at the outset, though they were aimed at getting an understanding of how the subject viewed the world. In particular, I was concerned with the role of religious ideas and identity in the way that they framed political issues, and their justification for the use of violence in social conflict. But rather than asking that directly, I usually began with a question asking them to provide some autobiographical background, to tell me how they came to their involvement in social activism. These accounts would often lead naturally to follow-up questions about religion, politics, and violence that probed the areas in which I was interested, but also illumined their view of the world and the way that these issues fit into the larger scheme of their personal concerns.

Relational knowledge

Though I had a general idea of the areas of interest that I wanted to probe in my interviews, as I've said, I did not have a list of questions. When I was in Myanmar in September, 2014, talking with the activist Buddhist monk, Wirathu, I began with questions about his involvement in the monastery and his interest in social issues (Juergensmeyer 2015). When he said that Buddhists should be engaged in society, this naturally led to questions about how they should do it and whether violence is ever justified. "Buddhism is nonviolent," he would insist repeatedly. Clearly this line of discussion was closed, from his point of view. But it did allow me to reframe the question from his point of view. If Buddhism needed to be engaged, and needed to defend itself, I asked him, from what and where were the threats coming? Immediately Wirathu snapped back that Muslim extremists were the threat, and that the very existence of Burmese Buddhism was in peril. This allowed us to move into the area of Buddhist-Muslim relations and to ask him the degree to which Buddhists were justified in defending themselves—even, if necessary, defending themselves in a situation that might lead to violence. Wirathu allowed for Buddhist violence in this context, though the subject would never have come up if I were not able to switch the direction of the conversation and reframe my questions depending on his previous responses.

This is not just a matter of being adroit in one's line of questioning, but also a matter of learning from what was said. It requires one to change ideas about what to ask depending on previous answers, and to let the conversations move in whatever direction seems appropriate. This is neither inductive nor deductive reasoning. Inductive reasoning assumes that one has a general idea or principle from which one makes sense of particular data. Deductive reasoning tries to build up the larger picture from accumulating particular information. The approach that I use might be called "relational reasoning," a form of understanding that emerges from the give and take of points of view in an interactive conversation. It is *relational* in that what is discovered depends upon the relationship between the conversation partners, with questions changing in response to the way previous questions have been answered. It is *reasoning* in that it aims at understanding the point of view of the subject, trying to make sense of the logic that informs a person's actions, including especially those actions that seem so inappropriate and unjustified in normal relationships, acts of violence.

Bracketing assumptions

The point of these conversations is to try to enter into the mindset of the interview subjects, to understand as best as possible how they see the world. This means that as much as possible we should try to bracket our own judgments about what is being said. It is a double bracketing in fact: we should try to reserve making value judgments, at least temporarily, about the truth or falsity of what they are saying, and to avoid making judgments about the truth or falsity of our own points of view (though needless to say, we think that we are always right). Sometimes both of these are difficult, especially when the issue at hand is the moral sanction for violence, or the unequal treatment of other people on the basis of their ethnicity, religion, or gender. Yet for the sake of the interviews we should keep our judgment about these matters at bay. There will be ample opportunity in the future to reflect on the conversation and condemn the subjects, if we feel that condemnation is warranted.

But in the heat of a conversation it is not easy to stay silent. I remember a conversation with the Israeli activist, Rabbi Meir Kahane, a cheerful character with a Brooklyn accent, who passed over the territorial claims of Palestinians as if they were trivial matters. From his point of view they were. After all, he believed that the Israeli claims over Eretz Israel—greater Israel, including the Palestinian West Bank of the Jordan River—were essential in order to lay the foundations for the coming of the Messiah. This is heady stuff in Jewish history, so it is understandable that if he fervently believed that the greatest moment of biblical prophecy was about to be fulfilled, territorial claims could seem to be a minor matter. Still, it was not a minor matter to Palestinians who were uprooted from their homes and who had their own claims to the region that Kahane thought was essential for Israel to occupy. "This is biblical land," Kahane told me, implying that the Palestinians did not belong there; "they should just leave," he said. It took all of my sense of self-control to keep from arguing with him, though I knew that there would have been no point to it if I did, his mind was closed on the subject. In a similar way, the Buddhist monk Wirathu in Myanmar was convinced that Muslims in his country were a corrosive force that would undermine Burmese culture and there would be no way to convince him otherwise.

My discussions with the Christian militant, Rev Michael Bray, probably involved the most give-and-take, since he was interested in talking about theology, and I knew the works of Reinhold Niebuhr and Dietrich Bonhoeffer that he admired. I clarified my own interpretations of their work, and Bray observed that they were different than his, which did not surprise him. He had already categorized me as a liberal Christian who would see scripture and theology differently from his point of view. So there was a tacit agreement to disagree, and there was no need to argue with him, he already knew my position. What I wanted to understand was his.

Perhaps the closest I came to getting into an argument in my interviewers was with the World Trade Center bomber, Mahmud Abouhalima. At one point in our discussion he was trying to make a distinction between his world of faith and the secular world around him. He pointed to me, and asserted that "you secularists" had no way of knowing what it was like to try to live faithfully in a secular society. I instinctively reacted, since I was raised in a churchgoing household, attended seminary before graduate school, and continued to be a regular member of a Protestant Christian congregation. Still, my protestations were brushed off by Abouhalima who insisted, "no, Mr. Mark, you are a secularist." And then he added, "I know your world, I've lived in it; but you haven't lived in mine" (Juergensmeyer 2017, 70).

Abouhalima was right, in fact. My religiosity was one that was comfortable with the secular, multicultural modernity of the contemporary West. This was the world that he was projected into after leaving Afghanistan where he had been a part of the Mujahidin militia fighting the Soviet-backed government, and before that in his native Egypt, where he was a member of an extremist offshoot of the Muslim Brotherhood, the Gamaa i-Islamiya. The world of New Jersey was certainly different, as was Germany where he lived for some years after leaving Egypt. So he did know my world. And it is also true that I didn't really know his, even though I lived for several years in India and have spent a considerable amount of time in Muslim-majority countries as well. But I have never really been out of my secular modernist element, and Abouhalima was right to remind me that I did not know his world as he knew mine. That did not mean that I condoned his interpretation of the commandments of his faith, nor did it alter my judgment that he was motivated as much by a kind of macho soldier-of-war adventurism as he was by piety. Still his point was well made, and I had to make the attempt to see the world as he saw it—or at least the way he wanted me to think that he saw it.

Entering their worldviews

This brings up another point—was I really probing into his mindset, or was I simply uncovering a version of himself that he wanted to sell? The point of my informed conversations was to let the subjects reveal their perspectives on the world around them, which is why I was careful not to dominate the conversations. One might object that this open-ended approach to interviews allowed the subjects to control the situation. Moreover, it would allow them to present themselves exactly as they would like to be presented. Especially since they were eager to talk with me, as I just mentioned, wouldn't they be eager to present a carefully choreographed image of themselves for my sake?

The answer to this question is yes, most likely. But even that is an interesting datum—it is useful to know how they would like to have themselves presented, and to contrast that with other information that I had gathered about their past and their social and political involvements. In every case I did not come to an interview cold, knowing nothing about the subjects; quite the opposite, I tried to learn as much as I could about what they had said and written, and how they had been perceived and described by others, both before and after interviewing them. I kept all of this knowledge in the back of my mind as a kind of corrective to what they might be saying and as a reminder, when I talked with them, to push them in certain directions.

In the case of Abouhalima, for instance, he never admitted to being involved in the attack on the World Trade Center even though he was tried and convicted in a US court for exactly that crime. Still, he was hoping to get out on appeal, and would not say anything that would implicate him directly in that incident. But in the course of the conversation I found that he was quite willing to talk about the Oklahoma City Federal Building bombing—after all, no one had implicated him in that crime, nor was there any possibility that he could have been involved in it since he was in prison at the time. This allowed me to ask him why some people, whoever they might be, would bomb buildings. He assured me that it was for a reason—Timothy McVeigh and his allies were not just bombing things for the sake of bombing them—they were trying to send a message. "What kind of message," I asked him, knowing that his answer would apply to his own convicted participation in the World Trade Center bombing as well as to McVeigh's Oklahoma City Federal Building attack. "They wanted to show you that your government is the enemy," he answered. He paused, and then added, "and now you know."

These are some of the guidelines that might be followed in attempting what Mona Sheikh and I have called "epistemic worldview analysis." They do not amount to a methodology, in the sense of a prescribed analytic approach. Rather they are general principles that are relevant in a variety of analytic situations—if one is involved in textual research, social survey studies or a more anthropological approach of entering into case studies. The greater involvement with the subjects of the study the better, though in the case of historical studies often the only evidence one has of their ways of thinking is in letters or writings or in others' commentary about them.

The degree to which scholars will want to immerse themselves in the milieu of their subjects depends in part on the purpose of the project: whether it is a broad comparative overview or a more intensive case study. Though I have done intensive case studies in other books, my project in *Terror in the Mind of God* was a broad comparative analysis of disparate activists in differing cultures and regions (Juergensmeyer 2017). There I attempted to find patterns in their ways of thinking and to identify some similarities in their understanding of the relation of religious images and ideas to contemporary social and political situations. Of course it would have been a more thorough project if I had known the languages of all of my subjects—Arabic, Hebrew, Burmese and Japanese, as well as those I have tried to master, Hindi and Panjabi. As it was, I was reliant on translators for many of the conversations. It would have been a deeper study if I had spent more time in each locale, come to know others within their circle, and relied not on a few interviews but on many. Yet this would have been a different book, or more likely a series of books. My purpose was to have comparative snapshots of a range of religious activists, and I feel fortunate to have had the remarkable conversations that I had. Though Abouhalima may still not believe it, I think that I was able to penetrate into his world and the worldviews of the many others with whom I spoke, for at least a bit, and that opening illumined much about why he and others did what they did, and why their worlds have been so very hard for us to understand.

About the author

Mark Juergensmeyer is distinguished professor emeritus of sociology and global studies and interim director of the Orfalea Center for Global and International Studies at the University of California, Santa Barbara, and William F. Podlich Distinguished Fellow and Professor of Religious Studies at Claremont McKenna College. He is a pioneer in global studies, focusing on global religion, religious violence, conflict resolution and South Asian religion and politics. He has published more than three hundred articles and thirty books, including the recent *God at War* (Oxford 2020), the award-winning *Terror in the Mind of God* (University of California Press, 4th ed, 2017), and his co-edited *Oxford Handbook of Global Studies* (Oxford 2018).

References

Brinkmann, Svend and Steinar Kvale. 2014. *InterViews: Learning the Craft of Qualitative Research Interviewing.* London: Sage Publications.

Juergensmeyer, Mark. 2017. *Terror in the Mind of God: The Global Rise of Religious Violence,* 4th ed. Oakland: University of California Press.

———. 2015. "Myanmar's Buddhist Terrorist," *Religion Dispatches,* posted March 10, 2015.

———. 1982. *Religion as Social Vision: The Movement Against Untouchability in 20th Century Punjab.* Berkeley: University of California Press.

Juergensmeyer, Mark and Mona Kanwal Sheikh. 2013. "A Sociotheological Approach to Understanding Religious Violence." In *The Oxford Handbook of Religion and Violence,* edited by Mark Juergensmeyer, Margo Kitts and Michael Jerryson, 620-643. Oxford: Oxford University Press. https://doi.org/10.1093/oxfordhb/9780199759996.013.0040

Lewis, James R., ed. 2017. *The Cambridge Companion to Religion and Terrorism.* Cambridge: Cambridge University Press. https://doi.org/10.1017/9781316492536

Sheikh, Mona Kanwal and Mark Juergensmeyer, eds. 2019. *Entering Religious Minds: The Social Analysis of Worldviews.* London: Routledge. https://doi.org/10.4324/9780429468810

Van Maanen, John. 2011. *Tales of the Field: On Writing Ethnography.* 2nd edition. Chicago, IL: University of Chicago Press. https://doi.org/10.7208/chicago/9780226849638.001.0001

Weiss, Robert. 1995. *Learning from Strangers: The Art and Method of Qualitative Interview Studies.* New York: The Free Press.

3

CONSPIRACY THEORIES ACROSS BORDERS

MICHAEL BARKUN

One of the most striking characteristics of conspiracy theories is their frequently transnational character. In previous centuries, such theories most frequently revolved around either the Catholic Church, the Masonic movement, or Jews. These traditional conspiracist networks were absorbed and superseded after World War II by conspiracy theories built around schemes for international cooperation. This evil elite and the conspiracy theories related to it were generally referred to as the "New World Order" and appeared in both religious and secular versions. A number of separate conspiracy theories arose at the same time that were consistent with the New World Order but were conceptually quite distinct from it. An examination of three of them is particularly instructive as a demonstration of the ability of conspiracy theories to cross borders. The three are, first, the Sovereign Citizen Movement; second, the followers of Anders Breivik; and, third, the QAnon movement. Sovereign citizens appeared in the United States as part of a highly deviant strain of legal and constitutional interpretation. Anders Breivik, the Norwegian mass casualty killer, claimed to lead an international movement but in fact had no followers at the time of his crimes. However, subsequently lone wolves in several European countries self-identified as his acolytes. Finally, the QAnon movement began as a web-based attack on the Democratic-liberal establishment and a representation of Donald Trump as a savior figure. Yet despite its American roots, it has spread as far as Europe and Japan.

Introduction

For at least the last few centuries, conspiracy theorists have often described plots that allegedly cross national boundaries. These supposed international networks of evildoers were said to be invisible to the untutored eye, but their machinations could be revealed to those with the requisite arcane knowledge, which conspiracy theorists alone claimed to possess. Conspiracy theorists have seemed peculiarly attracted to ideas of international evil, presumably because the broader the territorial scope of malevolence, the greater the danger it poses, and the more valuable the knowledge about it. Thus someone who claimed to know about secret evil within a village might have local status and power, but someone who claimed to know about secret evil that might threaten the world possessed an altogether greater potential influence. Even if this knowledge claim is false (as most conspiracy ideas prove to be), it translates into an individual sense of empowerment and influence vis-à-vis others to the extent that belief in it spreads.

For convenience sake, one may distinguish between two major types of alleged cross-national conspiracy networks: The first may be termed the *traditional networks*. These formed the basis of conspiracy theories from at least the late eighteenth century and in many cases much earlier. The second may be called the *modern networks*. These appear in conspiracy theories beginning in the aftermath of the Second World War and extending into the present day.

The traditional networks

Traditional trans-national conspiracy theories most frequently revolved around one or more of three elements: the Catholic Church, the Masonic movement, and Jews. All three lent themselves to conspiracist speculation because they had members in numerous countries and they either had certain secret teachings or ceremonies, or the ignorance of outsiders about them made them appear to operate secretly. They also, particularly in the case of conspiracism about Catholics and Jews, were reinforced by deep pre-existing prejudice and doctrinal hostility. Anti-Catholic conspiracism focused principally upon the Church's most politically active order during the Counter-Reformation, the Jesuits. While Masonry was in its structure a secret society, conspiracism claimed that evil designs were sought by both the Freemasons in general and the quasi-Masonic Illuminati of Central Europe in particular. The extraordinary force of Illuminati conspiracism was initially due to two books, John Robison's *Proofs of a Conspiracy* (1798) and Abbe Barruel's *Memoirs, Illustrating the History of Jacobinism* (1803), both of which argued that it was the Illuminati who were responsible for the French Revolution, rather than an upswelling of anger by a tyrannized population. Anti-Semitic conspiracy theories, of course, ran far back into medieval history and before. They thus were the common property of Europeans and Americans through both religious teaching and folk culture, episodically emerging in pogroms, blood libels, expulsions, ghettoizations, discrimination, and other manifestations.

This highly abbreviated description may lead one to think of the traditional conspiracy networks as purely pre-modern phenomena. Indeed, their origins did in fact lie in European societies before the dominance of the urban-industrial order. However, it is essential to recognize that despite their roots in the past, they have retained their vigor into the modern period. Thus fear of a potential Catholic conspiracy was very likely the decisive factor in the defeat of Al Smith in the 1928 Presidential election, and the belief in its potency almost certainly retarded the emergence of Catholic presidential candidates for some years afterwards. The belief in the Illuminati—even though they had been completely suppressed by European governments by the 1780s—was actually enhanced in the twentieth century by two British writers, Edith Starr Miller (aka Lady Queenborough) and Nesta Webster (Miller, n.d.; Webster, n.d.). Writing in the inter-war period, they argued that not only did the Illuminati survive past the French Revolution, but the Illuminati supposedly went on to wreak havoc for decades afterwards, including responsibility for the Russian Revolution. Miller's and Webster's works continue to circulate in right-wing and conspiracist circles on both sides of the Atlantic. Belief in Illuminati machinations has played a particularly significant role in the John Birch Society, beginning in the 1960s.

While anti-Semitism was to take many lurid and hateful forms in the modern period, none was perhaps more influential than its codification through the literary pastiche forged by the Czarist secret police in 1905, *The Protocols of the Elders of Zion* (Landes and Katz 2012). Translated into English in 1920, it was popularized in America in the '20s through Henry Ford's weekly newspaper, *The Dearborn Independent.* These elaborations of old themes allowed traditional cross-national conspiracism to persist into the twentieth century. Nonetheless, new motifs were added as political, social, and economic conditions changed.

The resulting conspiracism was therefore *layered*, with strata that had accumulated over centuries. Unlike certain areas of human culture—medicine, say, or science—where older material is discarded and replaced by ideas and practices that are new and deemed to be superior, conspiracism operates through a process of the gradual accretion of ideas. That is to say, centuries' old conceptions of trans-national conspiracy manage to maintain followings even as new plots develop alongside them.

The modern networks

These new motifs—what I have termed the modern networks—developed rapidly after the end of the Second World War and were particularly tied to evidence of postwar international cooperation. Thus the United

Nations and related organizations were prime targets of conspiracists, as were such private international ventures as the Bilderberg conferences, the Trilateral Commission, and the World Economic Forum at Davos. The common thread in conspiracism after the middle of the twentieth century was the belief that some elite group was preparing to seize global power, perhaps using the UN as a screen, perhaps through international financial machinations, or perhaps by first grasping control of the United States and using its power to subdue the rest of the world. In some largely secular versions, the aim was economic gain, while in others it was said to be part of the Anti-Christ's plan for the Last Days, as foretold in the Book of Revelation. Although the scenarios differed in details, there was general agreement that the cabal existed and was well on its way toward world hegemony. The phrase conspiracy theorists of all stripes adopted for this plot was the "New World Order," a term that seems to have gained currency beginning in the 1980s (Barkun 2013, 66-69). As the foregoing section suggests, this material coexisted with but did not supplant the traditional conspiracism that had developed in earlier periods. Thus the modern networks may be seen as strata laid down over the beliefs about traditional plots. At other times, they appear to absorb some of the older networks, partially assimilating anti-Catholic, Illuminati, and anti-Semitic motifs.

New World Order (NWO) theory might well be termed ecumenical for its capacity to incorporate a variety of different forms of conspiracism. It has been flexible enough to incorporate Jesuits, Illuminati, and Jewish international bankers along with Bilderbergers, Trilateralists, and the United Nations. In addition to the traditional forms, NWO theory had the ability to bridge the secular-religious gap among conspiracists. Thus one of the most widely read NWO tracts (indeed, it was entitled *The New World Order*) came from the American evangelist, Pat Robertson, published when he was at the height of his political influence (Robertson 1991). Yet even though it placed the conspiracy in the framework of end-time events, the evidence it adduced and the claims it made about the conspiracy's actions were generally similar to those held by non-religious conspiracy believers. The opposite was true as well. That is, religionists mined secular NWO literature for evidence that the plans of Satan and the Anti-Christ were coming to fruition.

NWO theories had advantages beyond creating a common conspiracy language shared by religionists and secularists. By absorbing different types of conspiracism, it provided a way of structuring conspiracy theories that reduced their complexity. By the late decades of the twentieth century the co-existence of traditional and modern networks meant that a very large number of separate plots were in circulation simultaneously. As has already been observed, those that were common in the nineteenth century continued to be cited and in some cases grew more fashionable. Alongside them were the modern networks, emphasizing international organizations of one sort or another, varying in emphasis or breadth, depending upon the nationality and taste of the conspiracist. This might have led to a chaotic welter of unrelated plots, were it not for the ability of New World Order conceptions to bring order through two techniques. One technique involved nesting smaller conspiracies within larger ones. Thus national cabals might be seen as components of regional plots, and regional plots as the pieces that composed the grand, global design. The second, somewhat vaguer technique was one of homogenization. That is, smaller conspiracies were simply assigned subordinate roles under the general guidance of some superior, over-arching intelligence. This was scarcely a new idea, since those obsessed with witches and demons in the sixteenth and seventeenth centuries saw the Satan and his minions in much the same way.

Reality and illusion

As long as conspiracists live in the domain of conspiracy theories, they exist primarily in the sphere of illusion. That is, they construct bricolages of facts and ideas that purport to represent reality. While some aspects of these assemblages may accurately map the world, for the most part these representations are incorrect. The pictures they present rarely match reality, at least as most people perceive it. The broader the conspiracy theory, the more likely this is to be the case. Therefore, conspiracy theories that claim an international reach are particularly prone to represent imaginary worlds.

Complications arise when those who believe in such representations seek to convert others to their point of view and/or to actually physically defeat the dark forces of the conspiracy. At this point, conspiracy theories move from speculation to action, and illusion and reality can intersect in strange ways. The manner of their intersection can depend on a number of variables: the international scope of the conspiracy theory, a factor already mentioned; the success of the conspiracists' proselytizing; and the political power conspiracy believers are able to acquire. In rare cases, such conspiracists have actually been able to secure political power and mobilize the machinery of the state against their imagined enemies. The totalitarian regimes of the twentieth century provide ample evidence of this potential. However, in the instances to be discussed below, the conspiracists possess few such worldly advantages. Nonetheless, one may still discern the strange confrontations that can occur when conspiracy ideas leave the confines of individual minds and enter the larger world.

Three cases of cross-boundary conspiracism

The discussion so far has focused on well-established conspiracism. Even the modern type consists of a sufficient number of instances over more than three decades so that its structure is no longer in no doubt. However, it would be both interesting and useful to find cases of conspiracism in the process of migrating across international borders. Consequently, the balance of this essay will be given over to an examination of three such cases. The first deals with the movement of "sovereign citizen" ideas from the United States to Australia; the second with the gradual creation within Europe of a conspiracist movement based on the actions of the Norwegian terrorist, Anders Breivik; and the third with the spread of the QAnon movement.

"Sovereign citizens"

The concept of "sovereign citizens" and the conspiracy apparatus that goes with it would seem to be relatively unexportable, given its rootedness in the United States. It grew out of radical movements on the American extreme right, and they, in turn, reflected peculiarities of the American political and legal systems. Although for convenience sake it will be called a "movement" here, it is, strictly speaking, more an ideological tendency than an organized group. It is, rather, a constellation of individuals who employ a common vocabulary and, most importantly, hold a common view of the political and legal system. As will be seen, its members' hostility to authority makes them unwilling to place themselves under hierarchical arrangements, even in pursuit of their own goals. However, there are sufficient common elements among writers, teachers, promoters, and "grassroots" followers so that a single term may be applied to all of them.

Sovereign Citizens can be traced back to an earlier movement, the Posse Comitatus in the 1970s (Lawless Ones 2010, 4). Posse Comitatus (literally, "the power of the county") was based on the idea that the county is the only legitimate legal and political unit, and that the Posse, defined as the armed adult males of a community, is its rightful enforcement arm. One Posse theorist went so far as to claim that "the County Sheriff is the only legal law enforcement officer in the United States of America" (Barkun 1997, 221). The Posse was particularly active in the mid-section of the country and, not surprisingly, before it began to disappear in the 1980s, its members were involved in several violent confrontations with state and federal authorities. Even though Posse Comitatus disappeared as a movement, it left a powerful legacy on the radical right. That legacy was in the form of beliefs that the commonly understood legal and constitutional structure upon which the American government had been raised was illegitimate, and that only the smallest political unit possessed legitimacy. This view, which I have elsewhere termed "radical localism" (Barkun 1997, 217–223) was to be taken even further by Sovereign Citizens several decades later. Their belief in the legal supremacy of the individual resulted in numerous clashes with officials carrying out what they regarded as perfectly normal duties. A corollary of Posse Comitatus that also reappeared among Sovereign Citizens was that lawyers and judges were involved in a vast conspiracy to prevent average Americans from learning their true rights, and instead had erected a false, complex, and arcane structure to obscure the genuine nature of the law.

Central to Sovereign Citizen beliefs is that the individual citizen is the only truly sovereign entity, thereby carrying radical localism to its ultimate extreme and in the process eradicating the claims of all governmental units. The intellectual apparatus created to support this position is mind-bogglingly complex and gives rise to a sub-culture that appears impenetrable to outsiders. It revolves around a revisionist history of American law and constitutionalism, according to which admiralty law was permitted to surreptitiously supplant the Constitution. In addition, and depending upon which version one chooses, either the 14th Amendment to the Constitution ratified after the Civil War, or the abandonment of the gold standard in 1933, became the perverse means for eliminating individual sovereignty. This sovereignty, the argument goes, must be reclaimed by penetrating the conspiracy.

In the first case, the 14th Amendment was said to have created a class of "citizens of the United States" rather than of independent states. Their rights, through a variety of legal instruments, are said to be illegitimate, since the federal government supposedly has no jurisdiction over them (Lawless Ones 2010, 4). The other, even more bizarre claim has it that the renunciation of gold as the basis for American currency caused the government to pledge its citizens as collateral and consequently to enslave them from birth. The birth certificate and Social Security number are said to be tools in the conspiracy to seize rights, which must then be "redeemed" if the individual is to achieve freedom (Sovereign Citizens Movement).

As the foregoing suggests, the Sovereign Citizen movement possesses characteristics that on the surface would appear to reduce the likelihood of its spread outside the United States. It is loosely rather than tightly organized, a set of atomistic coteries grouped around individuals who claim to be able to teach legal techniques that will free people from the supposed fetters of the legal conspiracy. Second, its teachings are strange. They contradict received ideas about politics and history, while encouraging acolytes to violate the law. Finally, even in its heresies, the Sovereign Citizen movement remains deeply rooted in America, since it claims to reveal the truth about the American Constitution and to right what it says is a monumental historic wrong in American history.

Yet despite these factors, Sovereign Citizen beliefs have spread to Canada (Sovereign Citizens Movement) and, more surprisingly, to Australia. The key links in the migration to Australia appear to have been through the activities of two American Sovereign Citizens, Winston Shrout and David Wynn Miller, both of whom have made multi-city tours of Australia holding seminars (Lawless Ones 2010, 15). Australian Sovereign Citizen sites also contain anti-Masonic and anti-Semitic material, as well as links to a variety of conspiracist websites (https://www.loveforlife.com.au).

Another Australian who appears to have been influenced by Sovereign Citizen ideas is Romley Stover. Stover, unlike American counterparts, claims to speak on behalf of an organization, the Australian Sovereign Council. A posted document about the Council mentions the names of three or four other individuals whom Stover says are either associated with or have been invited to join the organization. The group's basis and goals seem largely consistent with American Sovereign Citizen ideology. However, the Council seeks to establish a fifteen-person "Assise," in order "to enable justice and remedy to compensate for the damage done to citizens of Australia..." (What is the..., 2012). This harks back to the Posse Comitatus and its founder, William Potter Gale, who was involved in attempts to empanel citizen grand juries to "indict" public officials.

Here we see the desire of both American and Australian radicals to reach back to some mythic legal past when the Common Law was uncontaminated by the lawyers' conspiracy. It is in part this shared myth of a recoverable past age of legal purity that has allowed Sovereign Citizen beliefs to flow across oceans and transcend historical and political differences. The proselytizers for the movement grasped the fact that notwithstanding substantial historical differences between the United States and Australia, both societies shared a Common Law heritage. It was possible, therefore, to tap into the idea that in some imagined distant past, that legal heritage existed in an uncontaminated form, before it had been polluted by the conspiracy.

The efforts by Sovereign Citizens to proselytize allegedly stems from their belief that many states tyrannize over subjects in the same manner they believe occurred in the United States. However, their cross-border activities have a sub-text. That is the situation familiar in social science in which beliefs (particularly deviant beliefs) are reinforced to the extent that others can be convinced of their validity. While this is most strikingly the case in cognitive dissonance, where the beliefs are contradicted by empirical evidence (Festinger *et al.* 1964), the same holds true when the beliefs are likely to attract scorn, ridicule, or, as in the case at hand, even potential legal sanctions. The demonstration that the same problems supposedly exist in other countries and the acquisition of converts there consequently strengthens the believers' faith.

On the surface, Sovereign Citizens have more in common with modern conspiracy theories than with traditional theories. It is difficult to find similar belief systems in earlier eras. Even though the Sovereigns pay no attention to organizations such as the United Nations, they share with other modern theories an intense distrust of governing powers. However, there are nonetheless still links with a traditional world in the constant evocation of the Common Law, as well as the belief that in some distant past, before lawyers assumed control of the system, that Law was comprehensible and usable by the average individual without the intervention of specialists.

Anders Breivik

The case of Anders Breivik presents a very different picture of the relationship between conspiracism and national boundaries. On July 22, 2011, Breivik detonated a large bomb outside Norwegian government offices in Oslo, causing the deaths of eight people. He then went to an island where a Socialist Party camp was located and, using firearms, took another 69 lives. However, before embarking upon these acts, he posted a 1516-page manifesto on the Internet in which he claimed to be a "Justiciar Knight" of a Knights Templar organization. In that document, entitled "2083: A European Declaration of Independence" (Berwick 2011), Breivik claimed that he participated with eight other people, each from a different European country, in the formation of the organization at two meetings in London in April 2002. This newly re-formed Knights Templar order was to "serve as an armed Indigenous Rights Organisation and as a Crusader Movement (anti-Jihad movement)" (Berwick/Breivik 2011, section 3.12).

However, investigations by the prosecution cast substantial doubt on Breivik's assertions. At the time in question, he was traveling to London in connection with diamond transactions and to the Baltic area for money laundering. Reconstructions of his trips suggest he would not have had time for the organizational meetings he claimed took place and for which no other evidence exists (Ravndal n.d.). Examination of his Internet and social media use shows that he made no mention of plans for violent attacks prior to the events of July 2011 (Ravndal 2013). In sum, there is no reason to believe that a pan-European Knights Templar conspiratorial organization primed for a religious war was anything but a creation of Breivik's imagination. That makes all the more remarkable the events that occurred after Breivik's arrest. For to a considerable extent, the organization that did not exist outside his mind earlier, was, in effect, called into existence semi-spontaneously by his subsequent acts.

There is in all of this more than a little millenarian flavor: "The end time has begun...The goal of 7/22 [the date of Breivik's attacks] was to identify the Soldiers of Christ and to identify the Soldiers of the Beast" (The end time 2013). Those who are said to be Knights Templar are a motley bunch: Peter Mangs, a Swede who allegedly shot several immigrants in Malmo in 2009-10; Brunon Kwiecien, a Pole who wanted to detonate a car bomb outside the Polish Parliament; Vojtech Mlynek, a Czech who was planning both a combined bombing and shooting; and Pavlo Lapshyn, a Ukrainian living in Britain, who detonated bombs at mosques. The linkage made with Breivik varies and is often dependent on the eye of the beholder. In some cases, it appears that an individual may have been an admirer of Breivik. But in other cases someone's supposed membership in the Knights Templar is based on the slenderest of circumstantial evidence. Thus in the case of Pavlo Lapshyn: "Based on the evidence Lapshyn was most likely a Knights Templar. I base this on the media silence in combination with the miss-information [sic] that was spread by the media" (Lapshyn 2013).

So far as a Breivik conspiracy is concerned, therefore, there was almost certainly none before the July 22, 2011, attacks. Subsequently, however, a *constructed conspiracy* may be said to have come into existence. That is, supporters and admirers of Breivik re-conceptualized individual attacks by lone wolves as organizational attacks even if there had been no communication between the attackers and Breivik or any other persons. This re-conceptualization allowed those who believed in the war against Islam portrayed in Breivik's manifesto to think that the war is in progress and that its putative instrumentality—the Knights Templar—is in fact a functioning organization that spans European borders.

Of course, all conspiracy theories are, virtually by definition, constructed. They are assertions of fact (often untested or untestable), arranged to present a particular view of events. However, the use of conspiracy theory by Breivik partisans is two-fold. First, Breivik himself seems to have believed in an Islamic conspiracy to overwhelm and take over Europe, a view absorbed by self-proclaimed followers. Second, these followers believe that in order to defeat the alleged Islamic conspiracy, a covert, violent counter-conspiracy must wage war against it. This is the Knights Templar, the once mythical organization described by Breivik. His sympathizers now slot into that picture the various attempted and actual lone wolf attacks against immigrants in various parts of Europe that seem to qualify for inclusion. The result is a double construction, in which one phantom conspiracy is seen to be at war with another, but in which the actual evidence for either's existence is, to put it kindly, tenuous. Mattias Gardell argues that this dynamic was in fact what Breivik intended; that his description of the Knights Templar was "performative" in the sense that it was less a description than a design that was expected to eventually create what it described (Gardell 2014, 147).

Theories built around Breivik have links to the traditional theories of the pre-World War II past in their hostility towards Muslims and their fear that the West will be overwhelmed. Indeed, the very choice of "Knights Templar," echoing the Crusades, makes clear the conscious link with ancient inter-cultural warfare. They traffic in a faux-medievalism, seeking a return to a lost Europe of Christian dominance.

QAnon

QAnon first appeared in the United States in 2017. In a dramatic premier, on October 28, 2017, Q predicted the imminent arrest of Hillary Clinton as the beginning of Donald Trump's massive assault on the liberal "deep state." The prediction, of course, proved inaccurate, as did a number of subsequent predictions. The interrelated questions, then, are how QAnon survived the problem of cognitive dissonance, and how this quintessentially American phenomenon struck roots in other countries. The answer lies in three factors.

The first factor is Q's strategic movement away from specific predictions. In their place, he (the male pronoun seems justified inasmuch as the likeliest candidates are both men [Kirkpatrick 2022]) began to post increasingly vague and cryptic messages. Like those of the Delphic Oracle long ago, these could be read in various ways. Indeed, Q himself referred to them as "breadcrumbs"; that is, mere clues to some larger meaning. (Comprehensive Guide n.d.). The result has been the movement of content development from Q to his followers. It is they who must do the research, solve the puzzle, follow the crumbs. In the process, they have added all manner of lurid features to the original conception of a Trump counter-coup, including anti-Semitism, Satanism, child trafficking, molestation, and sacrifice.

The effect of this shift has been to empower Q's followers. They are called upon to make sense of Q's crumbs, to give them meaning by doing their own research, however that might be construed. This "crowd sourcing" (Argentino and Amarasingam 2021, 20) has opened the QAnon material to a vast array of conspiracist ideas, some only distantly related to the early posts from Q himself. This no doubt makes the movement attractive, especially outside the United States, inasmuch as it vests power in the rank-and-file. There has never been a QAnon organization or leadership.

The second factor encouraging international spread has been the linkage of QAnon with Covid-related themes. QAnon appears to be stimulated by hostility toward measures aimed at controlling the virus, such as masking, vaccination, and lockdowns (Argentino and Amarasingam 2021, 23). Since these issues have appeared in many countries, they provide an opening for the spread of QAnon internationally.

Finally, QAnon has been spread to nations such as Canada, Britain, Germany, Japan, and Australia through the conspiracy-friendly Omega Kingdom Ministries. Rather than operating through traditional ecclesiastical structures, the Ministries facilitates the creation of numerous small home congregations (Amarasingam and Argentino 2020, 39; Omega Kingdom Ministry).

Conspiracy belief and conspiracy scope

Although these cases have very different roots, they have all expanded across borders. They also share another similarity, namely, a link between their trans-national character and the investments believers make in them. If it can be shown that those in other countries also share one's own threat and view the world in comparably conspiracist ways, then despite scoffing and disbelief, one's perspective must in fact be correct. The heart of conspiracism lies in its claim to possess special knowledge, more valid and complete than that which circulates in the general culture. Consequently, its possessors see themselves as members of an elite.

Like many self-identified elites, conspiracy believers also often see themselves as persecuted by those who have allegedly been duped, brainwashed or coopted by the conspiracy. Hence conspiracists always live on a kind of knife-edge, at once claiming to possess powerful knowledge, but also believing themselves to be an embattled minority facing immensely powerful enemies. Their vision usually contains some ultimate, quasi-millenarian idea of future victory, but there is a suppressed undercurrent of fear that the conspiracy might somehow eventually prevail and overwhelm them.

QAnon is a case in point, particularly in its early days. It presented itself as the last hope against the power of the Deep State. Only the messianic leadership of Donald Trump could stave off the triumph of pedophilic, Satanist liberals, and produce the desired reign of virtue. Although the Trumpian cast of QAnon has been somewhat diluted in its later phases, the sense of an ultimate battle between good and evil remains.

In the meantime, while conspiracists remain an embattled minority, their contacts with non-believers are likely to be either unpleasant encounters or outright defeats. The three cases described above emphasize strategies for dealing with both. Sovereign Citizens have proven to be virtuosi in managing interactions with civil authorities. These relations have the potential for considerable unpleasantness, since Sovereigns reject the legitimacy of virtually all governments. They have sought to manipulate or sabotage the system in various ways: by utilizing false documents that appear to be official but are of their own creation; by questioning the legitimacy of officials by reference to arcane legal arguments; and by the mass filing of legal documents that have little substantive value but considerable capacity to bring routine bureaucratic operations to a temporary halt. Nonetheless, as has already been noted, Sovereign Citizens have also sometimes reacted to official inquiries with lethal violence. Yet Sovereign Citizen violence is an unintended byproduct of the interactions. Central to them are the Citizens' blizzard of paper, reflecting, as it were, an alternate legal universe.

The Breivik network has reacted differently to defeat, yet in a manner other, similar organizations have done in the past. They have begun to create a martyrology, with Anders Breivik himself at the center. Surrounding him are the numerous lone wolves whose usually bungled operations have placed them in the judicial systems of various European countries. Yet because theirs and Breivik's missions are seen as a holy cause, the collective defeats have been celebrated rather than mourned. Each individual effort to attack the conspiracy generates a new martyr, ironically if unconsciously mimicking the "martyrdom operations" of the jihadists they claim to fight.

In all the cases, some conspiracy theorists therefore come to eerily resemble their enemies. They seem to create, or at least to live in, a mental universe that is a mirror image of their adversaries. The greater the conspiracy's international sweep, the greater the potential for counter-conspiracists to create its reflection, whether on paper or in some organizational structure. The result—at least in the conspiracist psyche—is a bifurcated, Manichean world of good set against evil. All too often this is deemed to be the prelude to an eventual apocalyptic clash between the opposed forces. This logic explains the frequent linkage of conspiracy theories with millenarian beliefs, since millenarian belief systems so often include a final battle between good and evil before a perfect world emerges. To the extent that conspiracists act out these beliefs, this scenario will often trigger violent confrontations with the forces of political and social order. If this occurs, their predictions become self-fulfilling.

About the author

Michael Barkun is Professor Emeritus, Department of Political Science, Maxwell School, Syracuse University, Syracuse, NY. His books include *A Culture of Conspiracy: Apocalyptic Visions in Contemporary America*, *Religion and the Racist Right: The Origins of the Christian Identity Movement*, and *Chasing Phantoms: Reality, Imagination, and Homeland Security Since 9/11*. His current research interests include conspiracy theories, millennialism, and the white supremacist right.

References

Amarasingam, Amarnath and Mark Argentino. 2020. "The QAnon Conspiracy Theory: A Security Threat in the Making?" *CTC Sentinel* 13 (July 2020): 37–44.

Argentino, Marc and Amarnath Amarasingam. 2021. "They Got It All Under Control: QAnon Conspiracy Theories, and the New Threats to Canadian National Security." In *Stress Tested: The Covid-19 Pandemic and Canadian National Security*, edited by L. West, T. Joneau and A. Amarasingam, 15–32. Calgary, AB: University of Calgary Press. https://doi.org/10.1515/9781773852454-003

Barkun, Michael. 1997. *Religion and the Racist Right: The Origins of the Christian Identity Movement*. Revised edition. Chapel Hill, NC: University of North Carolina Press.

———. 2013. *A Culture of Conspiracy: Apocalyptic Visions in Contemporary America*. 2nd edition. Berkeley, CA: University of California Press.

Berwick, Andrew (pseud. Anders Behring Breivik). 2011. "2083: A European Declaration of Independence." London https://sites.google.com/site/knightstemplareurope/2083 (accessed March 18, 2014).

Festinger, Leon, Henry W. Riecken and Stanley Schachter. 1964 *When Prophecy Fails: A Social and Psychological Study of a Modern Group That Predicted the Destruction of the World*. New York: Harper.

Gardell, Mattias. 2014. "Crusader Dreams: Oslo 22/7, Islamophobia, and the Quest for a Monocultural Europe." *Terrorism and Political Violence* 26 (January-March 2014). https://doi.org/10.1080/09546553.2014.849930

Landes, Richard and Steven T. Katz, eds. 2012. *The Paranoid Apocalypse: A Hundred-Year Retrospective on The Protocols of the Elders of Zion*. New York: New York University Press.

Lapshyn, Pavlo (aka Pavel Lapshin). 2013. "The Knights Templar European Report." November 14, 2013. https://knightstemplareurope.wordpress.com/page/2/ (accessed December 16, 2013).

Miller, Edith Starr (aka Lady Queenborough). nd. *Occult Theocrasy* [sic]. Reprint, n.d. Los Angeles: Christian Book Club of America.

Ravndal, Jacob Aasland. 2012. "A Post-trial Profile of Anders Behring Breivik," Combating Terrorism Center at West Point. http://www.ctc.usma.edu/posts/a-post-trial-profile-of-anders-behring-breivik (accessed October 25, 2013).

———. 2013. "Anders Behring Breivik's use of the internet and Social Media," *Journal EXIT – Deutschland* Bd. 2 (2013). http://journals.sfu.ca/jed/index.php/jex/article/view/28 (accessed October 25, 2013)

Robertson, Pat. 1991. *The New World Order.* Dallas: Word.

Webster, Nesta H. *Secret Societies and Subversive Movements.* Reprint nd. Los Angeles: Christian Book Club of America.

Anonymous publications

"A Comprehensive Guide to QAnon, the Final Boss of Conspiracy Theories." https://www.vice.come/en_ca/article/ywex8v/what-is-qanon-conspiracy-theory (accessed June 19, 2018).

https://www.loveforlife.com.au (accessed November 1, 2013).

"Sovereign Citizens Movement." Southern Poverty Law Center. http://www.splcenter.org/get-informed/intelligence-files/ideology/sovereign-citizens-movement (accessed March 1, 2012).

"The end time has begun." The Commander Breivik Report, October 11, 2013. https://breivikreport.wordpress.com/ (accessed October 25, 2013).

The Lawless Ones: The Resurgence of the Sovereign Citizen Movement. Anti-Defamation League Special Report, August 9, 2010.

"What is the: Australian Sovereign Council? And what is it trying to achieve?" September 26, 2012. http://romstover.wordpress.com/2012/09/ (accessed October 11, 2013).

4

LOST CAUSE:
THE RISE AND FALL OF A SYMBOLIC CRUSADE MOVEMENT

DAVID G. BROMLEY

> New religious groups by their very nature pose some degree of challenge to the social order within which they emerge as they involve alternative ways of imagining and organizing. The sources of contention are some combination of movement provocation and societal control imposition. In a few cases, movement-societal conflict rises to the level of violence, in which each side concludes that peaceful coexistence is impossible. While there has been considerable research on the dynamics of such conflicts, there is less understanding of how movements that have been vanquished in battle with the forces of social control re-form, reorganize, and re-establish themselves. This chapter examines the loosely-coupled Lost Cause Movement following the end of Civil War hostilities. Three primary reconstitution tactics are identified: creation of an alternative social-cultural power base, narrative accounts challenging delegitmating depictions of slavery, and restoration of legitimacy through sacralization of southern culture. These tactics proved to be remarkably successful in repositioning the Confederate states over the next century.

While new religious and spiritual groups appear continuously in open societies, major periods of societal transformation are particularly favorable moments for the appearance of a set of movements precipitated by the unsettled times. They resist the changes attending the transformative moment and seek to re-establish a usually idealized version of the receding culture and social institutions that represent for them the "natural order of things." A variety of overlapping concepts have been employed to analyze these movements: moral crusades, symbolic crusades, social scares, moral panics, and culture wars (Bromley and Shupe 1981; Victor 1993; Gusfield 1986; Hunter 1992; Eder 1985). In the U.S., there have been several of these movements in recent history that have sought to combat "cults," "satanists," and, most recently, the "deep state." In this chapter,

I draw upon an earlier example, the Lost Cause Movement (LCM), to identify the core characteristics and strategies of these movements, which I shall analyze as symbolic crusades.

The emergence of the lost cause movement

Major social and cultural transformations are referred to here as destructuration/restructuration (elsewhere described by Gilles Deleuze and Félix Guattari as "deterritorialization–reterritorialization," Deleuze and Guattari 1977). These movements appear when traditional social and cultural moorings are upended and power relations across the social and institutional landscape are reconfigured. Individuals and groups impacted by such transformations are essentially living in two incompatible social worlds, with the former order receding and the emerging order enveloping their former way of life. Traditional ways of living and coping lose their legitimacy and effectiveness, and, at least for the most highly impacted segment of the social order, the connection between day-to-day life and the larger social order becomes more remote and opaque. The result is a sense of chaos and loss of control. This was precisely the situation in the years leading up to and during the U.S. Civil War. The result was what has been referred to as the Lost Cause Movement, which sought moral redress in the wake of not only military defeat but also social and cultural collapse.

Prior to the Civil War (1861–1865), the United States was hardly united. As Alan Taylor (2021) has observed, The U.S. was better understood through its history as "rival regions," exacerbated by an "ambiguous constitution." There was a significant and growing tension between North and South. The tensions centered around the interrelated issues of economic base and slavery. Even though the importation of slaves ceased in the early 1800s, this made the internal slave trade and natural increase in the domestic slave population even more important. The development of the cotton gin increased cotton production dramatically, creating the need for a larger, stable labor force, and the rapid development of industrializing cities in England, such as Manchester, represented a market for the produce (Stallard 2023; Younge 2023). The enormous profitability in a cotton-based economy created great wealth for some plantation owners, which served to further served to solidify the southern economy. The growth of the enslaved population necessary to support increased cotton production created potential instability as enslaved individuals came to constitute a majority of the total population in some areas of the South.

There was also North-South economic division between a developing urban-industrial order in the North and a rural-agrarian order in the South. So, for example, protective tariffs were in the interest of emerging northern industrial firms but not favorable to the southern economy based on exportation of agricultural products and imported manufactured goods. Efforts to diffuse mounting tensions were unsuccessful. For example, in the Nulification Crisis of 1833, tensions escalated sharply when Georgia refused to recognize new federal tariffs before a compromise was finally reached. In 1850, another compromise resulted in California being accepted into the Union as a free state; however, at the same time fugitive slave laws were strengthened and slave trade but not slave ownership was banned in Washington, D.C. Neither side was satisfied with these patchwork measures as the slavery question fundamentally impacted every other segment of the social order. A decisive moment occurred in 1860 when Abraham Lincoln was elected the sixteenth president of the United States and its first Republican. The Republican Party generally opposed the extension of slavery into U.S. territories. Signaling the deep political division in the nation, Lincoln was elected with less than forty percent of the popular vote and did not receive significant support in any state that would become part of the Confederacy. By the time Lincoln was inaugurated in March 1860, seven southern states had seceded, the Confederate States of America had been formed, and within a month the Civil War had commenced with the southern naval attack on Fort Sumter.

These various issues notwithstanding, in the North the core issue was culturally and legally embedded slavery, ownership of humans as property by other humans. That could not serve as a blueprint for an industrial economy. It would impact the functioning of every other institution, it would undermine the basic role of a constitutional republic (citizen), and it would delegitimate the moral underpinning of a nation presenting itself as in pursuit of a "more perfect union." For the South, a caste-like racial hierarchy was built into every aspect of life, and the economic engine of southern economies, the plantation system, could not be sustained absent a coercively organized labor force. By the time the Civil War began, there were around 4,000,000 slaves in the South. Southern states drew a line in the sand, insisting that states' rights were enshrined in the constitution and slavery was not explicitly prohibited. As Taylor has observed (2021, 146), slave labor was an "essential foundation" preserving the status of whites.

In the aftermath of the Civil War, the eleven secessionist states faced massive dislocation as a product of military defeat, mass loss of life (well over 300,000 military deaths and probably twice that number of total casualties), political submission, a no longer viable economy (an agricultural plantation system and captive labor force), infrastructure (roads, bridges, harbors, railway systems) that had collapsed, and a way of life that was in chaos. The North, by contrast, was largely spared war-related damage; its infrastructure remained intact. During the latter half of the nineteenth century there was a thoroughgoing transformation of the American social order as the industrial revolution, which began in the North, gained momentum, creating major urban centers, a rapidly expanding market economy, and increasing population diversity resulting from internal migration and external immigration. Indeed, by 1920 half of the American population lived in rapidly growing cities, making them centers of political and economic power. Urban-rural conflict intensified, both within and between states, as the political and economic power of urban centers rapidly expanded.

The year 1877 was a watershed with the implementation of the informal Compromise of 1877, which resolved an impasse in the 1876 presidential election, removed remaining federal control over southern states, and resulted in solid democratic dominance in the former states of the Confederacy. What followed was what has been referred to as the Jim Crow era in which racial segregation replaced slavery as a political form of control.

The rise of LCM

The end of military engagement did not redress North-South divisions. Lacking the capacity for continued large-scale armed resistance, the former Confederate states sought to reconstitute a power base. At the national level, the former Confederate states constituted a formidable minority coalition. The Supreme Court's 1896 acceptance of "separate but equal" in Plessy v Ferguson legitimated racial separation at the highest judicial level.

Following a decade long Reconstruction Period (1865-1877), the former states of the Confederacy replaced slavery with Jim Crow laws (segregation of all public facilities), increased voting restrictions (strict registration processes, poll taxes, literacy tests), and white control of state governments. For example, the state constitution in Virginia was amended in 1902 to impose poll taxes and require literacy and understanding provisions for voting eligibility. Mob violence and lynching functioned as an extra-legal mechanism. It is estimated that there were about 4,000 lynchings between 1877 and 1950 (Wolfe 2021; Equal Justice Initiative 2017). In addition, a coercively controlled labor force was buttressed by sharecropping and convict leasing (prison labor was exempted from the Thirteenth Amendment) to various commercial enterprises. These measures were punctuated by white mob violence. For example, just a year after Civil War hostilities ended, a mob attacked a black residential community in Memphis, Tennessee. The attack left forty-six residents dead, over seventy wounded, five women raped, twelve churches and four schools burned (Ash 2013). In May 1921, a white mob attacked an affluent black residential community in Tulsa, Oklahoma and left over 300 residents dead and the community in ruins. While institutionalized segregation recreated white political control, it did not produce legitimacy for a segregated, repressive social order. The South addressed the legitimacy issue through a loosely organized Lost Cause movement. This remarkably successful, largely symbolic movement sacralized southern culture and its armed resistance to "northern aggression." The South may have been subjugated militarily, but the Lost Cause narrative asserted that the South had in fact won a moral victory that demonstrated the superiority of its culture and way of life. While LCM projects were largely centered in the South, many were carried out elsewhere and had national impact. A loosely-coupled set of groups (United Daughters of the Confederacy, Confederate Memorial Literary Society, and United Confederate Veterans, Confederated Southern Memorial Association, Confederate Veterans, United Sons of Confederate Veterans) pursued a legitimation strategy both regionally and nationally.

The foundation of the LCM was the Lost Cause Narrative, which was constructed around three major components. First, the narrative asserted that the North-South conflict was not about *slavery* at all. Rather, secession was a constitutionally legitimate process, a protection of states' rights. The Civil War became a "war between the states" that was precipitated by "northern aggression." From this perspective the Civil War could be compared to the original American revolution, a struggle against tyranny. As one Confederate veteran put the matter, "If we cannot justify the South in the act of secession, we will go down in History solely as a brave, impulsive but rash people who attempted in an illegal manner to overthrow the Union of our Country" (Williams 2017). Indeed, if slavery could be defended on constitutional grounds, then the Civil War was a war of aggression and the South was illegally and immorally occupied by a northern military force.

Second, LCM mythology reinterpreted the meaning of slavery. In fact, slavery was benevolent and slaves were content with their status and faithful to their masters. They were not prepared to function as independent citizens and therefore were protected within plantations. There they could be civilized and Christianized, the objects of a southern religious mission. This position was reinforced through claims that slaves were siding with their owners in combat with Union forces (Levin 2019).

Third, Confederate soldiers were lionized as valiant and heroic defenders of their way of life, with General Robert E. Lee being its sanctified leader. He ascended to secular sainthood particularly following his death in 1870. Lee was included in a blanket pardon for supporters of the "insurrection" by President Andrew Johnson in 1868. Statues subsequently were erected across the country for Lee, with the premier location being on Monument Avenue in Richmond, Virginia. For their part, women in the Confederacy were saintly figures who made enormous sacrifices for the cause (Janney 2008, 2021). Women were particularly prominent and critical to the LCM since so many men were serving in the Confederate army or had been killed in battle.

Advancement of the LCM mythology was accomplished through several overlapping projects: comingling Confederate symbolism in sacred space in Christian churches, creating museums that presented the Confederate view of historical events, influencing the presentation of the South and the Civil war in library collections and school textbooks, and memorialization of Confederate leaders across the nation.

Churches were an important component of legitimating Lost Cause mythology. During the war, Jefferson Davis became a member of the congregation of St. Paul's Episcopal Church in Richmond, Virginia. Robert E. Lee also worshiped there. Most of the St. Paul's congregation at that time were involved in the slavery economy in some fashion as "the Episcopal church was the church of the antebellum planter class" (Wilson 2009, 35).

Confederate imagery continued to be represented in church sanctuaries across the south during the last half of the nineteenth century and the first half of the twentieth century. At St. Paul's, for example, it became popular during the 1890s to memorialize family members with wall plaques in the sanctuary, some of which featured Confederate battle flags (Kinnard 2017).

Museums created another means of narrating Lost Cause as an authentic presentation of historical events. As DeLucia (2018, 326) points out, museums constitute "memoryscapes," which she defines as "constellations of spots on the land that have accrued stories over time, transforming them from seemingly blank or neutral spaces into emotionally infused, politically potent places." The foremost museum, of course, was the Richmond museum that originated as the Confederate Museum (Coski 2021; Davenport 2019). Davenport reports that the early museum initially was closely linked to Lost Cause:

> Opened as the Confederate Museum in 1896, what later became the Museum of the Confederacy emerged directly from the Lost Cause propaganda machine, which itself had largely been steered from Richmond. Lost Cause organizations, like the all-female Confederate Memorial Literary Society, which funded and operated the Confederate Museum, campaigned to shift public opinion to a more sympathetic, pro-Confederate understanding of the South's "true" reasons for fighting the Civil War.

Other memorial museums were scattered around the nation, although predominantly in former Confederate states (Wilson 1980).

A major campaign by Lost Cause proponents was to control the secular presentation of the Civil War history in textbooks and library collections. Early in the twentieth century, the United Daughters of the Confederacy (UDC) and United Confederate Veterans (UCV) created a "Historical Committee," which had as its mission to combat both "long-legged Yankee lies" and to "select and designate such proper and truthful history of the United States, to be used in both public and private schools of the South," as well as to "put the seal of their condemnation upon such as are not truthful histories" (McPherson 2004, 87). Elements of the Lost Cause narrative continued to be represented in American popular culture and in educational materials well into the next century (Thompson 2013a, 2013b; Greenlee 2019; Coleman 2017). Indeed, by 1940 the Lost Cause narrative dominated textbooks throughout the U.S. (Ford 2017).

By far the most active and pervasive impact of LCM was achieved through various forms of memorialization: monuments, cemeteries, holidays, street and building names, and battle re-enactments that sacralized the Confederacy, its history and its leaders. Statues (and other forms of sculpting) were one of the most common means of memorialization (Anderson 1983; Hobsbawm and Ranger 1983). There have been well over 1,000 LCM-sponsored memorials of various kinds created in the United States since the end of the Civil War. These memorials have often been constructed using public funds and erected in public spaces. Memorials placed in public spaces presumptively represent and speak for the community. Palmer and Wessler (2018) report that between 2008 and 2018 over $40,000,000 of public funds was spent on such projects and the groups that organize them. Two of the most important projects were Stone Mountain outside of Atlanta Georgia and Monument Avenue in Richmond Avenue. Both were popular tourist attractions. Stone Mountain allowed KKK cross burnings through the early 1960s. It became a state park in 1958 and featured a 1972 carving of Robert E. Lee, Jefferson Davis, and Stonewall Jackson astride their horses (Lowery 2021). The U.S Postal Service issued a commemorative postage stamp in 1970. Richmond's Monument Avenue was a segregated upper-status residential development project in Richmond's West End. The first memorial statue, Robert E. Lee on his horse Traveller, was dedicated in 1890. Monuments subsequently were added to other military leaders of the Confederacy: J.E.B. Stuart and Jefferson Davis in 1907 and Stonewall Jackson in 1919. Special Confederate cemeteries were created as sacred space for fallen heroes.

The fall of LCM

Many elements of that remarkably successful southern heritage building, racial suppression system and Lost Cause narrative largely remained in place and unopposed until the 1960s when its social and political base began to erode. The overturning of Plessy in Brown v Board of Education in 1954 was followed by passage of the Civil Rights Act and Voting Rights Act in 1964 and 1965 and formation of a more active and assertive Civil Rights Movement.[1] A greater sense of urgency and a broader coalition emerged after 2010, particularly with the violent deaths of blacks at the hands of whites. In 2012, seventeen-year-old Trayvon Martin was killed by George Zimmerman in Florida. Zimmerman was subsequently acquitted of criminal charges. In 2013, the Black Lives Matter movement emerged, with Trayvon Martin's death as a major impetus. Martin's death was followed by the deaths of African Americans Eric Garner and Michael Brown Jr. in encounters with police the following year. 2015 was a flashpoint year as white teenager Dyllan Roof killed nine parishioners during a Bible study at the Emanuel African Methodist Episcopal Church in Charleston, South Carolina. Photographs later emerged of Roof, who was convicted of the crimes, carrying a Confederate flag. The murder of forty-six year-old George Floyd by police officer Derek Chauvin, who was convicted and incarcerated, added even greater momentum to an already inflamed situation.

The resistance to LCM that formed during this period resembled the LCM itself in its composition as a loosely-coupled movement. Some elements of the opposition were already functioning, some were new, and some incorporated race as an additional component of their work. Primary sources of opposition to LCM came from groups as diverse as police reform groups, museum "decolonization" groups, restorative justice groups, indigenous peoples rights groups, gun control groups, academic groups, and religious denominational groups. The overarching theme uniting these various projects was promotion of equal rights, diversity and inclusiveness.

The process of removing Confederate-themed symbols gathered momentum after 2010 with widespread removal of interior décor and renaming of public and private buildings, public streets, statues and monuments on public and private land, and public libraries (Anderson and Svrluga 2021). The most significant opposition formed around memorialization. Over 160 Confederate Symbols of all kinds were removed, renamed or relocated in 2020 following the murder of George Floyd that year. The total number of removals was greater than the four previous years combined. Because Virginia, and Richmond in particular, was a center of Lost Cause organization and activity, the growing opposition to Lost Cause was particularly visible there. In 1965, the City Planning Commission had described Monument Avenue as "a bridge from the past into the present" and proposed adding statues in 1965 (Black

---

1. Those de jure measures did not, of course, eliminate racial divisions such as segregation in schools.

and Varley 2003). By 1996, the city had dedicated a statue along the avenue to Arthur Ashe. In 2010, Virginia's governor renamed Confederate History Month to Civil War History Month. The Robert E. Lee statue on Monument Avenue was removed in 2021. That same year in neighboring Charlottesville the Lee statue was removed from a public park in the wake of a violent Unite the Right rally, killing one and injuring nineteen.

Other sites that celebrated Confederate history, such as museums and parks, were similarly impacted. Race became one element of the museum decolonization movement (which involves expanding the number of voices and traditions in displays and interpretations, particularly by reducing the influence of a white, colonial-based perspective) (Museum Association website 2023; Lonetree 2021; DeLucia 2018). For example, the most significant museum promoting the Lost Cause had been The Confederate Museum (later the Museum of the Confederacy). In 2013 it became The American Civil War Museum and was formed through a merger between the American Civil War Center and the Museum of the Confederacy. The earlier Lost Cause orientation of the museum was criticized both by the new museum itself and also in articles published in the prestigious Smithsonian Museum's periodical (Davenport 2019; Palmer and Wessler 2018). The Confederate memorial on Stone Mountain in Georgia went into steep tourist and financial decline after being a major tourist site since its origin. A KKK gathering permit request was denied in 2017. Georgia gubernatorial candidate Stacey Abrams made Stone Mountain a campaign issue, referring to the sculpture as a "blight upon our state" (Fausset 2018). By 2022 the site's viability was at best uncertain (Fausset 2018; *Shah* 2018; King and Buchanan 2020).

A number of religious denominations, primarily liberal leaning, have responded to their own histories of direct support for Lost Cause mythology or their implication in slaveholding. The Episcopal Church has been the most highly visible in this campaign as it established the National Cathedral in Washington, D.C. and St. Paul's Episcopal Church in Richmond, Virginia, which was popularly referred to as the "Cathedral of the Confederacy." In 2006, the General Convention of the Episcopal Church issued a resolution requesting that denominational churches, which are predominantly white and progressive, undertake studies of how they benefitted from the practice of slavery. The Episcopal Church followed this up in 2018 with a three-year audit of church leadership. St. Paul's was in the forefront of those efforts (St. Paul's n.d.). Other predominantly white denominations in several states followed suit, including the Presbyterian Church and the Evangelical Lutheran Church. Both passed resolutions (in 2004 and 2019, respectively) to study the denominations' role in slavery and have begun the process of determining how to make reparations.

Once the federal government had decided to pardon rather than criminally prosecute Confederate leaders following the end of armed hostilities, LCM activists successfully advocated for naming naval vessels and army bases in their honor. It became U.S. Army policy by 1917 to name bases on which troops were predominantly southern to be named after Confederate officers. One component of the de-memorialization movement was to rename military bases and naval vessels. The first renaming took place in 2023 when the U.S. Army base named for George E. Pickett was renamed in honor of Colonel Van Barfoot a Native American Medal of Honor recipient from World War II (Cameron 2023). That was closely followed by the renaming of Virginia's Fort Lee as Fort Gregg-Adams in honor of two Black officers who were pioneers in promoting racial inclusivity within the military (Olivo 2023).A number of colleges and universities across the U.S. and Britain have gone beyond statements of regret or apology to undertake reparation or restorative justice initiatives of various kinds. These diverse initiatives are intended to provide redress both for slavery and its long-term, continuing consequences for the institutions and for the descendants of slaves. In the U.S., for example, Brown University issued a report in 2004 that "made a number of recommendations, which included memorialising the past, creating a research centre for the study of slavery and providing support—financial and otherwise—to local communities negatively affected by Brown's past." Harvard University released a report in 2022 after three years of investigation that "pledged $100m (£80m) to carry out the report's recommendations, which included building relationships with the descendants of enslaved people who laboured within the university, or were enslaved by Harvard associates" (Otele 2023; Bromley 2021). The governor of Virginia signed legislation to establish the Enslaved Ancestors College Access Scholarship and Memorial Programs for five colleges and universities across the state, including the University of Virginia.

While there have been significant reversals for the LCM over the last decade, there has also been continued resistance that reflects the deep divisions in the contemporary U.S. For example, the remarkable pace of memorialization removal notwithstanding, many Confederate symbols remain in place and a number of states have taken steps to protect them against local removal actions (McGreevy 2021; Anderson and Svrluga 2021). A review of artwork in the Capitol showed that one-third depicted enslavers or Confederates (Brockell 2022). Eight busts of Confederate leaders, with two busts being selected by each state, remain in place in the U.S. Capitol. Correspondingly, at least thirty-six states, including all of the cessationist states, have taken steps to limit teaching material related to race and racism. By contrast, only seventeen states have expanded teaching material in these areas (Leonard 2022). A particular focal point has been attempts to control acceptance of critical race theory, which emerged in the 1970s as perspective to interpret institutional racism. This issue remains one of the most active areas of contestation.

Conclusions

Symbolic crusades like the LCM develop in different versions. As is the case for most new movements, many symbolic crusades have relatively brief lifespans as they constitute responses to shorter-term instability. More informative theoretically are longer term, more fully developed movements as they offer an opportunity to identify structural sources and developmental characteristics more clearly. LCM is particularly interesting because it has been unusually successful for a full century and its successes have been primarily of the symbolic variety. Based on an analysis of LCM history, several more general characteristics of longer-term movements of this type of movement emerge as indicators of long-term success and influence: moral positioning, oppositional organization, multi-centered organization, and appropriation of public space.

At the core of symbolic crusades is a campaign to simultaneously lower the moral standing of their opponents while elevating their own. Typically this involves an interactive escalation process that can lead to a sacralization-demonization dynamic. The LCM particularly emphasized sacralization of its own cause. In the LCM's telling, the South was the party which insisted on the inviolable rights of each state that were promised in the sacred governing document of the nation, and which took on the moral obligation of protecting, civilizing and Christianizing a backward race. This message of moral victory despite military defeat was intensely pursued through memorialization of Confederate heroes, placement of Confederate symbolism in church sanctuaries, presenting LCM historical accounts museums and educational institutions, and assuming the role of martyrs in battlefield re-enactments that became tourist attractions. Northerners were summarily dismissed as infidels, atheists, and an illegal occupying force.Moral crusades gain strength through unity in opposition. They simply bond around what they are against and deny alternatives. Denial is not simply forgetting elements of a complex history; it is a purposeful suppression of contradictions and discrediting information. The LCM's remarkable success, notwithstanding, there is convincing evidence that compromises the assertions in its narrative. For example, despite claims that the Civil War was fought over states' rights, slavery is presented as the reason for secession in several Confederate states' articles of secession. Black military units came to represent about ten percent of the Union forces and suffered heavy casualties; blacks were present in the Confederate military but were there as slaves in support roles. The claim that blacks were accepting of their status as slaves ignores the evidence of ongoing passive resistance, escape attempts, and organized rebellions.

Organizationally, successful moral crusades often contain multiple loosely-coupled entities that pursue group-specific objectives within the context of the broader movement. This was the case for the LCM with its memorial statue groups, museums, textbook lobbying groups, and veterans' groups. The constituent groups simply affirmed the central LCM tenet, the moral superiority of the southern cause and culture. This affirmation was not a policy position; it was a sacred totem that valorized their culture. This oppositional strategy has had the added benefit of allowing the LCM to add allies and incorporate new issues as opportunities have presented themselves.

A key measure of the success of moral crusades is their ability to not only pursue their objectives but also to create a legitimate public presence. The LCM was extraordinarily successful in not simply creating memorials but in placing Lost Cause symbolism in the public domain: public parks and squares, government grounds and in buildings, on the signage for army bases and naval vessels, in church sanctuaries. There are few, if any, other cases in which leaders of organized, armed opposition to the United States are widely celebrated in public spaces.

Perhaps the most impressive indicator of LCM success is its continuation in the currently polarized environment in the U.S., albeit in a somewhat more subterranean form. The calls for secession, insurrection, voting restrictions, white-Christian privilege, which now are found in the QAnon movement, all contain echoes of the past. These themes offer convincing evidence that the U.S. continues to experience a new iteration of a destructuration-restucturation process that began over a century ago.

About the author

David G. Bromley is Founder/Director of the World Religions and Spirituality Project (https://wrldrels.org) and Professor of Religious Studies at Virginia Commonwealth University in Richmond, Virginia. His primary interest is in the emergence, organization, and development of contemporary religious and spiritual movements. His most recent work is on Q'Anon and related conspiracy theory-based movements.

References

Anderson, Benedict. 1983. *Imagined Communities*. London: Verso.

Anderson, Nick and Susal Syrluga. 2021. "From slavery to Jim Crow to George Floyd: Virginia universities face a long racial reckoning." *Washington Post*, November 26. https://www.washingtonpost.com/education/2021/11/26/virginia-universities-slavery-race-reckoning/?utm_campaign=wp_local_headlines&utm_medium=email&utm_source=newsletter&wpisrc=nl_lclheads&carta-url=https%3A%2F%2Fs2.washingtonpost.com%2Fcar-ln-tr%2F356bfa2%2F61a8b7729d2fdab56bae50ef%2F597cb566ae7e8a6816f5e930%2F9%2F51%2F61a8b7729d2fdab56bae50ef

Ash, Stephen. 2013. *A Massacre in Memphis: The Race Riot That Shook the Nation One Year After the Civil War*. New York: Hill and Wang.

Blight, David W. 2001. *Race and Reunion: The Civil War in American Memory*. Boston, MA: Harvard University Press. https://doi.org/10.4159/9780674022096

———. 2002. *Beyond the Battlefield: Race, Memory, and the American Civil War*. Amherst: University of Massachusetts Press.

Brockell, Gillian. 2022. "Art at Capitol honors 141 enslavers and 13 Confederates. Who are they?" *Washington Post*, December 27. https://www.washingtonpost.com/history/interactive/2022/capitol-art-slaveholders-confederates/?itid=mr_4

Bromley, Anne. 2021. "New Law, Signed at UVA, Focuses on Reparations for Descendants of Enslaved Workers." *UVAToday*, May 5. https://news.virginia.edu/content/new-law-signed-uva-focuses-reparations-descendants-enslaved-workers#main-content

Bromley, David and Anson Shupe. 1981. *Strange Gods: The Great American Cult Scare*. Boston, MA: Beacon Press.

Cameron, Chris. 2022. "How Army Bases in the South Were Named for Defeated Confederates." *New York Times*, December 2. https://www.nytimes.com/2022/12/02/us/politics/army-base-names-south-confederates.html?login=email&auth=login-email

———. 2023. "Army Base Renamed for Native American War Hero, Replacing Confederate." *New York Times*, March 24. https://www.nytimes.com/2023/03/24/us/politics/army-base-pickett-barfoot.html on 10 April 2023.

Coleman, Arica. 2017. "The Civil War Never Stopped Being Fought in America's Classrooms. Here's Why That Matters." *Time*, November 8. https://time.com/5013943/john-kelly-civil-war-textbooks/

Davenport, Andrew. 2019. "A New Civil War Museum Speaks Truths in the Former Capital of the Confederacy." *Smithsonian Magazine*, May 2. https://www.smithsonianmag.com/history/civil-war-museum-speaks-truths-former-capital-of-confederacy-180972085/

DeLucia, Christine. 2018. *Memory Lands: King Philip's War and the Place of Violence in the Northeast.* New Haven, CT: Yale University Press. https://doi.org/10.12987/yale/9780300201178.001.0001

Domby, Adam. 2020. *The False Cause: Fraud, Fabrication, and White Supremacy in Confederate Memory.* Charlottesville: University of Virginia Press. https://doi.org/10.2307/j.ctvvsqcqb

Eder, Klaus. 1985. "The "New Social Movements": Moral Crusades, Political Pressure Groups, or Social Movements?" *Social Research* 52: 869–890.

Equal Justice Initiative. 2017. *Lynching in America: Confronting the Legacy of Racial Terror.* Equal Justice Initiative. https://eji.org/reports/lynching-in-america/

Fausset, Richard. 2018. "Stone Mountain: The Largest Confederate Monument Problem in the World." *The New York Times*, October 18. https://www.nytimes.com/2018/10/18/us/stone-mountain-confederate-removal.html

Ford, Matt. 2017. "What Trump's Generation Learned About the Civil War." *The Atlantic*, August 28. https://www.theatlantic.com/education/archive/2017/08/what-donald-trump-learned-about-the-civil-war/537705/

Deleuze, Gilles and Félix Guattari. 1977. *Capitalism and Schisophrenia.* New York: Viking.

Greenlee, Cynthia. 2019. "How history textbooks reflect America's refusal to reckon with slavery." *Vox*, August 26. https://www.vox.com/identities/2019/8/26/20829771/slavery-textbooks-history

Gusfield, Joseph. 1986. *Symbolic Crusade: Status Politics and the American Temperance Movement.* Urbana: University of Illinois Press.

Hobsbawm, Eric and Terence Ranger, eds. 1983. *The Invention of Tradition.* Cambridge: Cambridge University Press.

Hunter, James Davison. 1992. *Culture Wars: The Struggle To Control The Family, Art, Education, Law, And Politics In America.* New York: Basic Books.

King, Michael and Christopher Buchanan. 2020. "'I'm in your house' | Armed group condemns systemic and overt racism, marches to Stone Mountain." *11 Alive*, July 4. https://www.11alive.com/article/news/local/stone-mountain/group-of-demonstrators-enter-stone-mountain-park/85-2ea0c153-8a88-46bd-bca7-faf19ec2c8ba

Kinnard, Meg. 2017. "Episcopalians struggle with history of Confederate symbols." *Associated Press*, September 18. https://gettvsearch.org/lp/prd-best-bm-msff?source=google display&id_encode=187133PWdvb2dsZS1kaXNwbGF5&rid=15630&c=10814666875&placement=www.whsv.com&gclid=EAIaIQobChMIl6eUipjp8wIVVcLhCh3mbgFkEAEYASAAEgIG4vD_BwE

Leonard, Bill. 2022. "'The Religion of the Lost Cause' is back, and it may be winning." *Baptist News*, May 13. https://baptistnews.com/article/the-religion-of-the-lost-cause-is-back-and-it-may-be-winning/#.YsHo1OzMIQY

Lonetree, Amy. 2021. "Decolonizing Museums, Memorials, and Monuments." *The Public Historian* 43: 21–27. https://doi.org/10.1525/tph.2021.43.4.21

Lowery, Malinda Maynor. 2021. "The Original Southerners: American Indians, the Civil War, and Confederate Memory." https://www.southerncultures.org/article/the-original-southerners/

McPherson, James. 2004. "Long-Legged Yankee Lies: The Southern Textbook Crusade." In *The Memory of the Civil War in American Culture*, edited by Alice Fahs and Joan Waugh, 64–78. Chapel Hill: University of North Carolina Press.

Olivo, Antonio. 2023. "U.S. Army renames Fort Lee in Virginia after two Black former officers." *Washington Post,* April 27. https://www.washingtonpost.com/dc-md-va/2023/04/27/fort-lee-rename-gregg-adams/

Otele, Olivette. 2023. "More than money the logic of slavery reparations." *The Guardian,* March 31. https://www.theguardian.com/news/ng-interactive/2023/mar/31/more-than-money-the-logic-of-slavery-reparations?utm_term=64394042d78d113cf0217ca8b19f6d44&utm_campaign=GuardianTodayUS&utm_source=esp&utm_medium=Email&CMP=GTUS_email

Palmer, Brian and Seth Freed Wessler. 2018. "The Costs of the Confederacy." *Smithsonian Magazine,* December. https://www.smithsonianmag.com/history/costs-confederacy-special-report-18

Pennyfarthing, Aldous. 2023. "Mississippi's GOP governor signs Confederate Heritage Month proclamation and dates it … April 31." *Daily Kos,* April 5. https://www.dailykos.com/stories/2023/4/5/2162217/-Mississippis-GOP-governor-signs-Confederate-Heritage-Month-proclamation-and-dates-it-April-31

Rawls, Margaret. 2017. *The Nature and Life of Contested History and Memorials: The Story of Charlottesville.* Charlottesville: University of Virginia.

Shah, Khushbu. 2018. "The KKK's Mount Rushmore: the problem with Stone Mountain." *The Guardian,* October 24. https://www.theguardian.com/cities/ng-interactive/2018/oct/24/stone-mountain-is-it-time-to-remove-americas-biggest-confederate-memorial

Stallard, Matthew. 2023. "Cotton Capital how slavery made Manchester the world's first industrial city." *The Guardian,* April 3. https://www.theguardian.com/news/ng-interactive/2023/apr/03/cotton-capital-how-slavery-made-manchester-the-worlds-first-industrial-city

St. Paul's Episcopal Church. n.d. "History and Reconciliation Initiative." https://www.stpaulsrva.org/HRI

Tarter, Brent. 2020. *Virginians and Their History.* Charlottesville: University of Virginia Press. https://doi.org/10.2307/j.ctvxkn6m7

Taylor, Alan. 2021. *American Republics: A Continental History of the United States, 1783–1850*. New York: W. W. Norton.

Thompson, Tracy. 2013a. *The New Mind of the South*. New York: *Simon & Schuster.*

———. 2013b. "The South still lies about the Civil War." *Salon*, March 16. https://www.salon.com/2013/03/16/the_south_still_lies_about_the_civil_war/

Victor, Jeffrey S. 1993. *Satanic Panic: The Creation of a Contemporary Legend*. Chicago, IL: Open Court.

Wolfe, Brendan. 2021. "Lynching in Virginia." In *Encyclopedia Virginia.* https://encyclopediavirginia.org/entries/lynching-in-virginia

Younge, Gary. 2023. "Lest we remember how Britain buried its history of slavery." *The Guardian*, March 29. https://www.theguardian.com/news/ng-interactive/2023/mar/29/lest-we-remember-how-britain-buried-its-history-of slavery?utm_term=64242849853c521d88f67112663d047a&utm_campaign=GuardianTodayUS&utm_source=esp&utm_medium=Email&CMP=GTUS_email

5

BY THE CLEANSING FLAMES OF FIRE: QUR'AN BURNINGS, RACIALIZED RELIGION AND POLITIZED NOSTALGIA IN SWEDEN

MATTIAS GARDELL

> This chapter focuses on the burning of the Qur'an and the Hebrew Bible and the relation between bibliocaust and holocaust. I will begin with the recent series of Qur'an burnings in Sweden and then revisit history, from the ceremonial Qur'an burnings in Grenada 1499 via the Nazi bonfires of 1933 back to our time and show how book burnings throughout this history have been used as a way of ridding society of the evil these books were seen as associated with and how this frequently included the people who read and cherished these books.

Between 2020 and 2023 ethnonationalist Rasmus Paludan staged more than one hundred public Qur'an burnings across Sweden, predominantly in areas with a visible Muslim population. Explicitly designed to denigrate Islam and Muslims that Paludan wanted to cleanse from society, the Qur'an burnings were celebrated in the anti-Muslim milieu, protected by the police, and seen as a "right" important to "defend" by mainstream politicians and media. Unsurprisingly, the Qur'an burnings were met by protests from the street, some of which turned into violent clashes with the police, which culminated in the "Easter Riots" of 2022. The public Qur'an burnings affected the national elections of 2022, won by a coalition of rightwing parties, the largest of which was the Sweden Democrats, a reformed national socialist party previously considered too extreme to cooperate with by all mainstream parties in the *Riksdag* (the Swedish Parliament). In the Spring of 2023 unease spread as the Qur'an burnings seemed to jeopardize Sweden's application for NATO membership by strengthening Turkey's President Recep Tayyip Erdoğan's effort to block Sweden from entry.

Typically treated in public debate as unprecedented singular events without history and richer political significance, the meaning of the public Qur'an burnings in Sweden is treated herein by situated them in the history of book burnings in the West and the transforming political realities of Swedish society. The final analysis agrees with William Faulkner (1951), "The past is not dead. It's not even past."

The history of book burnings

"Books are sacred to free men for very good reasons," Kurt Vonnegut (1973) wrote in a letter, pointing out that "wars have been fought against nations which hate books and burn them." The letter was addressed to Mr. (Charles) McCarthy, chairman of the school board at Drake High School in North Dakota that had demanded that all copies of Vonnegut's antiwar classic *Slaughterhouse-Five* (1969), used in the school's English class, should be seized and burned in the school furnace as "obscene." The war Vonnegut referred to was the Second World War in which he served in the US Army deployed in Europe until he was captured by the Germans in the Battle of the Bulge and detained in a forced labor camp in Dresden housed in an old slaughterhouse, *Schlachthof-fünf* (Slaughterhouse 5), where he survived the devastating bombing of Dresden at the end of the war by hiding in an underground meat locker.

The burning of books Vonnegut called attention to was the public bonfires of "harmful" literature that symbolized the aim of the National Socialist regime to resurrect the Aryan racial nation, cleansed from "un-German" elements. In April 1933, the German Student Union (*Deutsche Studentenschaft*) that had come under the influence of the National Socialist German Students' League (*Nationalsozialistischer deutscher Studentenbund*), launched a "campaign of enlightenment" against "cultural Bolshevism" and "Jewish intellectualism." The campaign would commence by purging the universities and public libraries from "corrosive" literature and end in a series of book burning spectacles, extensively covered by the media and praised by politicians and nationalist members of faculty as "courageous" (Lewy 2016).

In 1933, ninety-three public book burnings were staged in seventy German cities across the country, with a peak of thirty-four on May 10. Arguably, the most spectacular book burning that day was organized in Berlin, and covered by national radio and cinematic newsreel. The day of May 10 began with the inaugural lecture of Alfred Bäumler, recently installed Professor of Political Pedagogy at the Friedrich-Wilhelm University of Berlin, urging the students to spearhead the cleansing of the Academy from the corrupt Literati by burning un-German books. That evening, a torchlight parade of students protected by the police marched alongside trucks carrying some 20,000 books of "condemned titles" to be handled by the flames of the bonfire at the Opera Square, among these works by Karl Marx, Sigmund Freud, Heinrich Mann, Karl Kautsky, Bertolt Brecht, Franz

Kafka, Erich Maria Remarque, Emil Ludwig, Heinrich Heine, Erich Kästner, Albert Einstein, and Ernest Hemingway (Lewy 2016; Whitfield 2002).

"The era of extreme Jewish intellectualism is now at an end," Joseph Goebbels, newly appointed Minister of Popular Enlightenment and Propaganda, declared in his *Feuerrede* ("fire speech") to the assembled crowd of some 40,000 onlookers. "The future German man will not just be a man of books, but a man of character!" Turning to the students, Goebbels exclaimed, "You do well in this midnight hour to commit to the flames the evil spirit of the past. This is a strong, great and symbolic deed ... From this wreckage the Phoenix of a new spirit will triumphantly rise" (Goebbels 1933).

The campaign of 1933 was not the end of book burnings in National Socialist Germany. The next major outburst came on November 9 and 10, 1938, now explicitly focused on Jewish sacred scripture, the Hebrew Bible and the Torah scrolls. The burning of the Hebrew Bible was a key element of the Kristallnacht pogroms that often is overlooked in later descriptions of the events, as pointed out by Alon Confino (2012, 2014). In hundreds of communities, not only in the big cities, but also small rural towns, the public desecration and destruction of the Jewish holy scripture by fire and other means was at the center of the Kristallnacht. "Key players were often children," Confino observes. "By allowing children to act in ways that go beyond the constraints of accepted cultural norms and behavior, adults reveal much about their own mentality." In Lichtenfels, children played football with the Jewish prayer book; in Fritzlar, Torah scrolls were rolled out on the streets for Hitler Youth to ride their bicycles on; in Berlin, children marched with shredded Torah scrolls as hats before an adult audience laughing and pointing; in Vienna's Jewish quarter, cheering spectators assembled to see children burning a pile of Arks and Torah scrolls brought out from ransacked synagogues (Confino 2012, 370).

A further transgression of previous norms of civilized decency was the public humiliation of Jewish people by forcing them to partake in the ceremonial elimination of what symbolized themselves. In Fürth, local Jews were brought to the synagogue in the middle of the night and forced to sing *Horst Wessel* and listen to the rabbi reading from *Mein Kampf*. They were then taken to the main square to watch local National Socialists hang the Torah scrolls on a pole and set the installation aflame. In Frankfurt, Jews were forced to tear the Torah in pieces and burn them; in Vienna, Jews were dressed in the ruined curtains of the Torah Ark and chased around the town with shredded Torah scrolls tied to their backs (Confino 2012).

Throughout the history of antisemitism is a glowing chain of burning books valued by Jews. "To wish this people ill was often expressed by incriminating, desecrating, and incinerating the books that Jews studied and cherished," Stephen J. Whitfield (2002, 2013) notes in his study of the role and function of book burnings in the history of antisemitism. "To set their sacred texts on fire was a way of accelerating the disappearance or extinction of those who read such works." Whitfield shows that there is an "intimate connection" between burning books and burning people. It rarely stopped by the burning of books. "That was only the prelude," Heinrich Heine wrote in 1823. "Where they burn books, they will ultimately burn humans too."[1]

Heine was one of the authors whose work was condemned to fire by the National Socialists in May 1933. His now famous words did not refer to book burnings foreboding anti-Jewish pogroms, but to the first major ceremonial Qur'an burning in history, in Granada 1499. Heine's tragedy *Almansor* (1823) is set after the fall of Granada 1492 during the *reconquista*, after which Spain became Catholic by excluding Jews and Muslims as inferior "races" (*razas*) of defiled blood (Hering Torres *et al.* 2012; Heng 2018; Geer *et al.* 2007). The protagonist Almansor escaped Granada before its fall, but clandestinely returns to search for Zuleima, the love of his life. He meets Hassan, the family's old servant, who tells him of the plight of the Moors after their forced conversion to Christianity. Learning about the public burning of the Qur'an, Almansor draws the gloomy conclusion cited above. Hassan informs him that his beloved Zuleima had been forcibly converted to Donna Clara and set to marry a Catholic nobleman. Alarmed, Almansor continues his search and finds Zuleima, who had believed him dead. The reunited young lovers make a daring escape on the day of Zuleima's wedding. They are spotted and pursued in a dramatic flight up the mountains that eventually ends at the edge of a huge ravine. With the shouting pursuers approaching, Almansor and Zuleima throw themselves over the cliff, perpetuating their love in death.[2]

To Heine, the doomed love of Almansor and Zuleima reflects the wider tragedy of the end of Moorish civilization and the *convivencia* of Muslims, Jews, and Christians in al-Andalus (Schonfield 2018). Following the fall of Granada in 1492, the Catholic monarchs Queen Isabel I of Castile and King Ferdinand II of Aragon issued an edict expelling all Jews who did not convert to Christianity from the territory they controlled. According to the Treaty of Granada, the integrity of the Moorish community was to be respected, and their mosques, laws and traditions preserved, in exchange

---

1. "*Das war ein Vorspeil nur. Dort, wo man Bücher verbrennt, verbrennt man am Ende auch Menschen.*"
2. In a further twist, the pursuers are not enemies but family who had called off the wedding when learning Almansor is alive.

for their allegiance to the Crown. The agreement was broken when Cardinal Ximénes de Cisneros, Queen Isabel's Confessor, was named Archbishop of Toledo and Grand Inquisitor of Granada. Horrified by Moorish presence on land sanctified as Christian, Cisneros in 1499 ordered the public burning of the Qur'an in Granada's market plaza. The affront provoked popular protest that was crushed by Christian soldiers in a commotion during which one of Cisneros' strongmen was killed. Enraged, Cisneros ordered the public mass burning of every Qur'an his armed forces could find in Granada's libraries, mosques, and homes, an estimated 5,000 volumes, an outrage that led to the first major Moorish rebellion.[3] Revoking the Treaty, the State banned Islam. In 1501, the Moors in Granada were given the choice between exile, conversion to Christianity, and death; an edict extended to all Moors in Castile 1502, Valencia 1525 and Aragon 1526 (Alaoui 2002; Boase 2002).

With the Purity of Blood Statues, first established in Toledo 1449 and extended throughout Spain in the 1500s, religion was further racialized by laws differentiating between a privileged race of pure-blooded Christians, and inferior races of impure Muslim or Jewish blood, named Moriscos and Marranos. Fearing that *conversos* and their descendants may secretly uphold Muslim or Jewish traditions, the regime established the Spanish Inquisition—which was a secular authority controlled by the State, not the Church—to interrogate suspected stealth Muslims and Jews by torture. A series of laws to enforce Christian homogeneity followed, banning the Muslim headscarf, Muslim holidays, bathhouses, festivals, traditions and music. In 1567, Arabic and Andalusi Arabic was prohibited in all forms, formal or informal, written or spoken, at home or in public. Moriscos were given three years to learn a Christian language, after which possession of books in Arabic was criminalized, and discovered texts publicly burned, which provoked a new rebellion[4] (Sicroff 1985; Perry 2005; Burk 2010, 2017).

No measure of enforced enculturation was enough to ease the administration's concern with its Morisco population. Fearing that Moriscos sought to replace Spain's pure-blooded Christian race by multiplying and conspiring with the Saadi or Ottoman Sultanates, King Felipe III in 1609 decided to expel the whole Morisco population, many of whom had been Christians for generations. Hundreds of thousands of Christians of Muslim "background" were forcibly expelled from the Catholic Monarchy between the years 1609–1614. In 1611, the Spanish envoy to the Holy See, Dominican friar Damián Fonseca, referred to the "just expulsion" of the Moriscos as *el agradable holocausto*, ("the pleasant burnt offering to God, completely

---

3. The First rebellion of the Alpujarras 1499–1501
4. The Second rebellion of the Alpujarras 1568–1571.

consumed by sacrificial fire"). Arguably the first time the term *holocaust* was used as a euphemism for genocide and racial cleansing of a territory claimed by a dominant group as its homeland, Fonseca saw the shedding of blood of racialized others as a cleansing act of repentance to avert the wrath of God for having allowed the followers of "the sect of Mahoma" to corrupt lands marked by conquest as Catholic and Spanish (García Arenal and Wiegers 2013; Jónsson 2007; Fonseca 1612).

Granada shows the connection between *bibliocaust* and *holocaust*, linking the desire to eliminate the culture of a stigmatized people to the desire of eliminating the people as such. Book burnings express an intention to eradicate the evil the burned text is held to contain, which historically has included the people associated with the book condemned to fire. This aspect was not lost to the instigator of the Qur'an burnings in Sweden 2020–2023 and their target, people in Sweden's already vilified Muslim community.

Cleansing the unwanted: Qur'an burnings as racist spectacle

The Qur'an burnings in Sweden were designed by the main instigator, Rasmus Paludan to attract national attention for himself and his vision of a world without Muslims. "The enemy is Islam and Muslims," Paludan (2018) said. "The best thing would be if there were not a single Muslim left on this earth."

In 2017, Paludan, already a lawyer convicted of hate crimes and reprimanded for violating the code of conduct of the Danish Bar and Law Society (Toft 2019; Retten 2020; Søndberg 2019), was expelled from the New Right (*Nye Borgerlige*) when his speech at a *For Frihed* (Danish PEGIDA) rally against the Great Replacement surfaced. "Our streets and alleys will be transformed to rivers of blood," Paludan shouted, "and the blood of the alien enemies will end in the sewer where it belongs" (Søgaard and Bloch 2017; Karker 2019). "*Rivers of blood*" refers to Enoch Powell's famous speech against non-white immigration to Britain, and the *Great Replacement* to the narrative that the "native" (white) populations of the global North currently are being replaced by non-white, predominantly Black and Muslim, "invaders"; both classic references in the radical nationalist milieu. In different versions, the Great Replacement has been recycled since the late nineteenth century, and reuses imaginaries rooted in post-reconquista Spain (Gardell 2021). The importance of the Great Replacement theory to radical nationalism was (re)discovered by mainstream media when the diverse digital underground of post-45 fascism and militias left their social media platforms to march under the motto *You Will Not Replace Us* in the Unite the Right rally in Charlottesville, Virginia, 2017.

Ousted from the New Right, Paludan opened shop of his own. His Hard Line (*Stram Kurs*) party centered on prohibiting Islam and expelling Muslims and non-Westerners from Denmark (*Politisk grundlag* 2019; *Udlændinge* 2019). The Hard Line campaign in the national elections of 2019 was based on livestreamed racist provocations, a technique here called *The Racist Spectacle*, staged in low-income, low-status areas with a high concentration of Muslim and Black residents, in Denmark known as "ghettoes." Knowing that YouTube's algorithms privileged videos with extreme and sensationalist content, later confirmed in several studies (Ledwich and Zaitsev 2019; Horta Ribeiro *et al.* 2020), the Spectacle followed a certain pattern. Introducing himself as "Rasmus Paludan, the Soldier of Freedom, the Protector of the Weak, the Guardian of Society, the Light of Denmark, the Hope of the Nordic,"[5] Paludan livestreamed himself hurling racist slurs at Muslims and Blacks, denigrating the Prophet Muhammad, and spitting on the Qur'an, throwing it to the ground, kicking it around, wrapping it in bacon, setting it aflame. Styled as "transgressive," the Racist Spectacle reenacted assaults of people already trampled upon in racist opinion, using offended residents held back by the police as part of the show. Cross-posted on social media platforms, including YouTube, Instagram, Facebook, Snapchat, and TikTok, Paludan's racism-as-entertainment videos attracted tens of millions of viewers, more than all the campaign videos of all other parties combined (Gjerding and Dahlin 2019). A key ingredient was Paludan's use of children, a detail reminiscent of the role of children during the transgressive public Torah scroll burnings in Germany 1938. In a trending YouTube film twelve young teenage boys gather around Paludan as he burns the Qur'an, cheerfully singing "They shall not be integrated; they shall go home" to the tune of the *She'll be comin' around the mountain* (Shakir 2019).

Taking the Racist Spectacle to at least forty-five locations, Paludan's election campaign peaked in the culturally diverse Nørrebro district of Copenhagen on Palm Sunday 2019. Staged a month after Brenton Tarrant brought renewed attention to the Grand Replacement narrative by livestreaming his massacre on Muslims in Christchurch, New Zealand, March 15, 2019, and distributing his *Great Replacement* manifesto, the Racist Spectacle provoked protests that turned into violent clashes with the police, and press coverage was immense. With 63,000 votes (1.79%), Paludan fell short of the two percent bar to the Danish parliament but found the keys to national attention. Discovered by Swedish media too, with ten to twenty articles on Paludan a day since the Copenhagen riots (Retriever Research

---

5. Jeg er Rasmus Paludan. Frihedens soldat, de svages beskytter, samfundets vogter, danernes lys, Nordens håb

2023), Paludan understood that the Racist Spectacle would work as easily across the Sound separating Denmark and Sweden.

Teaming up with hate-crime-convicted National Socialist "street artist" Dan Park (Gardell 2015a; Park 2009; Expo 2020), Paludan in August 2020 announced he would burn the Qur'an in Malmö but was denied entry. A handful of supporters followed through on their own, first burning the Qur'an in the low-income, low-status area of Rosengård, and then moving the Spectacle to a second location; now playing football with the Qur'an at a downtown square. As in Nørrebro, protests transformed into clashes with the police (Herkel and Brundin 2020), and Paludan vowed to continue (Stram Kurs 2020).

In October 2020, Paludan launched the Church of Saint James, the Muslim Slayer (*Sankt Jakob Maurerdræberens Kirke*), named after *Santiago Matamoros*, the Patron Saint of Spain, who according to legend is James the Great (Santiago in Spanish; Jakob in Danish/Swedish), one of the Twelve Apostles of Jesus the Christ, and the first Christian martyr. During the Spanish *reconquista*, the legend goes, James the Great miraculously reappeared as a heavenly fighter to assist the crusaders in cleansing Spain from Muslims, thus earning the epithet Muslim Slayer. It is precisely this capacity that makes him venerable to Paludan. "We are inspired by Saint James, who drew his sword when necessary. So, it's a bit of a crusade" (Christoffersen 2020). The Church, in which Paludan is Archbishop, is part of the Racist Spectacle with online "worship services." It allows Paludan to construe his mission in terms of a "crusade" and a "new reconquista," a claim familiar to actors in the wider radical nationalist milieu. "The crusades refuse to remain in the past," Horswell and Awan (2019) observe in their study of the ways in which crusading rhetoric frame and justify political violence in the present. Similarly, the concept of reconquista has returned as a call to purge "white territories" from Muslim "invaders." "There will only be two options" for white Europeans, identitarian alt-right ideologue Guillaume Faye (2016) says: "our historic disappearance, or a *reconquista*." "Muslims will be expelled from Europe yet again after major bloodshed and millions of dead across the continent," Anders Behring Breivik (2011, 741) the "Knights Templar Crusader" stated in the call to arms he distributed on the day of his 22/7 terror attacks in Norway. Ethnonationalist Brenton Tarrant (2019, 50) echoes: "Remove the invaders, retake Europe."

Seeking the best place from where to launch the reconquista, Paludan first opted for France, Belgium and Germany but was everywhere detained, kicked out or banned. He then decided to retry Sweden. To pave the way, Paludan applied for Swedish citizenship, which was granted in October 2020 on the grounds that his father was Swedish. He then became a member of the ethnonationalist Alternative for Sweden, a party obsessed with the Great Replacement that seeks to forcibly expel people of Muslim, African, and Roma "background" (AFS 2018, 2022). Paludan was now all set to "help the Swedish people" (Åkesson and Nordblad 2020).

Bringing the Racist Spectacle to Sweden

When Paludan brought the Racist Spectacle to Sweden, he took it to a society seeking to understand its transformation from the most equal to one of the more unequal societies in the world. At the end of the cold war, Sweden took a neoliberal turn that gradually undermined the Swedish *Folk Home* model (Thörn and Larsson 2012). Communal institutions (schools, healthcare institutions, homes for elderly and disabled etc.) were privatized and run for profit on a deregulated market for education, medical and healthcare and social welfare. Infrastructural facilities (including public transportation and real estate) were sold to private entrepreneurs who let the public rent them back at a higher cost. A new cast of multibillionaires was born. By 2022, Sweden had 542 multibillionaires, one percent of all multibillionaires in the world (in which Swedes are one permille). Constituting 0.05 percent of the Swedish population, this cast owns more than eighty percent of the nation's assets, which means that the middle-class share of wealth is relatively low (Cervenka 2022; Suhonen *et al.* 2021; Lapidus 2023, 2019). Compared to other OECD countries, income inequality grew exponentially, and by 2018 Statistics Sweden reported the greatest gap between the country's rich and poor since the measurement began (OECD 2015; Heggeman 2018).

Sweden became the most segregated society in Europe (Thörn and Thörn 2017). Housing segregation is based on class, but as class co-varies with structural discrimination on the basis of racialized ethnicity, religion, and culture, class distinctions increasingly acquired a racialized dimension. (De)linked to Swedish cities are geographically and discursively separated underclass areas, in media and political discourse named "areas of exteriority" ("*utanförskapsområden*"), as if they were islands of non-belonging within the national borders. With a high concentration of residents with a non-Western, often Muslim and Black African, migrant background, these areas were increasingly abandoned by the welfare state, and replaced with police and private security (Sernhede *et al.* 2016; Wolgast *et al.* 2018; Agerström *et al.* 2012; Arai *et al.* 2008; Schclarek Mulinari 2020; Neergaard *et al.* 2017; Larsson *et al.* 2012).

Transforming social realities contributed to rising tensions, aggravated by media portraying migrants as a problem (Strömbäck 2017). In 2017 alone, Swedish media published 23,478 negative articles on migrants

(Söderein 2017). "Alternative facts" on migrants and crime flooded radical nationalist social media while contrafactually insisting such news reports were censured (Merrill 2020). Especially exposed to negative media attention were Swedish Muslims (Axnér 2015; Ekman 2015; Horsti 2017). Anti-Muslim discourse co-occurred with raising levels of anti-Muslim hate crime. By 2018, six out ten (59%) of Sweden's mosques had been exposed to physical violence (Gardell 2015b; 2018).

In radical nationalist discourse, the "areas of exteriority"—in police jargon ranked "vulnerable" and "especially vulnerable" areas—are known as "no-go zones" and depicted as alien controlled territories. As such, they have repeatedly been used as settings for media stunts by radical nationalist politicians and influencers. The protagonist typically shows up in bullet-proof vest, sometimes in helmet, with a crew of photographers and security back-up at a busy plaza in a vulnerable area, picking a fight with locals as the lone representative of white civilization in the unruly waters of savage wilderness. The scene itself makes good content, and should the white hero manage to provoke angry reactions from local residents the better it gets. Paludan's Racist Spectacle conformed to this model.

Yet, it was not an instant success. In May 2021, Paludan sought permission to burn the Qur'an in Rosengård, but was assigned to a windy field at the foot of the Öresund Bridge between Sweden and Denmark. On site everybody turned their backs at Paludan. The police to keep an eye on protestors, and protestors to take exception from Paludan (Olsson and Rydén 2021). Following summer break, Paludan began marketing a Stockholm tour in September. He was to burn the Qur'an in seven areas of exteriority and speak at an Alternative for Sweden (AFS) Church election rally in a downtown city section of upscale shops and expensive residential quarters. It all became a great disappointment.

A few days ahead of his Stockholm tour, Danish reporters infiltrated Paludan's chat forum "Danish Youth" on the Discord platform and revealed that he spent long nights talking about hardcore homoerotic sex with young boys down to thirteen years of age. At password-protected sub-forums, Paludan led conversations on rape, torture, and violent sex, and showed pics of BWC's (Big White C*ks), fetish attire and torture tools (Andersen and Kopping 2021).

The AFS canceled his talk, and Paludan relocated to an adjacent square, seeking in vain to gain the attention of a handful of passersby businesspeople and tourists. The sex scandal disturbed Paludan's touring of Stockholm's racialized underclass areas too. Initially, it went by the script. The police escorted Paludan on his busy Racist Spectacle schedule: 09.00–09.45 Husby; 11,00–12.00 Rinkeby, and so on. "This doesn't feel especially Swedish," Paludan says into the camera, livestreaming in Rinkeby with locals as backdrop. "This feels like Afrika." However, reporters were more interested in his sex chats, and Paludan looked disappointed when dropping off. Similarly, online comments were more about grooming than expelling Muslims (Stram kurs Facebook 2021; Video 2021; Flashback 2021).

Expelled from Alternative for Sweden, Paludan registered Hard Line Sweden (*Stram Kurs Sverige*). "We are more libertarians," Paludan said. "We think that one should be allowed to talk about sex with children" ("Vi står..." 2021). In February 2022, Paludan announced he would run in the Swedish general election of September 11 (of all dates) that year and kick off the campaign by a "King's Tour," burning the Qur'an in Malmö, Jönköping, Linköping, Gothenburg, Stockholm and, oddly, Oslo, Norway (Sinnbeck 2022; Stram Kurs 2022), in March 2022. It became another failure. In Malmö people did not show; in Jönköping, Christian and Muslim congregations said they would turn their backs at Paludan, who called in sick; in Gothenburg, a "Swish reporter" long working the same niche as Paludan turned up to livestream himself at the Spectacle, adding his Swish and Bank transfer data,[6] thus stealing the show (Almkvist and Wennerberg 2022; Oldberg 2022; Lamotte 2022).

Paludan kept on going, knowing that all the ingredients for inflaming accumulating social tension were there. All he had to do was "fan the flames" as the tactic has been called in white radical nationalist revolutionary theory for the past fifty years (Gardell 2021, 24–26, 38). If Paludan continued to "pick them in the eye," the situation would eventually explode. He was proved right during the Holy Week in April 2022, when he staged the Racist Spectacle during the holidays from Maundy Thursday (April 14) to Easter Sunday (April 17). Escorted by the police, Paludan crisscrossed six/seven locations, some of them twice: Jönköping, Linköping (twice), Norrköping (twice), Rinkeby, Örebro, and Landskrona/ Malmö. Paludan succeeded in burning the Qur'an at two of these locations (Jönköping, Malmö) but was either stopped by violent protests (Linköping, Norrköping, Örebro), forced to change location (Landskrona), abrupted halfway (Rinkeby) or left due to violent protests (Linköping II, Norrköping II) in the others.

However, in terms of media impact Paludan got what he looked for. In April 2022, Swedish media published 5,432 pieces on Paludan and the Qur'an burnings (Retriever Research 2023), predominantly centered on

---

6   Swish is a mobile payment system that transfers money in real time through smartphones. A "Swish reporter" livestream events and adds his/her swish transfer number to get paid. Swish-reporters may specialize in producing news by provoking behavior and then livestream reactions, such as racist media stunts in areas of exteriority

the violent protests and clashes with the police named the Easter Riots (*påskupploppen*) or the Qur'an Riots (*korankravallerna*). The images were dramatic: Police officers in riot gear against a background of raging flames of fire towering black night skies, burning police vans, masked rioters, wrecked riot fences, flying stones, debris and molotovs, sirens, bangers, policemen aiming guns, burned-out cars, streets of violence, ruins of war.

In the immediate aftermath, official police records counted twenty-six severely hurt police officers; fourteen civilians seriously wounded, three protestors shot by the police, and twenty damaged police vehicles (Hagström 2022); numbers rose significantly during the post-riot assessment of events. The police part of the bill for Paludan's Spectacle came to forty-seven million, later updated to eighty-four million (SR 2022, 2023). Paludan cheerfully promised to return again the coming weekend. "I will burn really many Qur'ans in front of various mosques across Sweden. And that'll be a lot of fun" ("Paludan kommer" 2022).

Us debating our society

The ensuing national debate on the Easter Riots was driven by actors who felt entitled to discuss problems "we" have in "our" society, typically excluding the voice of protestors. The police investigated what went wrong in the locations where they lost control in an assessment led by the former head of Military Intelligence that overlooked the issue of why the officers who shot into the crowd (supposedly) did not wear body cameras (Polisen 2022; UG 2023). Who shot whom and why is still not really known.

The police seemed baffled by the rage of the protestors. "These were not ordinary counter-protestors" but "criminal gangs" seeking to "attack the society ruled by law," National Police Commissioners Anders Thornberg (2022, 2022b) claimed. Michael Östlund at the Swedish Psychological Defence Agency pointed at extreme Islamism and "antidemocratic movements" from abroad, "such as al-Qaida" ("Terrorgrupper"). The Minister of Justice readily combined both allegations that echoed across party lines (Svensson and Granlund 2022; Press Conference 2022; Aktuellt 2022). In a Tolkienesque argument, Tobias Andersson (2022) of the Sweden Democrats warned of the "slumbering evil" growing in the deep shadows of our parallel societies. The rioters were not "troublemakers" fighting the police, but "domestic terrorists of all ages" attacking "Sweden as such."

With massive documentation of evidence from drones, surveillance cameras, police body cameras, and thousands of citizen films, the police had arrested at least 149 individuals as of March 2023. Based on pre-trial records and convictions of 125 individuals held for crimes connected to the Easter Riots, most of the allegations above were disproved in a report by Acta Publica (2023). Only seven individuals had connections to criminal gang activities. Seventy had no prior crime records at all. Most were young. Thirty-three individuals were less than eighteen years, sixty-six were below thirty, and only eleven above forty. No Islamist extremists or touring rioters were found. Almost everyone lived in the local community in which the riot took place. A small minority of ten individuals came from a neighboring community; only two lived elsewhere and one had no registered address. A majority of sixty percent were foreign nationals, had double or no citizenship.

Almost all cases were tried for "blue-light sabotage" (endangering emergency operations), a new crime as of January 2022 which sentences a violator to imprisonment of at least two and at most eighteen years to life if grossly guilty. In March 2023, the Supreme Court lowered the time of imprisonment in two cases (both from Örebro) from six, and five-and-a-half years, to three years and three months, and three years, arguing that offenders could not be held responsible for what others did in the riot as a whole, only for crimes for which they, themselves, had been found guilty (Högsta domstolen 2023).

Significantly, few if any were active in Islamic congregations or regular mosque-goers. People in the mosque movement in Örebro, for instance, were not seen throwing rocks at the riot, but came out afterwards, cleaning the streets, giving flowers to neighbors. Also absent were Muslim civil society associations that have a record of favoring non-violent means of protest. In the areas where the riots took place, the Young Muslims of Sweden (*Sveriges unga muslimer*) had been active for years, urging young Muslims to participate in Swedish democracy as Muslims and Swedes. However, by 2022, the Young Muslims of Sweden was no more, as ill-funded allegations claiming they had infiltrated Swedish society as part of a Muslim brotherhood conspiracy had forced them out of business (Norell *et al.* 2016; Karlsson Minganti 2019; Marbinah 2021).

Most protestors felt they had responded to an attack from a racist who was arriving with police protection to question their existence. Many went to the scene out of curiosity or to protest and were drawn into the violence. Much as the National Police Commissioner (Thornberg 2022b) was "damned pissed off" (*jävligt förbannad*) by the violence of the protestors, protestors were enraged by the violence of the police. Footage shows carnivalesque moments of triumph when the police backed off (Acta 2023; UG 2023; TRB2769-22; B9257-22; TB1003-23).

All leaders of Sweden's mainstream parties saw the Qur'an burnings as protected by the freedom of expression (Politikernas svar 2022). "In Sweden, expressing one's views, tasteful or distasteful, is part of our democracy," Prime Minister Magdalena Andersson (2022) laid down. "It's obvious that we in Sweden have groups that haven't really understood what kind of country they live in, and that haven't accepted the far-reaching freedom of expression we have here," Minister of Justice Morgan Johansson said (Grahn 2022). "One of the most important tasks of the police is to secure that people can use their constitutional rights to demonstrate and express their opinions," the National Police Commissioner emphasized (Rikspolischefen 2022).

Another standard argument brought up the rights to blasphemy (e.g., Avellan 2022; Neuding 2022). The most interesting aspect of this argument is not that it was another case of "defending the unthreatened" as no one suggested to outlaw blasphemy, but that it overlooks a key principle of that which it claims to defend: *blasphemy, like apostacy, is relative to the religion of the subject.* The sin of blasphemy is directed against the God that you honor, not the God of others. To become an apostate, you leave the religion you once had, not some religion you never had.

Burning the Qur'an means different things in different contexts. A Muslim burning the Qur'an during a protest in Teheran against the regime of the Islamic Republic of Iran has not the same meaning as a Christian ethnonationalist burning the Qur'an during an anti-Muslim demonstration in Sweden.

The effort to legally frame the Qur'an burnings as freedom of expression is a misinterpretation of Swedish and European law, according to Göran Lambertz, former Chancellor of Justice and (retired) judge on the Supreme Court. Burning the Qur'an is by Swedish law considered incitement of hatred/hate speech if the act is done in a context of expressing aversion against Muslims as a group of people. In this case, Lambertz argues, Paludan has explicated his negative views on Muslims so many times that it can hardly be any doubt that he burns the Qur'an as a way to incite hatred of Muslims. In such a context, burning the Qur'an is not protected by the freedom of expression statues in the Swedish constitution, nor by the European Convention on Human Rights (Lambertz 2023), but is a hate crime.

If Paludan's public burning of the Qur'an is a hate crime, should the police have refused to grant him permit to demonstrate, knowing the demonstration was called to commit a crime? No, Lambertz argues. The freedom of assembly and demonstration cannot, by law, be infringed by the police with reference to any other consideration than obstacles to secure public order and safety. However, the right to demonstrate does not give immunity from criminal liability if a crime is committed during a demonstration for which there is a permit. Hence, Paludan may call for a demonstration to burn the Qur'an but may also be arrested for committing a hate crime if proceeding by burning the Qur'an (Lambertz 2023).

The Language of Riots and Hot Dogs

"Ours is the time of riots," Alain Bertho (2018) observes in his study of urban uprisings. Since the turn of the new millennium, the number of urban riots in the world has quadrupled. Every year from 2013 onwards, more than 2,000 riots have shaken the grounds somewhere in the world. The reason of course varies. Much like the riots in the French banlieues and the Black American urban riots, the Easter riots in Sweden 2022 were explosions of racialized tension accumulating for years. While seen as shocking, unexpected, and unprecedented by the Swedish political class, media, and the police, it was not the first time such riots shook Sweden, as evidenced by the 2013 Stockholm riots and the 2008 Rosengård riots (De los Reyes and Hörnqvist 2017). The riots signal an unfolding collapse of the system of representative democracy. Substantial parts of the Swedish population are excluded from being part of the people from whom all public power in Sweden proceeds, and are instead formally and/or discursively and practically set apart from the people and often concentrated in areas of exteriority. The discrepancy between the official image of Sweden as a harmonious nation of social equality beyond racism on the one hand, and lived experience of racial injustice on the other, creates accumulating frustration, similar to the discrepancy between the official American image of "one nation, indivisible, with liberty and justice for all" and Black American experience of lived realities in the hyper-segregated inner-city ghettoes, and the French national motto of Liberté, égalité, fraternité and lived experience in the banlieues. For years, the population of the Swedish areas of exteriority have kept heads low and worked hard to make ends meet and done their part of the social contract, as well as articulated frustrations and life experience through literature, poetry, arts, community upbuilding programs, civil society associations and civil rights movements. For years, the representatives of the people in the Riksdag, municipalities and regions have observed but not seen, talked but not said much, thought, but not really understood. Only thus can a riot in the areas of exteriority be unexpected.

"A riot is the language of the unheard," Martin Luther King (1968), said, talking about the riots of the long hot Summer of 1967 and those that lay ahead should racial justice fail to come. As one of the rioters of the Parisian banlieues quoted by Bertho (2018, 26) said: "It wasn't politics; we just wanted to tell the state something." The reply to violent rebellion has historically been massive repression, which, of course, was the logic Paludan hoped to invite by burning the Qur'an.

Ebba Busch (2022), leader of the Christian Democrats, questioned why the police did not use live bullets during the Easter riots. "Why don't we have at least 100 wounded Islamists, 100 wounded criminals, and 100 wounded insurrectionists?" Busch did not stand alone. "She put the finger on a feeling I also had," (conservative) Moderate party's Spokesperson of Justice said (Fernstedt 2022). "How could this even be controversial?" Jimmie Åkesson, leader of the Sweden Democrats asked. "Ebba is correct. The police should shoot sharp when Islamists try to take their lives" (Åkesson 2022). Tweeting Police Officer Peppe Larsson seconded. "You had been able to shoot straight into that mass of people attacking and got away with it no matter who you'd hit" (Peppe 2022). The police should be legally "entitled to shoot insurgents to death," and "especially trained" to that end, an editorial of *Samtiden* wrote, calling for the creation of a paramilitary force to "defend society" (Erixon 2022).

On April 21, the Sweden Democrats (2022) presented *Thirty Propositions in Response to the Assault on Sweden*. Understanding the Easter Riots as a systemic threat by an alliance of Islamism and criminal clans/gangs united in their hatred of Swedes and everything Swedish, the Propositions went beyond the principles of the legal order it claimed to defend. Besides conventional tough-on-crime demands (more police, harder punishments, more prisons, weaponize the police, employ the military, declare emergency laws) and anti-Muslim policies (close mosques, Muslim schools, civil society associations, restrict Muslim immigration) SD called for collective punishments. Should a "culturally burdened" family-member disrespect Swedish norms and values, engage in criminal activities or assault society, the whole family should be fined, lose their social rights, the custody of their children, and their rights of residency. The SD proposed that the possibilities to annul the citizenship of individuals guilty of "socially subversive" crime should be investigated.

The suggestions to solve the problem of accumulating tensions in the areas of exteriority by eliminating the racialized other, rather than the racial injustice that produced the tension, fitted nicely to the politicized nostalgia that permeated the national elections of 2022. Responding to popular concern with the dismantling of the Swedish Model of social equity, the Sweden Democrats had for years pointed to visible minorities as evidence of the betrayal of the political class, nostalgically envisioning a restored Folk Home for native (white) Swedes only. Using the Easter riots as a sign that time was running out, the Sweden Democrats promised to return to a society that "feels good again," that "builds cars, not burns them" (SD 2022).

Paraphrasing Trump, *Make Sweden Good Again* became the motto of the Sweden Democrats' election campaign of 2022 (SD 2022b; 2022c). Nostalgia marked the appearances of all the rightwing parties during the election campaign, which also signaled who was entitled to feel at home in the country that would be good again, and who was the problem. Dog whistle politics (Haney Lopez 2015) and banal nationalism (Billig 1995) celebrated triumphs in the party leaders' constant consumption of Swedish sausage. The hot dog is reminiscent of the 1950's, of dansband and "people's park" (*folkpark*), a folk tradition as Swedish as IKEA, which could not raise the price of the hot dog without popular protest. Swedish hot dogs consist of pig and beef and pig-fat and is food to "real Swedes" that are not Muslim or Jewish. In her campaign, Ebba Busch underlined Swedishness by going onstage waving Falu Sausage (*falukorv*) which has a Traditional Speciality Guaranteed recipe protected by European law, and always contains pig fat of not less than twenty-three percent.

With twenty-one percent of the vote, the Sweden Democrats became the largest party of the rightwing coalition that was formed at Tidö Castle, built during the Swedish Era of Great Power by the statesman Axel Oxenstierna who was the de facto ruler of the Empire of Sweden when the monarch, the underage Queen Kristina, was regent on paper only. Withdrawing the cordon sanitaire from the Sweden Democrats, *The Tidö Agreement* (2022) gives the reformed national socialist party a similar position of dictating politics from behind the scenes in the new government formally led by Ulf Kristersson (Moderate) as Prime Minister and Ebba Busch (Christian Democrat) as Vice Prime Minister, with Johan Pehrson (Liberal) as Minister of Employment and Integration.

To "solve Sweden's huge social problems" without rolling back the neoliberal reforms that allow welfare entrepreneurs to drain resources from the common, the Tidö Agreement focuses on monitored acculturation and detention/deportation of unassimilable elements. Foreigners "enjoying Swedish hospitality" are "bound to respect foundational Swedish values" and cannot "offend the population by their behavior." Exactly what this means is not specified, although the document clarifies that grounds for expulsion include "remarks on their ways of life" and "association" with "clans" and "milieus" that threatens the (unspecified) "foundational Swedish values" (Tidö 2022, 37f). Access to welfare and healthcare should be restricted to Swedish and European citizens. Citizenship will be harder to obtain and require proof of "decent morals," self-sufficiency, and adequate skills in Swedish language, history and culture. Constitutional change to make citizenship revokable will be initiated (Tidö 2022, 38f).

The past is not dead, but part of the present which forms the future. For the past five hundred years, books have been burned to eliminate the evil these books are said to represent. Since the Qur'an burnings of Granada this has also been a way to intimidate the people associated with the burning books and speed up their disappearance. This was the objective of the series of Qur'an burnings initiated in Sweden 2020 as explained by its main instigator who sought to repeat the pattern of book burning—protest—repression that led to the prohibition of Islam, forced conversion, bans of Moorish culture, clothing and language, and, ultimately, the expulsion of the Moriscos, Spanish Christians with Muslim background.

The outcome of the recent Qur'an burnings in Sweden is of course open, and no repetition of a cyclical pattern is identical, including the most well-rehearsed. Following the Easter riots, Paludan performed at least eighty more Qur'an burnings that formed the background noise as the Tidö team moved to implement its Agreement. On January 21, 2023, Paludan experienced his second largest peak of national and international attention by burning the Qur'an outside the Embassy of Turkey. When Turkey's President Recep Tayyip Erdoğan vowed to block Sweden's application for membership in NATO, Prime Minister Kristersson (2023) promptly declared: "Freedom of expression is a fundamental part of democracy. *But* what is legal is not necessarily appropriate." Burning the Qur'an is "deeply disrespectful," Kristersson continued, expressing his "sympathy for all Muslims" offended by "what happened in Stockholm today."

This shift in the point of gravity by switching around the order of the sentence—from "the message may be condemnable, yet freedom of expression is commendable" to "freedom of expression may be commendable, yet the message is condemnable"—became the official Swedish position on the Qur'an burnings since they began threatening interests the government found important. It was repeated as international Muslim calls to boycott Swedish contacts and severe diplomatic ties grew.

"Expressions of racism, xenophobia and related intolerance have no place in Sweden," the Swedish foreign ministry (UD 2023) assured the world community after a new Qur'an burning (this time not by Paludan) occurred at the doors of the Grand Mosque in Stockholm during the celebration of Eid al-Adha June 28, 2023. The following day, the government (Regeringen 2023) declared the establishment of "remigration centers" to speed up deportations.

And so it goes, as Vonnegut said.

About the author

Mattias Gardell is Nathan Söderblom Professor in Comparative Religion, and researcher at the Centre for the Multidisciplinary Studies of Racism at Uppsala university, Sweden. Working with ethnographic methods and text analysis, Gardell explores the complex terrain shaped by the intersections of religion, politics, racism and violence. His fields of research include radical nationalism, esoteric fascism, Islamophobia, political Islam, human bombs, torture history, hate crime, politicized nostalgia, the entangled history of racism and religion, fascist cultural production, and white racist lone wolf tactics. His list of publications may be found at https://www.cemfor.uu.se/about-us/researchers/publications-gardell/

References

Acta Publica. 2022. *Upploppsmakarna*, Stockholm: Acta Publica Report.

AFS. 2018. "Återvandring." *Alternativ för Sverige*, https://web.archive.org/web/20180906235718/https://alternativforsverige.se/atervandring/

AFS. 2022. *Valfilm 2022, Alternativ för Sverige*, https://alternativforsverige.se/valfilm-2022/

Agerström, Jens, Björklund, Fredrik, Carlsson, Rickard and Dan-Olof Rooth. 2012. "Warm and Competent Hassan = Cold and Incompetent Eric: A Harsh Equation of Real-Life Hiring Discrimination." *Basic and Applied Social Psychology* 34(4): 359–366. https://doi.org/10.1080/01973533.2012.693438

Åkesson, Jimmie. 2022. "Ebba har rätt", *Tweet*, April 25, https://twitter.com/jimmieakesson/status/1518613900186501120 Alaoui, Youssef El 2002 "Inquisición, moriscos y desemitización." In *Autour de l'Inquisition: études sur le Saint-Office*, edited by Rica Amran 75–90. Paris: Indigo.

Åkesson, Lovisa and Viktor Nordblad. 2020. "Rasmus Paludan begär skadestånd av Sverige", *Expressen/Kvällsposten*, 9.

Aktuellt. 2022. "Efter helgens upplopp—så vill partierna stoppa våldet." April 19.

Almkvist, Jonas and Joel Wennerberg. 2022 "Vändningen: Rasmus Paludan ställer in" *Jönköpings-Posten*, March 4.

Andersson, Magdalena. 2022. "Magdalena Andersson fördömer upploppen", Statement to TT/*Aftonbladet*, April 15.

Andersen, Mathias and Kasper D. Kopping. 2021. "Paludan i grov sexsnak med børn." *Extrabladet*, August 27.

Andersson, Tobias. 2022. "Protokoll från debatten." *Särskild debatt om påskhelgens kravaller*, Anf. 1 and 2, Stockholm: Sveriges riksdag, May 6.

Arai, Mahmood and Peter Skogman Thoursie. 2008. "Renouncing personal names: An empirical examination of surname change and earnings." Stockholm: Mimeo, Department of Economics, Stockholm University. https://doi.org/10.1086/593964

Avellan, Heidi. 2022. "Koraner får brännas, polisbilar inte," Helsingborgs Dagblad, April 30.

Axner, Martha. 2015. *Representationer, stereotyper och nyhetsvärdering*. Stockholm: Diskrimineringsombudsmannen.

B 9257–22, Dom, Stockholms Tingsrätt. Dec 8.
Bertho, Alain. 2018. *The Age of Violence*. Verso.
Billig, Michael. 1995. *Banal nationalism*. Sage.
Boase, Roger. 2002. "The Muslim Expulsion from Spain." *History Today* April 21–27.
Breivik, Anders Behring. 2011. *2083: A European Declaration of Independence* self-published, July 22.
Burk, Rachel L. 2010. "Salus Erat in Sanguine: Limpieza De Sangre and Other Discourses of Blood in Early Modern Spain." Unpublished PhD thesis, University of Pennsylvania.
———. 2017. "Purity and Impurity of Blood in Early Modern Iberia." *The Routledge Companion to Iberian Studies*, edited by Muñoz-Basols, Javier, Lonsdale Laura and Manuel Delgado, 173–183. London: Routledge.
Busch, Ebba. 2022. "Varför har vi inte minst 100 skadade islamister?" Sveriges Radio: Ekot, April 22.
Cervenka, Andreas. 2022. *Girig-Sverige*. Natur and Kultur.
Christoffersen, Philip. 2020. "Rasmus Paludan grundlægger kirke og vil selv være ærkebiskop." *Kristerligt Daglad*, Oct 10.
Confino, Alon. 2012. "Why Did the Nazis Burn the Hebrew Bible?" *The Journal of Modern History* 84, June, 369–400. https://doi.org/10.1086/664662
———. 2014. *A World Without Jews*. New Haven, CT: Yale University Press.
De los Reyes, Paulina and Magnus Hörnqvist, eds. 2017. *Bortom kravallerna*, Stockholm: Stockholmia.
Ekman, M. 2015. "Online Islamophobia and the politics of fear." *Ethnic and Racial Studies* 38(11): 1986–2002. https://doi.org/10.1080/01419870.2015.1021264
Erixon, Dick. 2022. "Polisen måste få skjuta för att döda." *Samtiden*, April 18.
Expo 2020. "Dan Park," *Expo Fakta*, https://expo.se/fakta/wiki/dan-park.
Faulkner, William. 2012 [1951]. *Requiem for a Nun*.Vintage.
Faye, Guillaume. 2016. *The Colonisation of Europe*. Arktos.
Fernstedt, Nora. 2022. "Åkesson backar Busch," *Aftonbladet*, 25.
Fonseca, Damián. 1612. *Justa expulsión de los moriscos de España*. Giacomo Mascardo.
García Arenal, Mercedes and Gerard Wiegers, Eds., 2013. *Los moriscos: expulsión y diáspora*, Editorial Universidad de Granada.
Gardell, Mattias. 2015a. *Raskrigaren. Seriemördaren Peter Mangs*, Leopard.
———. 2015b. "What's Love Got to Do with It? Ultranationalism, Islamophobia, and Hate Crime in Sweden." *Journal of Religion and Violence* 3:1, 91–116. https://doi.org/10.5840/jrv20155196
———. 2018. *Moskéers och Muslimska församlingars utsatthet och säkerhet i Sverige 2018*. CEMFOR and SST.
———. 2021. *Lone Wolf Race Warrior and White Genocide*, Cambridge University Press. https://doi.org/10.1017/9781108609760

Gjerding, Sebastian and Ulrik Dahlin. 2019. "Rasmus Paludan er større på YouTube end alle de andre partier tilsammen," *Information*, June 11, 2019.

Goebbels 1933. "Speech to the students in Berlin." In Bartrop, Pauk R and Michael Dickerman, Eds. 2017. *The Holocaust: An Encyclopedia and Document Collection*, ABC-CLIO.

Grahn, Hanna. 2022. "Morgan Johansson," *Borås Tidning*, April 29.

Hagström, Per. 2022. "Kollegorna bildade mänsklig sköld," *Polistidningen*, April 20.

Haney López, Ian. 2015. *Dog Whistle Politics*. Oxford University Press.

Heggemann, Hans. 2018. *Inkomsterna ökade 2005-2016*, SCB, January 31.

Heine, Heinrich. 2015 [1823]. *Almansor*, Hofenberg.

Heng, Geraldine. 2018. *The Invention of Race in the European Middle Ages*. Cambridge University Press. https://doi.org/10.1017/9781108381710

Hering Torres, Max, Martínez, María Helena, and Nirenberg, David, Eds. 2012, *Race and Blood in the Iberian World*, Lit.

Herkel, Peter and Lars Brundin. 2020, "Det var det värsta upplopp som jag varit med om under mina 15 år som polis," *Helsingborgs Dagblad*, August 31.

Högsta domstolen 2023. *Högsta domstolens dom. Mål nr B 6185-22*, March 14.

Horsti, Karina. 2017. "Digital Islamophobia." *New Media and Society* 19:9, 1440–1457. https://doi.org/10.1177/1461444816642169

Horswell, Mike and Akil N. Awan, Eds. 2019. *The Crusades in the Modern World*, Vol 2, Routledge. https://doi.org/10.4324/9781351250481

Horta Ribeiro, Manoel, Ottoni, Raphael, West, Rober, Almeida, Virgílio and Wagner Meira Jr. 2020. "Auditing Radicalization Pathways on YouTube." *Conference on Fairness, Accountability, and Transparency*. January 27–30, 2020, Barcelona. https://doi.org/10.1145/3351095.3372879

Jónsson, Már 2007. "The expulsion of the Moriscos from Spain in 1609–1614," *Journal of Global History* 2(2): 195–212. https://doi.org/10.1017/S1740022807002252

Karker, Andreas. 2019. "Paludan smidt ud af Nye Borgerlige", *BT*, May 6.

Karlsson Minganti, Pia. 2019 "Studera uppåt: myndighetshantering av statsbidrag till en muslimsk ungdomsorganisation", *Eftertankar*, Björklund, Anders, Blehr, Barbro and Simon Ekström, Vulkan, 112–145.

King, Martin Luther. 1968. "The Other America." *Grosse Point Historical Society*, March 14.

Kristersson, Ulf. 2023. "Tweet on burning books", @SwedishPM, https://twitter.com/SwedishPM/status/1616927938368229376

Lambertz, Göran. 2023. "Bränna koranen är hets mot folkgrupp," *Svensk juristtidning*, April 4.

Lamotte, Joakim. 2022. "Livrapportering," https://www.facebook.com/watch/live/?ref=watch_permalink&v=1073609089883846, Feb 27.

Lapidus, John. 202 3. *Den sjuka debatten*, Verbal.

———. 2019. *The Quest for a Divided Welfare State*, Palgrave Macmillan/Springer. https://doi.org/10.1007/978-3-030-24784-3

Larsson, Bengt, Lentell, Martin and Håkan Thörn, eds. 2012. *Transformations of the Swedish Welfare State*. Palgrave. https://doi.org/10.1057/9780230363953

Ledwich, Mark and Anna Zaitsev. 2019. "Algorithmic Extremism." *arXiv:1912.11211*. Cornell University.

Lewy, Guenter. 2016. *Harmful and Undesirable*. Oxford University Press.

Marbinah, Rosaline. 2021. "Unga muslimer, fortsätt organisera er!" *LSU*, February 1.

Merrill, Samuel 2020. "Sweden then vs. Sweden now." *First Monday* 25:6. https://doi.org/10.5210/fm.v25i6.10552

Neergaard, Anders, Ålund, Aleksandra and Carl-Ulrik Schierup, Eds. 2017. *Reimagineering the Nation*, Peter Lang Verlag.

Neuding, Paulina 2022. "Påskkravallerna blottar det svenska tillståndet", *Svenska Dagbladet*, April 18.

Norell, Magnus, Carlbom, Aje and Pierre Durrani. 2016. *Muslimska Brödraskapet i Sverige*, Myndigheten för samhällsskydd och beredskap, Dnr 2017-1287.

OECD 2015. *Income inequality data update: Sweden*, OECD.

Oldberg, Erika 2022 "Malmö stad polisanmäler Paludan," *Sydsvenskan*.

Olsson, Gustav and Hanna Rydén. 2020. Lugnt under Paludans manifestation i Malmö, *Dagens Nyheter*. May 20.

"Paludan kommer." 2022 "Paludan kommer till Sverige i helgen—ska bränna "jättemånga" koraner," Fria Tider, 29 April 2022.

Paludan, Rasmus. 2018. "Advarsel," New Jersey: *Paludan YouTube*, December 12. https://web.archive.org/web/20190903100349/https://www.youtube.com/watch?v=Ml62afEvRXY

Park, Dan. 2009. *Sieg*. Stockholm: Bokbål förlag.

Peppe. 2022. 1/3 Tweet, @Peppe_Larsson, April 23, https://twitter.com/Peppe_Larsson/status/1517970017186426882

Perry, Mary Elizabeth. 2005. *The Handless Maiden*. Princeton University Press

Polisen. 2022. *Förbättrad förmåga att förebygga och hantera våldsamma upplopp*, Stockholm: Polismyndigheten Rapport, Dnr A279. 989/2022, December 14.

"Politikernas svar efter påskhelgens upplopp." 2022. Expressen, April 22.

"Politisk grundlag." 2019. *Stram Kurs*, Vores politik.

Press Conference. 2022. *Regeringens pressträff efter påskupploppen*. Swedish Government, April 18.

Regeringen. 2023. *Uppdrag att inrätta återvändandecenter*, Ju2023/01593, June 29.

Retten i Næstved. 2020. *Dom om overtrædelse af straffelovens racismebestemmelse § 266b*, Sag.nr. SS 3185/2020, Dom afsagt: June 25.

Retriever. "Rasmus Paludan" 2023. *Retriver Research Mediearkivet/Media Archive*. Uppsala University.

Rikspolischefen. 2022: "Upploppen förkastliga," *Security User*, April 16.
Samnytt. 2019. "VIDEO: Invandrargäng attackerade dansk politiker med fyrverkerier—polisen tvingades fly", *Samnytt*, February 10.
Schclarek Mulinari, Leandro. 2020. *Race and Order*, Stockholm University, Diss.
Schonfield, Ernest. 2018. "Heine and Convivencia," *Oxford German Studies* 47:1, 35-50. https://doi.org/10.1080/00787191.2018.1409508
SD 2022 *Inte som alla de andra.*
SD 2022b. *Sverigedemokraternas valfilm—Sverige ska bli bra igen*, September 2,
SD 2022c. *Vad vi vill.*
Sernhede, Ove, Thörn, Catharina and Håkan Thörn *2016.* "The Stockholm Uprising in Context." *Urban Uprisings.* Eds Mayer, Thörn and Thörn. Palgrave.
Shakir, Kevin. 2019. "Dansk högerextremist radikaliserar barn på YouTube", *Opulens*, March 8.
Sicroff, Albert A. 1985. *Los Estatutos De Limpieza De Sangre. Controversias Entre Los Siglos XV y XVII.* Taurus Ediciones S.A.
Sinnbeck, Peter. 2022 "Rasmus Paludan stiller op til svensk valg", *B.T.*, February 17.
Söderin, Eigil. 2017. "Stor ökning av de negativa artiklarna om invandring", *ETC*, Feb. 5.
Søgaard Rohde, Thomas and Cathrine Bloch. 2017. "Han ville se »fremmede fjenders blod i kloakken«: Nu er han fortid i Nye Borgerlige", *Belingske*, February 17. https://doi.org/10.7146/spr.v17i52.102823
Søndberg, Astrid and Mikkel Walentin Mortensen. 2019. "Landsretten stadfæster: Rasmus Paludan dømt for racisme," *tv2dk*, July 4.
SR 2022. "Paludans möten kostade 43 miljoner," *Sveriges Radio*, Aug 15.
SR 2023. "Polisinsatserna i samband med Paludans aktioner kostade 84 miljoner," *Sveriges Radio*, March 22.
Stram Kurs. 2020. "Vi kommer fortsätta bränna koraner i Rosengård," *Fria Tider*, August 30.
Stram Kurs. 2021. *Rasmus Paludan indtager SVERIGE*, Stram Kurs Facebook, August 27.
———. 2022. "Den 4-6 mars fortsätter Paludan sin Eriksgata," *Stram Kurs* Facebook.
Strömbäck, Jesper and Andersson, Erika. Eds. 2017. *Misstron mot medier*, Stockholm: Institutet för mediestudier.
Suhonen, D., Therborn, G. and Weithz, J. 2021. *Klass i Sverige.* Arkiv and Katalys.
Svensson, Olof and John Granlund 2022 "Ministern: Kravallerna underblåstes av utländska islamister," *Aftonbladet*, April 20.
Sweden Democrats. 2022. *Thirty Propositions in Response to the Assault on Sweden*, The Sweden Democrats, April 21.
Tarrant, Brenton 2019. *The Great Replacement.* Self-published 15 March.
TB 1003-23, *Dom*, Lunds Tingsrätt, May 3.

"Terrorgrupper hetsade vid påskupploppen: 'Hör till al-Qaida'", *P4, Sveriges radio*, April 27, 2022.

Thornberg, Anders. 2022. "Polisens presskonferens efter påskupploppen", *SVT Live*, April 18.

———. 2022b. "Rikspolischefen efter kravallerna," *TV4* April 18.

Thörn, Catharina and Håkan Thörn. 2017. "Swedish cities now belong to the most segregated in Europe." *Sociologisk forskning* 54(4): 293-296. https://doi.org/10.37062/sf.54.18224

Thörn, Håkan and Bent Larsson. 2012. "Re-Engineering the Swedish Welfare State," *Transformations of the Swedish Welfare State*. Larsson, Lentell and Thörn, Eds. 2012. Palgrave. https://doi.org/10.1057/9780230363953_17

Tidö Agreement, The. 2022. *Tidöavtalet*, October 14.

Toft, Emma. 2019. "Rasmus Paludan idømt flere bøder for at tale grimt om politiet", *DR*, 6. maj 2019.

TR B 27969–22, *Dom*, Södertälje tingsrätt, Jan 25.

UD 2023. "Här är hela uttalandet från utrikesdepartementet," SR, 2 July 2023.

"Udlændinge" 2019. *Stram Kurs, Vores politik*.

UG 2023. *Påskupploppen*. Uppdrag Granskning, I-IV, SVT Grävredaktion.

"Vi står för mer frihet," *Expo* 2021 # 3, 9

VIDEO 2021: Rasmus Paludan i Rinkeby och Tensta—"Känns lite afrikanskt," *Samnytt*, March 9.

Vonnegut, Kurt. 1969. *Slaughterhouse-Five*, Delacorte Dial Press

———. 1973. "Letter to Mr. McCarthy." *Letters of Note*, Chronicle Books, 2014.

Whitfield, Stephen J. 2002. "Where They Burn Books…," *Modern Judaism* 22, 213-233. https://doi.org/10.1093/mj/22.3.213

Wolgast, Sima, Molina, Irene and Mattias Gardell. 2018. *Anti-Black Racism and Discrimination in the Labor Market*. Länsstyrelsen 2018: 22.

II

New Religious Movements

6

JAMES R. LEWIS AND JONESTOWN STUDIES

REBECCA MOORE

The extensive writings of James R. Lewis provide a number of insights that illuminate studies of Peoples Temple and Jonestown. Sometimes these insights directly relate to the tragedy in which more than 900 people lost their lives, such as his analysis of the mental and physical states of those cult leaders who led their followers to death. At other times, insights come indirectly. These include Lewis's concept of "monolithic inferences," which features his observation that scholars, including he himself, tend to assume that everyone belonging to a new religion has the same knowledge and information as everyone else. Another, and related, example is Lewis' insistence that scholars differentiate between religious groups, noting salient differences and similarities, rather than squeezing them into ideal types. A final, implicit insight concerns the way, or ways, in which the Jonestown tragedy has shaped the study of new religious movements. Lewis sees Jonestown as a pivotal moment in the growth of this field. I agree, but at the same time—and using Lewis' own arguments—I argue that Jonestown is largely an anomaly, and ultimately somewhat irrelevant to the study of new religions.

It is a daunting task to attempt to read everything that Jim Lewis produced as author, co-author, editor, and mentor during his lifetime. However, a review of more than two dozen articles, chapters, and books reveals a number of insights that illuminate studies of Peoples Temple and Jonestown. Sometimes these insights directly relate to the tragedy, such as his analysis of the mental and physical states of cult leaders who led their followers to death. Lewis demonstrates clear parallels between the cases of Jim Jones of Peoples Temple, Joseph Di Mambro of the Order of the Solar Temple, and Marshall Applewhite of Heaven's Gate. He challenges traditional explanations that attribute the catastrophes to either apocalypticism or isolation, looking instead at the health of the leader.

At other times, insights come indirectly. These include, for example, Lewis' concept of "monolithic inferences," which appears in an article about Aum Shinrikyo. In this instance, he observes that scholars tend to assume that everyone belonging to a new religion has the same knowledge and information as everyone else. This point helps us understand the compartmentalization of tasks and power not only within Aum Shinrikyo, but also within Peoples Temple. In the latter case, a leadership cadre carefully planned a literal revolutionary suicide, which, for the most part, the rank and file believed was rhetorical and metaphorical.

A third, implicit insight concerns the ways in which the Jonestown tragedy has shaped the study of new religious movements. Lewis sees Jonestown as an important moment in the growth of new religions studies as an academic discipline. Related to this is his insistence that scholars differentiate among religious groups, noting salient differences and similarities, rather than squeezing them into ideal types. To this, we might add, the acceptance of cult stereotypes that lead to further tragedies, such as framing the Branch Davidians within the events of Jonestown. I strongly agree with Lewis' claim that it is a mistake to lump all new religions together, seeing them as potential mass suicides. Moreover, and perhaps somewhat paradoxically, I would like to argue that Jonestown is largely an anomaly and somewhat irrelevant, or at least misleading, in the study of new religions.

This article, therefore, addresses three key contributions Jim Lewis has made to Peoples Temple and Jonestown studies. First, it assesses the health of the leader and the role that may play in violent outcomes. Next it considers the monolithic inferences scholars erroneously make about the nature of life within new religions. Finally, it argues, along with Lewis, for clarifying differences, rather than conflating similarities between groups. The development of ideal types to understand new religious movements can be helpful, except, as I will demonstrate, in the case of Peoples Temple.

The pathology of the leader

Even before the Jonestown murders–suicides of 1978, historians, sociologists, psychologists, and cult watchers attributed great and compelling power to the group leader. New religions scholar Massimo Introvigne noted that in the Middle Ages, Europeans viewed the prophet Muhammad as "a dangerous psychopath" (Introvigne 2022, 6). Deprogrammer Ted Patrick called all cult leaders "crooks" and "totalitarians" (Patrick 1976, 20, 260). Cult critics Carroll Stoner and Jo Anne Parke asked if society "has a responsibility to regulate totalitarian groups that require obedience to a living godhead" (Stoner and Parke 1977, xvii). And prominent anticult attorney Richard Delgado asserted that "It is clear that cult leaders have absolute control over their followers, who would willingly carry out any order, legal or otherwise" (Delgado 1977, 34).

After the tragedy, both popular and scholarly explanations focused on the charismatic leader, with journalists characterizing Jim Jones as demented, deranged, and mad (Moore 2023). Almost every analysis of incidents of mass murder and suicide, including that in Jonestown, "assume that the charismatic authority of the religious leaders facilitated the onset of violence" (Dawson 2006, 4). According to cult watcher Steven Hassan, "In the Peoples Temple mass suicide–murder in Guyana, a single cult leader could preside over the literal dispensing of existence—or, more precisely, nonexistence—by means of a suicidal mystique which he himself had made a part of the group's ideology" (Hassan 2020, 35). Psychiatric and psychological analyses of events claimed that Jim Jones' followers so identified themselves with their leader, that they would do whatever he demanded (e.g. Galanter 1989). Jones was either a mother figure (Nesci 1999, 2017) or a father figure (Zee 1980; Ulman and Abse 1983). In either case, members were reduced to possessing a child-like mental state, incapable of resisting their leader's dictates.

While some scholars took this approach, others emphasized the apocalyptic or catastrophic millennial outlook of Peoples Temple (e.g. Hall 1987; Chidester 1988; Wessinger 2000). In expectation of a global nuclear holocaust, the group emigrated from the United States to Guyana, an English-speaking nation on the north coast of South America. Its fears of another type of catastrophe—a fascist takeover in the United States—also prompted the move. These concerns fed what sociologist Constance Jones calls a "Manichean dualism" in the group, which consequently divided the world and its inhabitants into good and evil. Jones thereby "crafted a worldview which made an impending apocalypse plausible" (Jones 1989, 212). The United States and its capitalist, racist system was beyond redemption, with its salvation coming only through its complete destruction. Barring that possibility, however, the residents would commit "an act of revolutionary suicide protesting the conditions of an inhumane world" (FBI Audiotape Q042).

Additional explanations for the eruption of violence in Jonestown concentrated on the isolation of the group in the jungles of Guyana; its totalistic organization; its suppression of individual rights; its persecution at the hands of US government officials; and its volatile interactions with critics. In several articles, Jim Lewis rightfully challenges all of these tropes, especially that of the all-powerful charismatic leader and the apocalyptic worldview (Lewis 2005, 2013, 2014a). He shifts the focus from all violent NRMs to "suicide cults," arguing that they comprise a special category of religious violence. In his view, Peoples Temple in Jonestown (1978), the Order of the Solar Temple in Switzerland and Quebec (1994-1997), and Heaven's Gate in San Diego (1997) have more in common with each other than do the groups involved in other violent incidents, such as the Branch Davidians in Waco, Texas (1993), Aum Shinrikyo in Tokyo (1995), and the Movement for the Restoration of the Ten Commandments of God in Uganda (2000).

Lewis argues that both millennialism and isolation are inadequate explanations for religious violence. On the one hand, he finds that Marshall Applewhite, the head of Heaven's Gate when 39 "class members" committed suicide, did not fit the charismatic leader stereotype. On the other, he notes that leaders of the three suicide groups shared some qualities with leaders of other violent groups—such as "an intolerance of any perspective other than their own" and a demand for total commitment from their followers (Lewis 2005, 309). Lewis does identify one quality unique to the leaders of the three suicide groups, however: they all believed that they were terminally ill. Applewhite thought he was dying of cancer; Di Mambro, who oversaw the deaths of 74 Solar Temple members, suffered numerous ailments and also assumed he had cancer; Jones either had a genuine physical illness or supposed that he did. He was certainly impaired due to his use of prescription drugs. Each of these individuals saw their groups in decline, but none had appointed a successor to lead the group in their absence. Thus, according to Lewis, a leader in failing health, in combination with other factors, may be one of the greatest predictors of violence in new religious movements.

It is clear that Jim Jones was indeed in failing health in Jonestown's final months. Notes of meetings between Temple leaders and officials at the Soviet Embassy in Georgetown, Guyana reveal repeated attempts to persuade a Cuban or Soviet doctor to go to Jonestown to treat Jones' medical problems (McGehee 2022). In August 1978, the group received word that the embassy would send its own physician to Jonestown, but as a guest, rather than in an official capacity. Yet in September, the doctor still had not come, even though Temple leaders made several more embassy visits; at one of them, a Temple visitor began to cry as she pleaded for help.

On another front, Temple members in San Francisco, including Jones' wife Marceline Jones, begged Jones' physician, Dr. Carlton Goodlett, to travel to Guyana to conduct an examination. He did so in August 1978, and found Jones looking "rather fatigued, pallid, and pale ... [with] a spiking temperature which fluctuated between 96 and 102.8 degrees. He also had a deep, nonproductive cough" (Goodlett 1989, 51). Goodlett concluded that Jones might have been suffering from a fungus infection of the lung. The community's leader was also taking a variety of psychoactive drugs, which may have contributed to his growing paranoia. "He's been ill," Jones' attorney Charles Garry said in the days immediately following the mass deaths. "He's been under a lot of medication. And I think he'd just lost his reason. A terribly, terribly emotionally sick person" (Russomano 1978). Goodlett stated that if reports like Garry's were true, Jones' drug use would have weakened him by the time Congressman Leo Ryan arrived in November to investigate Jonestown. "To that degree, then, Jones' physical health during the last few months of his life may have contributed as much as anything else to the terrible decision to destroy everything he had built" (Goodlett 1989, 51). This is precisely what Lewis asserts.

Monolithic inferences

Jim Lewis introduces the concept of monolithic inferences in a special issue of the *Journal of Religion and Violence* devoted to assessing religious terrorism (Lewis 2019). In a self-reflexive assessment of his personal experiences with members of Aum Shinrikyo, he says he saw a side to the group that others had missed. Personal interactions and conversations with ordinary disciples prompted him to view them far more sympathetically than those focused on the individuals responsible for the 1995 sarin gas attack in Tokyo that left thirteen dead and thousands injured. Indeed, he admits that he made generalizations about the entirety of Aum Shinrikyo and its leaders from those few experiences with the rank and file. After listing factors that led him to doubt official accounts of the disaster, Lewis confesses that he believed "that the ordinary [Aum] members with whom I was interacting were good, honest people who sincerely believed that AUM Shinrikyo was not involved in the subway attack" (Lewis 2019, 50). As a result, he publicly declared that the movement was not responsible for the violence. As he goes on to note, he subsequently regretted this statement many times.

Yet the criticism that followed alerted him to the problem of monolithic inference—the conviction that "all members shared the same views and had essentially the same access to knowledge of internal decisions." The fact is, however, two levels of membership existed within Aum: "an inner circle of trusted devotees clustered around the guru and a larger body of ground level members who were not privy to sinister decisions made at the inner level" (Lewis 2019, 52). While most scholars assumed that the leadership reflected the views of the entire group, Lewis had taken the opposite view, assuming that ordinary, lower-level adherents reflected the position of the group's leaders. By viewing Aum as homogeneous—that is, as monolithic—he concedes an error in judgment, an acknowledgment we should all appreciate. It was a small group of high-level insiders, rather than the thousands of devotees, who perpetrated the 1995 Tokyo attack. In that respect, Lewis is correct in claiming that Aum was innocent.

This nuanced approach to understanding group dynamics clarifies what happened in Jonestown and, more broadly, illuminates what I call the charisma of the cadre—the power and authority of an inner circle that implements the mandates of the leader (Moore 2021a). A small body of high-level followers maintains its own charisma by imparting the leader's teachings and directives (down from the top) and mediating access to the leader (up from the bottom). This group reveals to ordinary members the extraordinary powers of the leader and initiates newcomers into the cult of personality (Barker 1993). Even before a process of routinizing the leader's charisma begins, "a small cohort of those intimate with the leader turns its attention to the practical matters of mundane operations in order to promote the supramundane message" (Moore 2021a, 279).

Although multiple examples illustrate the power of the leadership cadre and that of everyday members, I focus here on Peoples Temple and just two of its successful, if tragic, endeavors: the immigration of a thousand members into Guyana and the realization of its plans for mass murder-suicide. In the first instance, a small group of pioneers built the Jonestown agricultural project from scratch, carving it out of dense rainforest. Designing and constructing an entire town to accommodate children, youth, adults, and seniors, the early Jonestown settlers worked with hopeful determination to create what they believed was going to be a heaven on earth. Ordinary members who made the move from one continent to another traveled in the expectation that their lives would improve in the new community. Dozens of Temple members in the United States made this mass migration possible by helping emigrants to obtain travel documents, health certificates, and other items necessary for moving to a foreign country (Shearer 2018). Once in Jonestown, hundreds of residents worked in a variety of professions—carpenters, cooks, laborers, teachers, nurses, tailors, mechanics, and many more—to keep the community going. The vast majority had little personal access to Jim Jones and even less participation in planning the mass deaths. Their knowledge of Jonestown was literally from the ground up.

Although Jonestown residents discussed sacrificial death frequently at community meetings and wrote imaginative scenarios describing the murder of their enemies and their own deaths, this was all part of a narrative of martyrdom prevalent in the 1960s and 1970s. "A discourse asserting the positive need to fight, and even to die, for the cause infused Peoples Temple" beginning in the 1960s and continuing throughout the 1970s, first in California and then in Guyana (Moore 2014, 73). This outlook arose as a result of the human liberation struggles of that era—Black, Latino/a,

Feminist, Indigenous, and anticolonialist—that presupposed violent death as an unavoidable consequence of resistance. The revolutionary must always be prepared to face death, hence the expression "revolutionary suicide" coined by Black Panther leader Huey P. Newton (Newton 1973, 7). Those living in Jonestown believed they were part of a radical vanguard, harassed by a conspiracy of enemies that included former members working with US government agencies. While such collusion did in fact exist, it was a conspiracy of insiders, not outsiders, who planned the mass deaths.

The scale and nature of the deaths in Jonestown gave birth to a plethora of conspiracy theories, but the conspiracy for which the most evidence exists is the collaboration of Jim Jones and the leadership circle in Jonestown. "A plan had been devised, cyanide had been acquired, and dress rehearsals occurred, all with the complicity of a number of individuals" (Moore 2018b). Several residents had suggested different ways to terminate the community (McGehee 2020), but eventually mass poisoning was selected as most effective.[1] Of course, others were needed to implement the plan—ordering the poison, unloading it from the community's ship on the Kaituma River, storing it, mixing it, and serving it. Still others were needed for crowd control as the deaths were occurring.

Jim Lewis' question regarding the innocence of the vast majority of Aum Shinrikyo devotees interrogates all explanations for the deaths in Jonestown. Children were murdered by their own parents, either by their active participation or their tacit acquiescence. Using the critique of monolithic inference, should only the leadership group be held accountable? Who is innocent? Who is guilty? These are far from rhetorical questions, since a debate continues to rage over the inclusion of Jim Jones' name on plaques memorializing those who died in Jonestown (Moore 2021b). If the leader's name were to be excluded, shouldn't the names of the leadership cadre be excluded as well, along with those of the young men who murdered Congressman Leo Ryan and four others as they attempted to leave Jonestown? Under the rubric of monolithic inference, scholars would assume that all are guilty.

Jonestown and the study of new religious movements

Even before the deaths in Jonestown occurred, scholarly consideration of "new religions" and the "new religious consciousness" had begun—a result, in part, of the 1960s counterculture interest in mysticism, self-realization, and Asian religions (Ashcraft 2018). The controversies surround-

---

1. In the interest of full disclosure, I need to state that my two sisters were part of the inner circle and were involved in this planning process; they both died in Jonestown.

ing the proliferation of new and alternative religions, however, focused on recruitment practices of the groups and lifestyle choices of the devotees. Parents and professional cult experts turned to extreme measures, such as kidnapping and deprogramming, to combat what they believed were the perverse effects of brainwashing on their (adult) children. In time, the controversies and conflicts drew the attention of sociologists. "By the time of the Jonestown tragedy in 1978, NRMs was a recognized specialization within the sociology of religion" (Lewis and Tøllefsen 2016, 2). Meanwhile, the nonsectarian study of religion was emerging as an academic field in its own right. It was not until the 1990s, however, that the religious studies academy "truly embraced" the field of NRM study (Lewis and Tøllefsen 2016, 2). This decade saw the violence at Waco, Texas (the Branch Davidians), Tokyo, Japan (Aum Shinrikyo), and San Diego, California (Heaven's Gate).

These tragedies provided scholars with comparative data by which to re-evaluate the deaths in Jonestown and other new religions. Little scholarly work on Jonestown had appeared between the 1970s and the 1990s, with the exception of two important volumes. Sociologist Thomas Robbins identified two waves in Jonestown research (Robbins 1989), a first wave comprising a single monograph, a collection of essays, and several scholarly articles; and a second wave, consisting of books by John R. Hall (*Gone from the Promised Land* 1987) and David Chidester (*Salvation and Suicide* 1988) (Robbins 1989). In 2000, I proposed adding a third wave, namely the comparative studies that came in the wake of the religious violence of the 1990s (Moore 2000).

At long last, the deaths in Jonestown could be considered in light of other tragedies. But as Lewis points out, the opposite was also the case: other tragedies, like those of the Branch Davidians, could be considered in light of Jonestown. "The government's interpretation [of Branch Davidian actions] assumes that, like Jonestown, the Davidians had actually planned a mass suicide" (Lewis 1994a, 117). In this regard, Lewis notes the influence of Davidian apostate Marc Breault, who told federal investigators that Mount Carmel was another Jonestown just waiting to happen. In other words, law enforcement officials and cult critics read Waco and the Branch Davidians through the lenses of Jonestown and Peoples Temple (see also Hall 1995). By framing the Branch Davidians as a "suicide cult," the FBI and other federal agencies could absolve themselves of responsibility for the deaths that occurred there (Lewis 2014b). Lewis criticizes the role that disaffected ex-members played in contributing to this framing, declaring that "had it not been for these outside forces, it is highly unlikely the community would ever have been engulfed in violence" (Lewis 2014b, 236).

Indeed, he describes the ways in which David Koresh, the leader, and the community seemed very much future-oriented and not suicidal. "If there is a lesson here," he observes, "it is that we should hesitate before unreflectively accusing other non-traditional religious groups of being potential Jonestowns" (Lewis 2014b, 245).

A great variety of new religious groups exists around the world, but only a few may be deemed destructive or, in the words of Introvigne, "criminal religious movements" (Introvigne 2018). As Lewis writes, "To collapse distinctions within this complex spectrum and imply that *all* such religions are potential Jonestowns/Branch Davidians is inaccurate, misleading, and dangerous" (Lewis 1994b, xv, emphasis in original). The fact is, however, that "Ever since Jonestown, part of the 'cult' stereotype has been that NRMs are volatile groups, ready to commit group suicide at the drop of a hat" (Lewis and Cusack 2014, 7).

At the time of the fortieth anniversary of the deaths in Jonestown, I addressed this very problem of using extreme cases, like Jonestown, to make predictions about other groups (Moore 2018a). Using Godwin's Law as the point of departure—which states, in brief, that all online arguments eventually end up raising the specter of Hitler and Nazism—I developed Jones' Corollary, which states that: "Discussions of new religions inevitably begin with a comparison to Jonestown" (Moore 2018a, 147). Whereas Godwin's Law describes the endpoint of the discussion (case closed!), Jones' Corollary depicts both the starting and ending point of analysis, since it presupposes the impossibility of objectively considering any new religious movement apart from Jonestown. It "reduces the known and the knowable all to Jonestown, without regard to distinction" (Moore 2018, 147). The greatest danger of appealing to Jones' Corollary is readily apparent in the deaths at Mount Carmel: it justifies state violence against religious groups. Or, to repeat what Lewis has said, the conflation of Jonestown with other groups is "inaccurate, misleading, and dangerous."

The danger is obvious, evident in the mishandling of the Branch Davidians. In the case of Peoples Temple, it is also inaccurate because it compares apples and oranges. The Temple had little in common with the Moonies, the Hare Krishnas, the Children of God, or any of the other groups that aroused the concern of professional cult watchers in the 1970s. These and other groups tended to attract a largely young, White, college educated, single, middle class membership, whereas Peoples Temple appealed to working class Blacks and Whites of all ages, and included a large cohort of families and children. Although a small group of White professionals joined and ultimately comprised the Temple's leadership cadre, by far the majority of members were African Americans who lived in the urban cores of Indianapolis, San Francisco, and Los Angeles. What they found in Peoples Temple was neither exotic nor unfamiliar; rather, they encountered traditional Black, spirit-filled worship services with a strong emphasis on implementing the Christian Social Gospel (Harrison 2004). They also discovered a political critique of American racism and capitalism, which eventually drew them out of Christianity and into a type of Humanism that Jones called "Apostolic Socialism" (Moore 2022). In short, Peoples Temple "differed in kind from other groups in terms of its membership, its ideology, its social geography, and its acute isolation" (Moore 2018a, 150). Thus, viewing other NRMs through the prism of Peoples Temple offers an inaccurate perspective.

It is also misleading to compare Peoples Temple with other groups because of the extraordinary nature of its ending. It is always dangerous to make comparisons with dramatic events, whether the Holocaust or Jonestown, because such evaluations present the extreme as the norm. "Raising the specter of Hitler, Nazis, and gas chambers stifles analysis rather than enhances it because everything is measured by a standard most people consider extreme, the Holocaust" (Moore 2018a, 146). In the same way, when cult experts invoke Jonestown to discuss all new religions, they are relying on Jones' Corollary to make a point: all cults are dangerous and even deadly. According to this view, violence is inherent in every new religion. Yet it is precisely the unusual, and even bizarre, deaths in Jonestown that make it exceptional and thus useless as a point of reference. The fact that a mere handful of groups ended by violence in the late twentieth and early twenty-first centuries, allows us to conclude that cult violence, especially that of Jonestown, appears to be the exception rather than the rule. To use Jonestown as a point of reference, then, is dangerously misleading.

Conclusion

There is more, much more, that Jim Lewis contributed to Peoples Temple and Jonestown studies. The breadth and depth of his research is astounding. His humility in the face of error is noteworthy. If there is one lesson to be learned from his vast opus, I would argue that it is his insistence on our consideration of the ultimate diversity and uniqueness of new religious movements.

He made this point very early in his career, in a paper devoted to analyzing continuities and discontinuities among six Native American prophets and shamans (Lewis 1988). His effort to construct an ideal type of Native prophet showed that they shared certain traits, but that no prophet had all of them. He concluded that if only those (six) traits he identified comprised the typical Native American prophet, "no single movement ever existed which was wholly 'typical' in the sense of embodying the entire pattern." Adding more characteristics would only reinforce this conclusion. "The principal difficulty is that out of any given set of traits, each new religion will have some but not all of them" (Lewis 1988, 222). Continuities and discontinuities exist not only across new religious movements, but also within them. This seems particularly true of Peoples Temple, thereby making broad generalizations of dubious value. I think Jim Lewis might agree with me.

About the author

Rebecca Moore is Emerita Professor of Religious Studies at San Diego State University. She serves as Series Editor for the Cambridge University Press series Elements in New Religious Movements. She is also reviews editor for *Nova Religio*, the quarterly journal on new and emergent religions published by University of Pennsylvania Press. She has written numerous books on Peoples Temple and the Jonestown tragedy. Publications include *Beyond Brainwashing: Perspectives on Cultic Violence* (Cambridge University Press 2018), and *Peoples Temple and Jonestown in the Twenty-First Century* (Cambridge University Press 2022).

References

Ashcraft, W. Michael. 2018. *A Historical Introduction to the Study of New Religious Movements*. New York: Routledge. https://doi.org/10.4324/9781315163321

Barker, Eileen. 1993. "Charismatization: The Social Production of an Ethos Propitious to the Mobilisation of Sentiments." In *Secularization, Rationalism, and Sectarianianism: Essays in Honour of Bryan R. Wilson*, edited by Eileen Barker, James Beckford, and Karel Dobbelaere, 181–201. Oxford: Clarendon Press.

Chidester, David. 1988. *Salvation and Suicide: An Interpretation of Jim Jones, the Peoples Temple, and Jonestown*. Bloomington and Indianapolis: Indiana University Press.

Dawson, Lorne L. 2006. "Psychopathologies and the Attribution of Charisma." *Nova Religio* 10(2): 3–28.

Delgado, Richard. 1977. "Religious Totalism: Gentle and Ungentle Persuasion under the First Amendment." *Southern California Law Review* 51(1): 1–98.

FBI Audiotape Q042. 1978. "Transcript by Fielding M. McGehee III." *Alternative Considerations of Jonestown and Peoples Temple*. https://jonestown.sdsu.edu/?page_id=29079.

Galanter, Marc. 1989. *Cults: Faith, Healing, and Coercion*. Oxford: Oxford University Press.

Goodlett, Carlton B. 1989. "Notes on Peoples Temple." In *The Need for a Second Look at Jonestown*. Edited by Rebecca Moore and Fielding M. McGehee III, 42–51. Lewiston, NY: Edwin Mellen Press.

Hall, John R. 1987. *Gone from the Promised Land: Jonestown in American Cultural History*. New Brunswick, NJ: Transaction Books.

———. 1995. "Public Narratives and the Apocalyptic Sect: From Jonestown to Mt. Carmel." In *Armageddon in Waco: Critical Perspectives on the Branch Davidian Conflict*. Edited by Stuart A. Wright, 205–235. Chicago, IL: University of Chicago Press.

Harrison, Milmon R. 2004. "Jim Jones and Black Worship Traditions." In *Peoples Temple and Black Religion in America*, edited by Rebecca Moore, Anthony B. Pinn, and Mary R. Sawyer, 123–138. Bloomington, IN: Indiana University Press.

Hassan, Steven Alan. 2020. "The Bite Model of Authoritarian Control: Undue Influence, Thought Reform, Brainwashing, Mind Control, Trafficking and the Law." Unpublished PhD thesis. Fielding Graduate University.

Introvigne, Massimo. 2018. "Xie Jiao as 'Criminal Religious Movements': A New Look at Cult Controversies in China and Around the World." *Journal of CESNUR* 2(1): 13–32.

———. 2022. *Brainwashing*. Cambridge: Cambridge University Press.

Jones, Constance. 1989. "Exemplary Dualism and Authoritarianism at Jonestown." In *New Religious Movements, Mass Suicide and Peoples Temple: Scholarly Perspectives on a Tragedy*, edited by Rebecca Moore and Fielding McGehee III, 209–230. Lewiston, NY: Edwin Mellen Press.

Lewis, James R. 1988. "Shamans and Prophets: Continuities and Discontinuities in Native American New Religions." *American Indian Quarterly* 12(3): 221–228. https://doi.org/10.2307/1184496

———. 1994a. "Fanning the Flames of Suspicion: The Case Against Mass Suicide at Waco." In *From the Ashes: Making Sense of Waco*, edited by James R. Lewis, 115–120. Lanham, MD: Rowman and Littlefield.

———. 1994b. "Introduction: Responses to the Branch Davidian Tragedy." In *From the Ashes: Making Sense of Waco*, edited by James R. Lewis, xi–xvi. Lanham, MD: Rowman and Littlefield.

———. 2005. "The Solar Temple 'Transits': Beyond the Millennialist Hypothesis." In *Controversial New Religions*, edited by James R. Lewis and Jesper Aagaard Petersen, 295–317. Oxford: Oxford University Press. https://doi.org/10.1093/019515682X.003.0013

———. 2013. "Sects and Violence." *Journal of Religion and Violence* 1(1): 99–121. https://doi.org/10.5840/jrv20131121

———. 2014a. "Violence." In *The Bloomsbury Companion to New Religious Movements*. Edited by George D. Chryssides and Benjamin E. Zeller, 149–162. New York: Bloomsbury. https://doi.org/10.5040/9781472594518.ch-016

———. 2014b. "The Mount Carmel Holocaust: Suicide or Execution?" In *Sacred Suicide*, edited by James R. Lewis and Carole M. Cusack, 233–250. Farnham: Ashgate.

———. 2019. "Monolithic Inferences." *Journal of Religion and Violence* 7(1): 44–54. https://doi.org/10.5840/jrv201941763

Lewis, James R. and Jesper Aagaard Peterson. 2005. "Introduction." In *Controversial New Religions*. Edited by James R. Lewis and Jesper Aagaard Peterson, 3–26. Oxford: Oxford University Press.

Lewis, James R. and Carole M. Cusack. 2014. "Introduction." In *Sacred Suicide*, edited by James R. Lewis and Carole M. Cusack, 1–8. Farnham: Ashgate. https://doi.org/10.4324/9781315607382-1

Lewis, James R. and Inge B. Tøllefsen. 2016. "Introduction." In *The Oxford Handbook of New Religious Movements*, Vol. II. Edited by James R. Lewis and Inge B. Tøllefsen, 1–14. Oxford: Oxford University Press. https://doi.org/10.1093/oxfordhb/9780190466176.013.38

[McGehee, Fielding M. III]. 2020. "Making Plans to Die." *Alternative Considerations of Jonestown and Peoples Temple.* https://jonestown.sdsu.edu/?page_id=108562.

———. 2022. "Peoples Temple Meetings with the Soviet Embassy in Georgetown, Guyana, 1978." *Alternative Considerations of Jonestown and Peoples Temple.* https://jonestown.sdsu.edu/?page_id=112381.

Moore, Rebecca. 2014. "Rhetoric, Revolution and Resistance in Jonestown, Guyana." In *Sacred Suicide*, edited by James R. Lewis and Carole M. Cusack, 73–90. London: Ashgate Publishing.

———. 2018a. "Godwin's Law and Jones' Corollary: The Problem of Using Extremes to Make Predictions." *Nova Religio* 22(3): 145–154. https://doi.org/10.1525/nr.2018.22.2.145

———. 2018b. "Jonestown at 40: The Real Conspiracy is More Disturbing than the Theories." *Religion Dispatches*. 16 November. https://rewirenewsgroup.com/2018/11/16/jonestown-at-40-the-real-conspiracy-is-more-disturbing-than-the-theories/

———. 2000. "Is the Canon on Jonestown Closed?" *Nova Religio* 4(1): 7–27. https://doi.org/10.1525/nr.2000.4.1.7

———. 2021a. "Apocalyptic Groups and Charisma of the Cadre." In *The Routledge International Handbook of Charisma*, edited by José Pedro Zúqete, 277–287. New York: Routledge. https://doi.org/10.4324/9780429263224-29

———. 2021b. "A Monumental Problem: Memorializing the Jonestown Dead." In *Beyond the Veil: Reflexive Studies of Death and Dying*, edited by Aubrey Thamann and Kalliopi M. Christodoulaki, 187–207. New York: Berghahn Press. https://doi.org/10.1515/9781800730656-012

———. 2022. *Peoples Temple and Jonestown in the Twenty-First Century.* Cambridge: Cambridge University Press.

———. 2023. "The Violence at Jonestown." In *Oxford Research Encyclopedia of Religion.* Oxford University Press. https://doi.org/10.1093/acrefore/9780199340378.013.1168

Nesci, Domenico Arturo. 1999. *The Lessons of Jonestown: An Ethnopsychoanalytic Study of Suicidal Communities.* Rome: Società Editrice Universo.

———. 2017. *Revisiting Jonestown: An Interdisciplinary Study of Cults.* Lanham, MD: Lexington Books.

Newton, Huey P. 1973. *Revolutionary Suicide.* New York: Writers and Readers Publishing.

Patrick, Ted, with Tom Dulack. 1976. *Let Our Children Go!* New York: E. P. Dutton.

Robbins, Thomas. 1989. "The Second Wave of Jonestown Literature: A Review Essay." In *New Religious Movements, Mass Suicide and Peoples Temple: Scholarly Perspectives on a Tragedy,* edited by Rebecca Moore and Fielding M. McGehee III, 113–134. Lewiston, NY: Edwin Mellen Press.

Russomano, Tony. 1978. "Guyana: How It Was." KSFO-radio, November 25. https://jonestown.sdsu.edu/?page_id=29011

Shearer, Heather. 2018. "'Verbal Orders Don't Go. Write It': Building and Maintaining the Promised Land." *Nova Religio* 22(2): 65–92. https://doi.org/10.1525/nr.2018.22.2.65

Stoner, Carroll and Jo Anne Parke. 1977. *All Gods Children: The Cult Experience—Salvation or Slavery?* Radnor, PA: Chilton Book Company.

Ulman, Richard Barrett and D. Wilfred Abse. 1983. "The Group Psychology of Mass Madness: Jonestown." *Political Psychology* 4(4): 637–661. https://doi.org/10.2307/3791059

Wessinger, Catherine. 2000. *How the Millennium Comes Violently.* New York: Seven Bridges Press.

Zee, Hugo J. 1980. "The Guyana Incident: Some Psychoanalytic Considerations." *Bulletin of the Menninger Clinic* 44(4): 345–363.

7

The Charisma of David Koresh

Catherine Wessinger

James R. Lewis has the distinction of publishing the first edited book, *From the Ashes: Making Sense of Waco* (1994), on the conflict between the Branch Davidians at Mount Carmel Center outside Waco, Texas, and federal agents in 1993. In 2014 Lewis published a chapter titled "The Mount Carmel Holocaust: Suicide or Execution?" He argued that the FBI Hostage Rescue Team's tank and CS gas assault on the Branch Davidians on April 19, 1993, which culminated in a fire, amounted to the execution of Branch Davidians for the deaths of four Bureau of Alcohol, Tobacco, and Firearms agents killed during a shootout on February 28, 1993. On the other hand, FBI agents, Justice Department attorneys, and other government representatives have argued that the deaths of seventy-six Branch Davidians of all ages in the fire were the result of a mass suicide. Based on sources accumulated during thirty years of research, Catherine Wessinger argues that there is evidence supporting both conclusions—mass suicide and massacre. She describes the social construction of the charisma of Vernon Howell/David Koresh (1959–1993), and how his narcissistic attachment to his charisma was an important factor in the interactions between FBI agents and the Branch Davidians. FBI behavioral scientists informed FBI decision-makers about Koresh's psychopathologies and how he was likely to react to an assault, but FBI officials opted for a tank and CS gas assault that would obviously end in deaths.

After the conclusion of the violent conflict between Branch Davidians, led by David Koresh (1959–1993), and federal agents between February 28 and April 19, 1993, with a total of 86 deaths at Mount Carmel Center located ten miles outside Waco, Texas, James R. Lewis (1949–2022) solicited papers and published an edited book titled *From the Ashes: Making Sense of Waco* (1994). In 2014 Lewis published a chapter titled "The Mount Carmel Holocaust: Suicide or Execution?" in which he argued for "execution" to explain the deaths of

76 Branch Davidians of all ages in the fire that concluded the FBI tank and CS gas assault on April 19, 1993. However, there is evidence that supports both conclusions—mass suicide and massacre. Branch Davidian survivor Graeme Craddock (1999) testified that during the assault he saw someone pouring fuel. Stuart A. Wright (1999) agrees with Lewis' conclusion that it was a "government massacre," because sixteen of the FBI's crisis negotiation guidelines were broken during the siege. The sabotage of the negotiations by the actions of the FBI's Hostage Rescue Team (HRT) operators, ordered by their superiors (Wessinger 2017), and the Branch Davidians' understanding of the HRT's aggressive actions as fulfilling Koresh's prophecies derived from the Bible, drove the conflict's trajectory toward the deaths on April 19, 1993. Surviving Branch Davidians who maintain faith in Koresh's teachings understand the deaths as martyrdom, not mass suicide (Wessinger 2018). After thirty years of research in a variety of sources, scholars are now better informed to analyze David Koresh's charisma constructed by the faith of his followers, and how Koresh's psychological attachment to his charisma factored into the interactive events in 1993.

Scholarly research has found that FBI decision-makers knew about the Branch Davidians' apocalyptic theology of martyrdom (Wessinger 2009; Wessinger 2017). Koresh and his students did not want to die, but they were committed to being obedient to God's prophecies in the Bible, as interpreted by Koresh, for their eternal salvation. A psychological assessment by the FBI's Behavioral Science Unit concluded that Koresh's personality had a statistically "low suicide rate," and that he was "more likely to arrange a 'suicide by cop' situation" (FBI 1993c). On April 19, 1993, a "suicide by cop" situation was prompted by HRT operators in a tank (Combat Engineering Vehicle) gassing the mothers and children, which was the point of no return in the assault. The actions of FBI agents eliminated a way for Koresh to be taken into custody while retaining charisma in the eyes of his followers, which was vital for his personal sense of importance.

The 1993 events at Mount Carmel Center were interactive. When Koresh was pressured, instead of coming out in a manner that would disprove to his followers his divinely inspired ability to interpret the Bible's prophecies, he was willing to give up the lives of everyone in the residence to fulfill his prophecies that they would be killed in a government assault, to be resurrected and carry out judgment against humanity on Earth and set up God's Kingdom in the Holy Land.

Mount Carmel Center conflict

The Branch Davidian community of about 120 people living at Mount Carmel Center became famous when agents with the Bureau of Alcohol, Tobacco, and Firearms (ATF) attempted to make a "dynamic entry" on February 28, 1993, to deliver an arrest warrant for Koresh and a search warrant to look for semi-automatic weapons that had possibly been illegally converted to automatic weapons. The "no-knock" raid turned into a shootout resulting in the deaths of four ATF agents and six Branch Davidians. FBI agents named the case WACMUR (Waco Murders) and arrived the next day to take over the siege. FBI agents who presided over the siege included the special agent in charge from San Antonio, Texas as the on-site commander; special agents in charge from other states to assist; several FBI negotiators working with police negotiators; behavioral scientists (profilers); and the FBI's Hostage Rescue Team and its commander. All the FBI teams in Waco reported to FBI officials in a command center in the Hoover Building in Washington, D.C. Beginning on March 12, 1993, FBI agents reported to the newly sworn-in Attorney General Janet Reno (1938–2016) (Wessinger 2017; K. Hall 2018).

Twenty-one children were sent out of the residence, and fourteen Branch Davidian adults came out. However, every time adults came out, HRT operators punished the remaining Branch Davidians: electricity was turned off, Combat Engineering Vehicles (CEVs) removed vehicles, high-decibel sounds were blasted through loudspeakers, and spotlights were shone during the nights. These "stress escalation" tactics undermined the efforts of negotiators, who were attempting to build trust to persuade adults to come out and be taken into custody and to send more children out (Noesner 2010, 94–132; Wright 1999). As described by retired FBI behavioral scientist Gregg O. McCrary, "The basic strategy is ... you punish the behavior you don't want, and you reward the behavior you do want. Tragically, we [the FBI] were doing just the opposite" (Bernard 2023, episode 2).

The Branch Davidian adults were waiting to see if they would be "translated" to heaven or perhaps killed by federal agents during Passover (April 5–13), after which they would be resurrected (Craddock 1999, 1: 29–30; FBI 1993d). When nothing happened during Passover, on April 14, 1993, Koresh sent out a letter describing his exit strategy. After he wrote his "little book" giving his commentary on the Seven Seals discussed in book of Revelation 5–8 in the New Testament, and the manuscript was given to two scholars, Drs. J. Phillip Arnold and James D. Tabor, for safekeeping, he would come out (Tabor and Gallagher 1995, 15–17). On April 16, Koresh reported he had completed his commentary on the First Seal, and Branch Davidians started asking for supplies for a battery-operated word processor so the manuscript could be typed. The supplies were not sent in until the evening of April 18 (Wessinger 2017, 221–22).

On April 19, 1993, starting at 6:00 a.m., HRT operators carried out an assault using CEVs to demolish portions of the building and spray inside

"CS gas," a tear gas intended for outdoor use only. Grenade launchers were used to fire in ferret rounds that release CS upon impact. CS is a powder suspended in a methylene chloride liquid base. CS burns the skin and is highly irritating to the respiratory system. The massive amounts of mucous stimulated by CS reduce oxygen intake and cause fluid to accumulate in the lungs. A person exposed to CS can quickly become disoriented, incapacitated, and suffocate. Burning CS turns into hydrogen cyanide if it comes into contact with water. CS particularly harms children, the elderly, and people with respiratory diseases, but it incapacitates healthy adults who are exposed to it for only a few seconds. In 1993, CS was banned by the Chemical Weapons Convention for use against enemy combatants, however, it continues to be used as an outdoor crowd control agent (Kaur 2020). Methylene chloride is a toxic solvent that is used in paint stripper. Short-term exposure harms the central nervous system, and lengthy exposure can cause death. As of 2023, the Environmental Protection Service is attempting to ban methylene chloride for consumer use (Puko 2023). The Branch Davidian adults had gas masks, whose filters quickly clogged up (Doyle with Wessinger and Wittmer 2012, 147), but the children had no gas masks. The 1,900 grams of CS gas utilized against the Branch Davidians is the largest reported quantity ever used in a law enforcement operation against civilians in the United States (Failure Analysis Associates 1995).

CEVs punched holes in the wooden building at locations that created air crosscurrents that would feed a fire (Gifford, Gazecki, and McNulty 1997; Wetherington 2000, 21; Failure Analysis Associates 1995). April 19, 1993 was a gusty day with winds up to 30 mph (Failure Analysis Associates 1995). FBI decision-makers knew the building contained kerosene for use with lanterns. A large propane tank was located behind the central tower. Anyone could see that a fire would likely result from a tank and CS gas assault. FBI agents testified in congressional hearings in 1995 that no "pyrotechnic" devices (explosive tear gas grenades) had been used on April 19, 1993, but in 1999 it was revealed that the evidence locker contained a pyrotechnic device, as well as four or five "flashbang" grenades (Wright 2009, 15). The Final Report of Special Counsel John C. Danforth exonerated FBI agents of using pyrotechnic devices close to the time that the first fire started (Danforth 2000, 29–32).

The mothers, young children, and two pregnant women who were taking shelter in a concrete room that had formerly been a vault, were gassed at 11:49 a.m. CS was sprayed through a nozzle mounted on the boom of a CEV driven through the front of the building toward the open doorway of the concrete room at the base of the central tower (FBI 1993a). CEV-1 was next driven into the front door of the building. Then CEV-1 moved to insert gas into the second-floor southeast corner front window (Craig 1994), and at 12:07 p.m. flames were seen inside that window. Flames originating in at least three areas of the complex quickly became a conflagration during which there was a massive explosion, probably caused by the propane tank behind the central tower (FLIR video at Grant 2021; FBI 1993b; Wetherington 2000, 7; Failure Analysis Associates 1995). Seventy-six Branch Davidians, including Koresh, died in the fire on April 19, 1993. Twenty-two children from babies to age thirteen died, including two fetuses still in the wombs of their pregnant mothers. Fourteen of these children were fathered by Koresh. Seven teenagers and forty-seven adults died. Eight adults and one teenager escaped the fire, suffering minor to severe burns (Wessinger 2018, 66). One woman brought out a floppy disk on which was saved the typed interpretation of the First Seal by Koresh (Tabor and Gallagher 1995, 20, 189-203). In addition, six Branch Davidians and 4 ATF agents died as a result of the shootout with agents of the Bureau of Alcohol, Tobacco, and Firearms on February 28, 1993.

Charisma

In 1993 and afterwards, reporters characterized David Koresh as a "cult leader" and his followers as "cultists" (Wessinger 2006). FBI agents in press briefings emphasized that Koresh was a "cult leader" who was a "liar" and "a classical sociopath" ("Barricaded Cult Leader" 1993). The news media and FBI agents stressed that Koresh had total control over his followers (Hinds 1993), illustrating what James T. Richardson has termed the "myth of the omnipotent leader" and the "myth of the passive, brainwashed followers" (Richardson 2021). No single leader can control all followers without complicit followers, secondary leaders, and guards who control whether or not persons can leave the group (see "charisma of the cadre" discussed in Rebecca Moore's chapter in this volume). There is no "omnipotent leader," although a leader may become authoritarian when there are secondary leaders who emphasize the leader's charisma to followers, and guards who enforce punishments and take other actions ordered by the leader. Followers make decisions about giving their allegiance to an individual, and when and why they may choose to give up their faith and leave (Barker 1993; J. Hall 1987; Moore 2009).

An alternative religious group frequently has a "charismatic leader," although a diffuse religious movement does not necessarily have to have one. "Charisma" comes from a Greek word that means "gift," referring to a gift of the gods or God. Sociologist Max Weber (1864-1920) defined charisma as:

> a certain quality of an individual personality by virtue of which he [or she] is set apart from ordinary [people] and treated as endowed with super-

natural, superhuman, or at least specifically exceptional powers or qualities. These are such as are not accessible to the ordinary person, but are regarded as of divine origin or as exemplary.... (Weber 1964, 358)

I define "charisma" as when people believe that someone or something has access to an unseen source of authority. People may attribute charisma to persons, scriptures, certain locations, natural or human-made objects. The unseen source of authority can be conceptualized in various ways as God, gods, Jesus, the Virgin Mary, the Holy Spirit, saints, angels, spirits, ancestors, or extraterrestrials—"all beings who are not normally visible or tangible to most people" (Wessinger 2012, 80–81).

Charisma is socially constructed by the faith of the believers. Eileen Barker argues that "charismatic authority can result, at least in part, from social processes that take place within the group which is headed by the person who is accorded the authority" (Barker 1993, 184). Judith Coney has pointed out that "developing faith in a charismatic leader is often like falling in love" (Wessinger 2012, 83; Coney 2013). People in the group's social context encourage others to manifest an attitude of love toward the leader. While charisma can be socially constructed to support a ruler's authority, anthropologists have noted that charisma may also "be the means by which talented but marginalized people—such as women, men of low social status or education, and children—gain authority, respect, and often a fulfilling religious career" (Wessinger 2012, 81).

When one person in a movement claims access to an unseen source of authority and gains followers, typically other people will claim access to the same or similar unseen source of authority. This is how new religious movements develop competing claimants to be a prophet, "an individual who is believed to receive messages from the unseen source of authority," or a messiah (the Hebrew word for "anointed"), who is "believed to be empowered by an unseen source of authority to create a collective salvation" that is expected in millennial movements. A messiah is a prophet, "but the attributed functions of a messiah go beyond those of a prophet" (Wessinger 2012, 82).

After reviewing studies of leaders to whom charisma was attributed, Lorne L. Dawson summarizes the qualities that often characterize them. Charismatic leaders "tend to be energetic people who exude self-confidence and determination" who "display a consistent faith in the fulfillment of their mission"; "their style of leadership is more visionary and emotionally expressive" and they "lead by example ... which entails a notable willingness to make the sacrifices they demand of others"; "they are known for their seeming sensitivity to the needs of others"; "they are known and admired for their superior rhetorical skills and their ability to manage impressions in face-to-face and larger group contexts"; and "charismatic leaders create the impression that they are extraordinary, and that they possess uncanny powers, by audaciously inserting themselves into the great historical and mythical scripts of their cultures" (Dawson 2011, 116–117).

"Responsible charisma" (Ji 2008) is when a leader utilizes charisma to benefit followers and others. According to Dawson (2006), when a charismatic leader suffers from psychopathologies, he or she may "mismanage" their charisma and make decisions that contribute to violence. I note that the mismanagement of charisma frequently occurs when a leader is trying to retain their charisma.

The charisma of Vernon Howell

Vernon Wayne Howell was born in Houston to an almost 15-year-old unwed mother, Bonnie Sue Clark, who after her second marriage became known as Bonnie Haldeman (1944–2009). The child's biological father was Bobby Wayne Howell (1939–2008), who was twenty when his son was born. In Texas at that time, it was legal for a girl of fourteen to marry with parental permission, but Bonnie and Bobby did not marry. During his first four years, Bonnie was frequently away and Vernon was raised by her mother, Erline Smith Clark (1924-2009), who took him to the Seventh-day Adventist Church Sabbath school for children. Vernon's paternal grandmother, Jean Holub (1924–2001), spent time with the child, but his father Bobby did not (Haldeman 2007, 5–9, 16).

Men in Vernon's family contexts drank heavily, beat their wives and children, were verbally abusive, and demanded that males be silent and tough, while Vernon talked a lot and cried frequently. His maternal grandfather Vernon Lee Clark (1922–1985) called him "that little bastard." After Bonnie married a man named Joe, she brought two-year-old Vernon to live with them. Joe gave Vernon hard spankings, and once he pressed the child's knees against the hot metal heat register on the floor. Bonnie's marriage to Joe quickly ended, and Vernon was sent back to Erline be raised (Talty 2023, 8–10, 12–13; Haldeman 2007, 9–10).

After Bonnie married Roy Haldeman, a former bar owner who became a carpenter, she went to bring four-year-old Vernon into her marital home. Vernon cried, "Don't take me from my mama. I don't want you to be my mama!" The Haldeman family moved into a rural home in Richardson, north of Dallas, and Vernon's younger brother, Rodger, was born. When Bonnie's parents and their kids came to visit, Vernon got to play with his younger aunt and uncle. When they departed, Vernon would get on his bicycle and pedal after them crying out, "Take me with you!" (Talty

2023, 14–17). Roy drank a lot, was violent toward Bonnie, and would whip Vernon or Rodger hard when angered. When Vernon cried, Roy shouted, "Be a man!" (Talty 2023, 24–25, 39–40).

When Vernon was five, one of Bonnie's male relatives "started touching Vernon sexually," which advanced to rape. This abuse continued for four years (Talty 2023, 27–28; Samples *et al.* 1994, 20–21). When he was six, an older girl molested him. Once some older boys chased Vernon and a friend through a field, where they "held the two boys down and violated them" (Talty 2023, 27–28).

Vernon was gregarious as a child and could not sit still. He had difficulty learning to read and had to take first grade twice. He was evaluated in second grade, and Bonnie was told he had a learning disability. In third grade he was put into a special education class, but at recess, Vernon was emotionally crushed when the other children shouted, "Here come the retards!" School bullies called him "Retard," and after third grade, he was called "Mr. Retardo" (Haldeman 2007, 15; Talty 2023, 17–18).

When Vernon was nine, Bonnie took him with her to attend a Seventh-day Adventist Church. He loved listening to the sermons. He also listened to radio preachers and watched television evangelists. He read the Bible and memorized sections of it. He read the Bible studies of William Miller (1782–1849), the Baptist Bible interpreter who started the Millerite movement that set dates for the Second Coming of Jesus Christ until the Millerites experienced the "Great Disappointment" on October 22, 1844. He read essays by Ellen G. White (1827–1915), who by means of her visions interpreted the Great Disappointment to indicate that Christ had started an important work of judgment in heaven on that date. Ellen White co-founded the Seventh-day Adventist Church and was regarded as its prophet by members (Talty 2023, 21–23).

Vernon doubted that he was loved. When he was twelve, he prayed, "Dear God ... dear Father ... I don't understand why I'm this way.... I know I'm stupid but ... please talk to me because I want to serve you..." (FBI 1993e, 26). One evening, Vernon was praying when he saw "a very beautiful, soft ... like explosion in the universe and this star." He heard a voice call his name (FBI 1993e, 28; Talty 2023, 28–29). As he became a young man, Vernon frequently heard what he believed was God's Voice.[1]

When Vernon was eleven, he decided to exercise because he did not "want to be a target anymore" (Talty 2023, 30). He joined the track team

---

1 Hearing voices apparently ran in Bonnie's family. Her younger sister Beverly, who had been diagnosed with schizophrenia, on January 23, 2009 stabbed Bonnie in the heart, killing her, when Bonnie arrived at the house to take Beverly to the doctor (Nailling 2018; Talty 2023, 44).

at school and became popular due to winning races. In his early teens, Vernon became interested in cars and learned how to fix car engines. After Roy and Bonnie purchased a home in Sachse, Texas, at thirteen, Vernon said he wanted to attend a Seventh-day Adventist school for junior high. Bonnie enrolled Vernon and Rodger at the Dallas Junior Academy, where they attended for a couple of years until it was time for Vernon to attend Garland High School. He dropped out of high school in the eleventh grade (Talty 2023, 30–34).

In 1976 Vernon, age seventeen, got a construction job. He and a 15-year-old girl named Linda became lovers. When Linda called to tell him she was pregnant, he replied, "I'm sterile." Subsequently, the Lord told Vernon in a dream that he should marry Linda, but when he went back, she informed him that she had gotten an abortion. She invited him over and they resumed their love affair. When Linda became pregnant a second time, her father drove Vernon off. Vernon told Linda that God had told him that she was to be his wife, but after the baby was born, Linda would not let him see their daughter.

Vernon was devastated by the loss of Linda and the opportunity to be a father to his daughter. By that time, his parents were living near Tyler, Texas. Vernon began attending churches in Tyler to see if any of them could provide answers to heal his grief. He bought a car to work on, but then set it on fire (Talty 2023, 39–43). He attended "Revelation Seminars" held by a Seventh-day Adventist preacher depicting the events predicted in the book of Revelation, but he found that the preacher did not discuss the meaning of the Seven Seals, which Vernon felt was needed to present a complete message of the Last Days. One night while sleeping in the back seat of his pickup truck, Vernon felt God's presence above his body, pulsing and pressing down on him. God spoke to Vernon saying, "Don't you know that for nineteen years I've loved you and for nineteen years you've turned your back on me and rejected me?" (Talty 2023, 39–49, quote on 49).

Vernon started attending the Seventh-day Adventist Church in Tyler. Now 20 years old, Vernon came to the pastor's home for Bible studies, and he noticed the pastor's 15-year-old daughter named Sandy. After the pastor baptized him, Vernon told Sandy that, as he went down into the water, he heard demons' voices shrieking to try to make him stop being baptized. He confided to Sandy that he battled Satan every day. Once Satan pressed him down on his bathroom floor for hours as he "begged God to help him." When she saw him after that episode, he was "exhausted, just wrung out" (Talty 2023, 50–53).

Sandy's father invited Vernon to come on the family's vacation to Minnesota. Sandy and Vernon sat in the car's back seat, reciting Bible verses to express their love to each other. Once in Minnesota, outside among trees, Vernon kissed her and said, "Sandy, God has told me that you are to become my wife." He immediately told her father that "God has revealed to me that I'm to marry Sandy...." Her father became angry and attempted to keep Sandy and Vernon apart for the rest of the trip (Talty 2023, 53-61). After returning to Tyler, Vernon continued seeing Sandy.

Once Vernon took over her father's pulpit during a service and preached about how he wanted to hear new prophecies from living prophets. He interrupted sermons in the church multiple times. Finally, men picked him up and carried him out of the church. Sandy broke up with him, but he began stalking her. Sandy agreed to meet Vernon in Dallas, but when he pulled up in his car, he told her that they were married in the eyes of God, and he "opened the trunk and told her to get in." She spent three hours persuading him to let her go (Talty 2023, 62-64; Bunds 2023d).

Vernon asked an older family friend named Harriet, "Where are the living prophets?" Harriet told him about Mount Carmel Center outside Waco, Texas, where there was a prophet named Lois Roden (1916-1986). In the summer of 1981, when he was 22, Vernon Howell went to Mount Carmel Center (Talty 2023, 64-65).

Social construction of Vernon Howell's charisma at Mount Carmel Center

Former Branch Davidian David Bunds has commented that when Vernon arrived in 1981, there was an "invisible 'Prophet Wanted' Sign" at Mount Carmel Center (Bunds 2023a; Bunds 2023b). The Branch Davidians, as an offshoot of an offshoot (the Davidians) of the Seventh-day Adventist Church, believe it is essential to be led by an individual possessing the "Spirit of Prophecy" to reveal "New Light" on the Bible's prophecies about the imminent Last Days. They believe in "present truth" (2 Peter 1: 12) (Lovelock 2023b) revealed for God's people today. Knowledge about Christ's appearing is regarded as being revealed progressively to "God's remnant people," those considered to be the "wave sheaf," the "first of the first fruits" of the coming harvest of souls (Tabor and Gallagher 1995, 48-49; Doyle with Wessinger and Wittmer 2012, 83-90).

Branch Davidians believe that individuals important for their lineage of prophets are the "seven angels" in Revelation 8-10, 14-18. The Seventh-day Adventist Church interpreted William Miller and Ellen G. White as fulfilling the messages of the first three angels in Revelation 14. Adventist Joseph Bates (1792-1872) taught that the message of the first two angels, "that the hour of the judgment had come" in 1844 and that Babylon would fall, had been fulfilled by Miller and his associates. The third angel was Ellen G. White and those who founded the Seventh-day Adventist Church with the message of God's requirement to observe the seventh-day Sabbath (Saturday) (Tabor and Gallagher 1995, 48–49). According to Branch Davidian interpretation, the fourth angel was Victor Houteff (1885-1955), the founder and prophet of the General Association of the Davidian Seventh-day Adventists in Waco, Texas in 1935. His message was that there "would be a literal, earthly Davidic Kingdom in Palestine." The fifth angel was Ben Roden (1902–1978), the prophet and founder of the General Association of Branch Davidian Seventh-day Adventists in 1955, who purchased the 77 remaining acres of property located outside Waco called Mount Carmel Center, formerly owned by the Davidians. He taught the observance of the Jewish feast days (Tabor and Gallagher 1995, 50). Prior to Ben's death, his wife Lois Roden in 1977 had a vision showing that the Holy Spirit is feminine, and with that message she became the sixth angel and second prophet of the Branch Davidians (Tabor and Gallagher 1995, 50; Talty 2023, 71–72).

Bunds states that as soon as Lois Roden was recognized as the sixth angel, everyone at Mount Carmel Center knew that there would be a seventh angel (2023a). Vernon Howell, a young man who believed that God's Voice spoke to him, and who battled Satan daily, found a culture at Mount Carmel Center that emphasized the need for the group to be led by a prophet inspired to interpret the Bible's secrets about the Last Days.

The Branch Davidians believe that an individual who is able to interpret the Bible's prophecies plausibly is a prophet inspired by God to interpret God's Word. Vernon Howell was accepted as the new prophet, succeeding Lois Roden, by 1984. The Branch Davidians consider the Bible, particularly the King James Version of the Bible, to be God's Word and therefore a repository of charisma. Only a prophet can adequately interpret the meaning of God's Word to reveal the events of the impending Last Days. Branch Davidians believe that figures described in the Bible are "types" that predict figures in the present or near future called "antitypes" (Newport 2006, 77–79, 216).

Gradually, Vernon learned the culture at Mount Carmel Center and the scriptures that he would teach to encourage Branch Davidians to regard him as the seventh angel, the antitypical King David, the antitypical King Cyrus who would defeat the Spirit of Babylon for our time (Lovelock 2023a), and the Son of God filled with the Spirit of Prophecy. By 1985 Vernon claimed to be almost every significant figure described in the Bible. He taught that he had cracked the code in the Bible to interpret its "present truth" (Bunds 2023f).

Soon after arriving at Mount Carmel Center, Vernon wanted to start giving Bible studies, but that decision was up to Lois Roden. First, Vernon had to study the prophetic literature published by Ellen White, Victor Houteff, Ben Roden, and Lois Roden, and also study the Old Testament prophets to learn how to give Bible studies that Branch Davidians would find plausible. In 2003 I asked Branch Davidian survivor Clive Doyle (1941–2022) how he discerned if someone was a prophet or not. Doyle told me that a true prophet will present a message that is consistent with the messages given by previous prophets (personal communication). Branch Davidian survivor Derek Lovelock (2023c) explains that a new prophet's teaching, while shedding "New Light" for present-day believers, must not contradict earlier prophets. The previous prophets include the prophets in the Seventh-day Adventist, Davidian, and Branch Davidian lineage, but they also include the prophets of the Old Testament.

When I interviewed her in 2003, Bonnie Haldeman did not remember the name of Vernon's learning disability, but she said it was not dyslexia (Haldeman 2007, 15). David Bunds reports that he saw Vernon switch particular letters, so he thinks Vernon had a type of dyslexia (2023f). However, when Vernon's attention was captured by something like the biblical prophecies about the Last Days, he was able to read. As observed by Debbie Kendrick at Mount Carmel Center,[2] Vernon spent a lot of time studying in his bedroom in a little house across from the Kendricks' house (Talty 2023, 79–81). He became adept at relating Bible passages to the Seven Seals passages in the book of Revelation to describe an apocalyptic scenario that was captivating to the majority of the Branch Davidians and attracted new members.

During this period, Lois Roden may have introduced Vernon to a book in the Waco Public Library named *Koreshanity* (Bartosh 1971) about the biblical interpretations of Cyrus R. Teed (1839-1908), who in the 1980s founded a community in Estero, Florida called Koreshan Unity. In 1892, Teed changed his name to Koresh, which is Hebrew for Cyrus. Cyrus the Great (d. 530 BC) was the ruler of the Persian Empire who in 539 BC conquered the Babylonian Empire, and decreed that the Jews who were being held in exile in Babylon could return to Jerusalem and rebuild the Temple, which had been destroyed by the Babylonian army in 586 BC. King Cyrus provided the funds for the rebuilding of the Temple (2 Chron. 36:23; Ezra 6: 3–8). In Isaiah 45: 1 Cyrus is called the Lord's anointed (*messiah* in Hebrew, *christos* in Greek). *Koreshanity* discusses Teed as being "the end-time David, the final Koresh, and the Lamb who opens the Seven Seals" (Arnold 2023, 102). The book argues that Koresh is the Rider on the White Horse (Rev. 6: 2), one possessing the "Spirit of Prophecy" (Bartosh 1971, 19, 137). J. Phillip Arnold argues that Vernon Howell did not "plagiarize" Teed, but may have

---

2   Deborah Kendrick would subsequently marry David Bunds and become Deborah Bunds.

been inspired by the *Koreshanity* book, either indirectly through teachings received from Lois Roden, or directly by reading the *Koreshanity* book. If he knew of Teed's Bible interpretations, Vernon would have made the Koresh messiah concept his own and placed it at the center of the theology that he crafted from the themes of prior Seventh-day Adventist, Davidian, and Branch Davidian prophets, to which he added his own interpretations. Arnold argues that there are no other examples in Christian history of a messiah taking the name Koresh, and to find "two Koresh figures in the same century" seems to be more than coincidence (Arnold 2023).

Lois Roden was being challenged for the role of prophet after Ben Roden's death by their son George Roden (1938–1998). George has been described as coarse, violent, and not well versed in the Bible or the literature produced by the earlier prophets in this lineage. He was armed, threatening, and sometimes hurt people. Lois did not consider him to be suitable for the prophet role (Talty 2023, 82–84).

Vernon gave his first series of Bible studies, titled "The Serpent's Root," beginning on September 8, 1983, and recorded on seven audiotapes. Clive Doyle's voice can be heard on the audio as he rigorously questions Vernon about his interpretations of Bible passages and his understanding of the teachings of Ellen White, Victor Houteff, and Lois Roden. Two decades later, Doyle reported, "I heard him speak two or three times and I was convinced that this was of God" (Doyle with Wessinger and Wittmer 2012, 75, 209n2). Vernon gave five Bible studies and then he and Lois left to travel to Israel. After their return, Vernon gave two more Bible studies in this series.

When Vernon was giving one of his Bible studies in 1983, Lois Roden remarked to Branch Davidian Perry Jones (1929–1993), "It looks like God has raised a son out of the earth" (Bunds 2023a). Perry told David Bunds (2023a) that he understood Lois as saying that Vernon was now her adopted son, the prophet after her, and therefore the seventh angel. But Vernon was more than a son to Lois, who in 1983 was 67. She fell in love with Vernon (24 in 1983), and he moved into her house. Vernon justified their relationship by citing Isaiah 8: 2: "And I went unto the prophetess; and she conceived, and bare a son." One day Lois announced to everyone that she was pregnant while waving around a pregnancy test. (Bunds points out that a pregnancy test in that period could give a false positive if instructions were not carefully followed [2023b]). Lois considered that she and Vernon were married (Tabor and Gallagher 1995, 41). After Vernon snuck off one night in January 1984 in Lois' van and legally married 14-year-old Rachel Jones (1969–1993), with permission of her father Perry Jones, Lois was hurt and angry (Bunds 2023c).

Passover 1984 marked the consolidation of Vernon's charisma among the Branch Davidians, but he also had to face Lois Roden's wrath in public. Catherine Matteson, who was Lois' secretary, reports that before Passover, Vernon gave her a letter for Lois to sign inviting Branches from all over the world to come to Mount Carmel Center for Passover to hear him give Bible studies. Lois did not want to sign it, but Catherine said, "Lois, you know you have to sign it, so why don't you just sign it?" (Matteson 2004). Lois signed the letter.

The Branch Davidians at Mount Carmel Center were concluding that the Spirit of Prophecy had moved from Lois Roden to Vernon Howell. According to Catherine Matteson, "One day [Lois Roden] said to me, 'I've lost my spirit of prophecy,'" and Catherine replied, "Yes, I know" (Matteson 2004; Pitts 2009). During one of Vernon's Bible studies during Passover 1984, Lois came in, sat quietly, but then stood up and described everything that she and Vernon had done together sexually (Bunds 2023b; Bunds 2023c). This was clearly an attempt to undermine Vernon's charisma in the eyes of the Branch Davidians, but the majority of the Branch Davidians had already decided that the Spirit of Prophecy was with Vernon, making him the seventh angel.

In 1986, Lois was diagnosed with breast cancer, but she did not have it treated by conventional means. She came to have Passover with Vernon and the Branch Davidians in a camp they had constructed in the piney woods near Palestine, Texas to escape George Roden's violence. She died on November 10, 1986.

Vernon Howell becomes David Koresh

In 1985 Vernon and Rachel, now pregnant with their first child Cyrus (1985–1993), went to Israel. Upon returning, Vernon reported that while he was standing on Mount Zion outside the Old City walls in Jerusalem, he saw seven angels, without wings, riding in a merkabah (flying four-wheeled chariots), who came down and spoke with him. He was flown in a merkabah past the constellation Orion, where he learned what he called the "Cyrus Doctrine." He was the Cyrus messiah, the Christ who would defeat present-day "Babylon" and create God's kingdom on Earth (Talty 2023, 104–105; Newport 2006, 181–183; FBI 1993f, 6–19; Lovelock 2023a).

When Vernon returned from Israel, he presented himself as the Son of God. He had a flyer printed for distribution to Seventh-day Adventists, signed V. W. H. Jezreel (c. 1986). Vernon, using his own initials with the name Jezreel, was emulating Victor Houteff, who wrote letters to members of the Seventh-day Adventist Church signed V. H. Jezreel (Houteff 2023). In the flyer, Vernon wrote as Jezreel in the book of Hosea, "the son of an unfaithful mother," to call the Seventh-day Adventist Church back to God (Bunds 2023e).

> I Am the Son of God. You do not know Me nor My name. I have been raised up from the north and My travels are from the rising of the sun.
>
> All the prophets of the Bible speak of Me....
>
> I have been rejected in the person of My prophets over and over.... My Name is the Word of God and I ride on a white horse (Rev. 19:11). I Am here on earth to give you the Seventh Angel's Message (Rev. 10:7).
>
> I Am the prophets; all of them.... I Am the Word of God. The key of David is in My hand.... My Name is Cyrus and I Am here to destroy Babylon (Rev. 9:14)....
>
> The young men will abuse My kindness. They will take My life, but I will arise and take theirs forever more....
>
> I Am the Word and you do not know Me. I ride on a white horse and My Name is secret....
>
> PREPARE TO MEET THY GOD

Initially Vernon's group was called the Davidian Branch Davidian Seventh-day Adventists (DBD Seventh-day Adventists). This name for the group was on a checking account (Kiyabu 2023a). During the 1993 conflict with federal agents, journalists found that the title to the Mount Carmel Center property listed the owner as the General Association of the Branch Davidian Seventh-day Adventists, so the group was called the Branch Davidians in news articles, and that name has stuck.[3] As Vernon Howell brought in new followers from California, Hawai'i, Australia, and the United Kingdom, they simply called it the study group for the students of the Seven Seals (Kiyabu 2023b).

A major support for Vernon's claim to be the Christ for the imminent Last Days was that he was able to "open" the Seven Seals in the book of Revelation. Since Rev. 5: 9 states that only the Lamb "as it had been slain" (Rev. 5: 6), who stands before the one who sits on a throne holding a book sealed with Seven Seals, is worthy to open the Seals, Vernon reasoned that he was the Lamb. He would be slain, and according to the Fifth Seal (Rev. 6: 9–11), some of the faithful in his group would be slain, and after a waiting period, the remainder would be slain. Afterwards, they would be resurrected, with David Koresh as the Rider on the White Horse, and with the Branch Davidians as members of the wave sheaf, the 200 million (Rev. 9: 16) martyrs of all the ages, they would judge humanity on Earth, before Koresh set up God's kingdom on a miraculously elevated Mount

---

3   The Branch Davidians must be distinguished from Victor Houteff's Davidians, and any other individuals or groups calling themselves Branch Davidians.

Zion, with the 144,000, and then the other souls to be harvested (Doyle, with Wessinger and Wittmer 2012, 89–98).

In 1986, Vernon began to take additional (extralegal) wives to bear his children since he carried God's seed. The children were God's children who would help rule God's Kingdom on Earth. Dana Okimoto Kiyabu, who was his sixth wife, reports that during this early stage, Vernon taught that if group members were attacked and killed, the children would survive. Vernon was not yet teaching that his children would be the twenty-four elders described in the book of Revelation who would assist in the judgment (Kiyabu 2023b).

Some of the young women whom he made his wives were fourteen years old, and apparently there was parental permission, or at least, no objection. Some were of legal age, which in Texas is seventeen or older. Two of the older young women—Robyn Bunds and Dana Okimoto—eventually decided to leave, taking three of Vernon's offspring. Michele Jones (1974–1993), Rachel's younger sister, was made his "wife" when she was twelve, and Aisha Gyarfas (1975–1993) when she was thirteen (England and McCormick 1993a, 1993b). Michele had three children with Koresh. Aisha had one child and was pregnant with her second child when she died with the other mothers and children in the concrete room on April 19, 1993.

In 1988, the Branch Davidians returned to live at Mount Carmel Center. In 1989, Vernon Howell, who would legally change his name to David Koresh in 1990, presented a "New Light" teaching that David Bunds terms the "doctrine of marriage nullification" (2023i). Koresh announced that all marriages in the group were annulled, because God had not sanctioned them, and all the women were Koresh's wives and all the men—except Koresh—were to be celibate. This caused a lot of consternation, with some people leaving the group. Several of the legally married women had children with Koresh.

In congressional testimony in 1995, Kiri Jewell said that when she was ten years old in 1991, her mother Sherri Jewell (1950-1993) and a female friend took Kiri to a motel room where they slept in the same bed with Koresh, and hung out for several days. When the women left to go shopping, he had sex with Kiri, after which he read the Song of Solomon (also called, Song of Songs) to her, thereby inducting Kiri into the House of David as one of his wives (House of Representatives 1995, 1:147-55; Kiyabu 2023c). Kiri Jewell was the subject of a custody dispute between her father, who was not a Branch Davidian, and her mother. In 1992 a judge in Michigan ruled that Kiri could not be taken back to Koresh, and Sherri could have supervised visitations (England and McCormick 1993a).

Koresh justified his "marriage" of young girls under fourteen by referring to Song of Solomon 8: 8: "We have a little sister, and she hath no breasts: what shall we do for our sister in the day when she shall be spoken for?" He understood "spoken for" as a marriage proposal, and he understood this to mean that he should "marry" Michele Jones (Talty 2023, 127) and other young girls. Koresh stressed that the youngest wives needed to be "protected," meaning that those "marriages" were kept secret (Kiyabu 2023c).

In 1992, the Branch Davidians were investigated for child abuse by Texas Child Protective Services. No evidence of abuse was found and the case was closed. Also in 1992, Koresh and his students moved into the large building that they had built at Mount Carmel Center. Toward the end of 1992, Koresh and the Branch Davidians were aware that their new neighbors in the house across the street were law enforcement agents. Koresh was told that an ATF agent was visiting his licensed gun dealer asking questions, and over the telephone Koresh invited the agent to come over and inspect his weapons, which was declined. The stage was set for the conflict between the Branch Davidians and federal agents in 1993.

David Koresh's charisma

Branch Davidian adult survivors say that even if they did not like him personally (Schroeder 2019), they found Koresh's Bible interpretations to be so convincing they were motivated to join the group. Many had Seventh-day Adventist backgrounds, but some of Koresh's students did not. With the possible exception of Steve Schneider, who is said to have earned a degree in Religious Studies at University of Hawai'i (Newport 2006, 4), the majority of them had not been exposed to the historical-critical method for studying the Bible and the social contexts in which its books were written and developed. According to David Bunds, Vernon never admitted he was mistaken on a biblical interpretation, except once when the two were studying the Bible together in private (Bunds 2023f).

According to Dana Okimoto Kiyabu, when she entered the room in Hawai'i where she first heard Vernon teach, "I felt what I believed to be the presence of God. There was a Spirit in the room that called to me, and said, 'Listen,' so I did." She reports, "His ability to paint the picture that was there [in the Bible] was amazing. He could bring the Bible to life." "He was showing me my part in God's words. We are written in the Book." When Vernon was not giving a Bible study, "He was just this goofy guy" (Kiyabu 2023b).

Julian Bonano's report (2023) on Koresh's charisma is interesting because of his non-member perspective. He was raised Catholic, became a Buddhist, and was attracted to the theology of the Seventh-day Adventist Church. While he was attending an SDA church in Hollywood, he met Kathy

Andrade (1968–1993). She invited him, in 1990 or 1991, to attend Koresh's Bible study being given in a house in Pomona, California. Julian was captivated by Koresh's presence and knowledge of the Bible. Koresh was quoting scripture after scripture, but did not pick up the Bible that was on a table. During a break, Julian told Koresh, "You are either an effective liar slash con artist, or you really know your Bible." Koresh said, "What if I'm both?" Julian said, "I don't know if that is a bad thing." Koresh asked, "Are you going to stay?" Julian replied, "I'll just stay and see if you really are a con artist." Koresh laughed and said, "Have a seat."

Julian liked what Koresh was teaching about the book of Revelation and the Last Days, and he judged that Koresh believed what he was teaching. Julian became a student of the Seven Seals, but he did not travel to Texas to join Koresh's group. Julian believes that Koresh was divinely inspired to interpret the Bible's prophecies, and that Koresh heard God speaking to him and followed God's lead.

I asked Julian Bonano if he found Koresh to be charismatic in light of how I define "charisma." Julian said that he felt Koresh's charisma when he walked into the room. He reported that Koresh had the "It Factor." He explained that in the entertainment industry the It Factor involves knowing your lines, being beautiful with a chiseled body, and being smart. He said, "David Koresh had that charisma, that 'It Factor,' that could have and would have taken him into places that he had never been before. Even though his ministry wasn't as long as most, it made a very, very indelible impression on many. I'm one of many" (Bonano 2023).

Conclusion

Vernon Howell was a high school drop-out from a modest working-class background in Texas. After multiple incidents of name-calling, torture, sexual abuse, and bullying in his childhood, and two rejections in love as a young man, in 1981 at age 22 he joined the Branch Davidian community at Mount Carmel Center. As someone who believed he heard the voice of God and was wrestling with Satan daily, among the Branch Davidians he was in a social context in which the devil was viewed as real and God was believed to inspire prophets. By 1984 Vernon had consolidated his role as the group's new prophet, the seventh angel. In 1985, he reported having an experience in Jerusalem revealing that he was the Son of God, the "Lamb" in the book of Revelation who can "open" the Seven Seals. He was the antitypical Cyrus—Koresh—who would defeat today's Spirit of Babylon.

David Koresh fit the pattern of a creative individual of low social status, who through the social construction of charisma became viewed by followers as having access to an unseen source of authority. As the Son of

God, the Christ for the Last Days, he was seen as being one with God and God's Word. Becoming David Koresh gave Vernon Howell self-confidence, significance within the Branch Davidian group, a new family of which he was the head, and love from his followers (Gifford, Gazecki, and McNulty 1997; Branch Davidians 1993; Doyle with Wessinger and Wittmer 2012; and Thibodeau with Whiteson 1999).

In a religious group led by a charismatic leader, it is typical for other persons to claim charisma and attempt to attract followers. Vernon Howell superseded the charisma of Lois Roden as prophet when the Branch Davidians decided that the Spirit of Prophecy had moved from her to him based on the quality of his teachings delivered in Bible studies. In 1987 George Roden dug up a casket from the Mount Carmel Center cemetery, and challenged Vernon to see which one of them could raise the dead. He was proposing a test based on charisma, power coming from God (Doyle with Wessinger and Wittmer 2012, 65–66). When Marc Breault converted to Vernon's message in 1986, Vernon was aware that Marc had visions. When Marc left the group in 1989, he pretended to be a prophet who could interpret the Bible better than Koresh to draw people away from Koresh (Talty 2023, 121–123, 195–198). After David Bunds and Marc Breault corrected or disagreed with his biblical interpretations, Koresh recorded a sermon in late 1989 or early 1990, which Bunds has named "Our Foundation," in which Koresh shouted: "God in the flesh! Do you know who I am? God in the flesh! The Word of God in the Book has been shown to you, the most powerful of all the prophets!"

Derek Lovelock explains that Koresh encouraged his students to look behind the man Koresh. He told them to look to the Lord, because when Koresh was teaching, it was the Lord talking. Koresh taught that anyone who hears the Lord's message and rejects it is "in jeopardy" (Lovelock 2023b). David Bunds stresses that fear was a major factor keeping people inside the group. They believed that the resurrected David Koresh, during the judgment of humanity on Earth, would kill them for rejecting the Truth. In the "Our Foundation" tape Koresh threatened, "Now go against that revelation of Truth, and I guarantee you, I'll kill you one day" (Bunds 2023h).

People who disagreed with Koresh's theology and his activities left the group, but leaving was easier for some than for others. It was harder for people from other countries to leave because their passports had been taken (Talty 2023, 220–221; BBC Radio 5 2018, fourth episode). It was difficult to decide to leave if a person did not have a job or financial resources (Bunds 2023j). Such factors constituted high "exit costs" (Zablocki 1997). Exit costs included emotional factors such as having given up a wife or daughters to be Koresh's wives, and not wanting to leave loved ones who intended to stay. A significant exit cost was people's fear that if they rejected Koresh's message, they would suffer death in the resurrected Koresh's judgment and thereby be "lost" to eternal life. On the other hand, if there were persons that Koresh judged as having the potential to diminish his charisma in the eyes of followers, he would evict or strongly encourage them to leave (Bunds 2023i; Haldeman 2007, 66–69).

Out of the qualities frequently found in charismatic leaders (Dawson 2011), the one that Koresh did *not* manifest was willingness to make the sacrifices demanded of others. All the men were required to be celibate, but Koresh was not. The Mount Carmel Center large residence was not air-conditioned, while Koresh's room was. People who worked at outside jobs were required to turn over most of their earnings as "tithes," while Koresh used their money to purchase sports cars, entertainment items, and to travel in the United States and abroad, in addition to using it to support the community.

Koresh may have recognized the aspect of his personality that was a con artist, but he believed what he was teaching. After he was wounded in the side and wrist during the shootout with ATF agents, he called his mother and left the following message:

> Momma? It's your boy. They shot me and I'm dying, alright? But I'll be back real soon, okay? I'm sorry you didn't learn the Seals, but I'll be merciful, okay? Tell Grandma, I tried [to call]. I'll see ya'll in the skies. Bye.
> (Koresh 1993a)

Koresh also talked to several media outlets to spread his message so people would have the opportunity for salvation when the time of judgment came. He waited several hours to be put on the air on CNN (Schechter 2023). Describing himself as "weakening," he spoke in the CNN broadcast for about twenty minutes. Koresh stated that he wanted to explain to the public the "foundation of our belief." He mentioned his encounter with seven angels in Jerusalem, and explained that since he could open the Seven Seals, he was the Lamb (Koresh 1993b).

When Koresh promised on April 14, 1993 to write his "little book" providing his commentary on the Seven Seals, the angel in Revelation 10 holding "a little book opened" was the "type" that he utilized, with himself as the "antitype," to validate his exit plan while maintaining his charisma in the eyes of his followers. Maintaining his charisma was the most important motivating factor for him. In terminology used by FBI and police negotiators, permitting Koresh to "save face" while coming out to be taken into custody could have saved a lot of lives. As Gregg McCrary summarized it, "Don't tip over the dignity domino. Their dignity must be respected" (Bernard 2023, episode 2).

Violence, Conspiracies, and New Religions

David Koresh had psychopathologies that prevented him from exercising his charisma responsibly. Dr. Todd L. Grande, licensed mental health counselor, does not think that Koresh had schizophrenia because his thinking was not disorganized. Instead, Grande suggests that Koresh had delusional disorder combined with narcissism. Grande explains there is a "grandiose narcissism" for people who are "extroverted, socially bold, self-confident, having a superficial charm, being resistant to criticism, and being callous and unemotional." There is also "vulnerable narcissism" "characterized by shame, anger, aggression, hypersensitivity, a tendency to be introverted, defensive, avoidant, anxious, depressed, socially awkward, and shy" (Grande 2020a), which appears to apply to Vernon Howell more than David Koresh.

According to Grande, FBI agents' tactical actions "did everything to feed David's delusion." Grande states:

> Many clinicians know that when you're working with somebody who's delusional, you really can't always refute the delusion directly—especially early in the relationship—and this is what we really see the FBI did. They refuted it. They made fun of David [in press conferences]. That was going to get them nowhere. A better tactic would have been to say, "Alright, tell me about what you think is going on here," and to really get invested to really, truly try to understand his point of view. Then maybe they could have used their intelligence to create a narrative within that framework—within the delusional framework—that perhaps could have had David release more people or even give up at some point. (Grande 2020b)

This is what Dr. J. Phillip Arnold and Dr. James D. Tabor understood as religious studies and Bible scholars. They contacted FBI agents to suggest ways negotiation strategies could be crafted to work within the worldview to persuade Branch Davidians to come out while remaining true to their ultimate concern of being faithful to God's will for them. When FBI agents refused to listen, on April 1, 1993, Arnold and Tabor directed a radio conversation to Koresh and the Branch Davidians discussing the Bible's prophecies and suggesting that the "waiting period" in the Fifth Seal would be more than a few months, and that Koresh could spread his message by coming out and writing his book explaining the Seven Seals in prison. On April 14, 1993, Koresh sent FBI agents his written exit plan, but this plan was derailed by the FBI tank and CS gas assault on April 19, 1993.

In a 2023 Facebook group discussion, Dana Okimoto Kiyabu wrote:

> I have no clue as to who started the fire on April 19, 1993, but I do know who picked the fight on February 28. As someone who would have been in that "concrete bunker" that I remember as where the walk-in refrigerator was, I lay the ultimate responsibility at the ATF's feet for not calling it off on Day 1. The rest is hubris, and people on both sides died. (Kiyabu 2023d)

On April 19, 1993, there was hubris on the part of David Koresh, who chose not to risk losing his charisma in order to bring the children and his followers out safely. There was hubris on the part of FBI officials and other government officials, who felt their image was being diminished by the length of the siege. Retired FBI negotiator Gary Noesner states that pressure on the FBI was mounting: "We were the big, bad FBI, but we were being made to look powerless" (HLN 2018). The anger felt by federal law enforcement agents toward the Branch Davidians for what they regarded as the murder of four ATF agents has to be taken into account (Wessinger 2017). A plan for a tank and CS gas assault had been drawn up, with input from Delta Force commanders, as early as March 10, 1993, but FBI officials had to wait to get approval to implement the plan from Attorney General Janet Reno, which was given on April 17 (Wessinger 2017, 222, 226).

The assault carried out by the FBI's Hostage Rescue Team and the resulting fire in which 76 people died was what sociologist David T. Bromley has called a "dramatic denouement," described as occurring "when a movement and some segment of the social order conclude that the requisite conditions for maintaining their core identity and collective existence are being subverted and that such circumstances are intolerable." "Parties on one or both sides ... undertake a project of final reckoning to reverse their power relations and to restore what they avow to be the appropriate moral order" (Bromley 2002, 11).

Due to his psychopathologies, Koresh mismanaged his charisma as he struggled to retain it in the face of pressures from FBI agents, but the Mount Carmel Center conflict consisted of interactions between multiple actors. The FBI had greater analytic resources and firepower than Koresh and his followers. It was FBI agents' jobs to collect intelligence and analyze it (which was done), and then utilize it to resolve the siege without further loss of life (which was not done).

Harvard University psychiatrist Alan Stone (1929-2022) was among scholars invited to investigate the events by the Justice Department and make recommendations for changes in the FBI. Stone wrote, "the FBI behavioral science experts had worked out a good psychological understanding of Koresh's psychopathology" (1993, 13), but FBI decision-makers did not follow their advice to refrain from tactical actions (Wessinger 2017). Stone concluded that "Koresh had an absolute need for control and domination of his followers that amounted to a mania" (1993, 14), but the FBI on-site commander and the HRT members also "tried to assert control and demonstrate to Koresh that they were in charge" (1993, 15). According to Stone, the FBI's tactical strategy pushed Koresh "to the ultimate act of control—destruction of himself and his group" (1993, 22; see also Wessinger 2009, 2017). In dealing with a critical incident, it is the responsibility of FBI supervisory officials "to override the group psychology of the agents ... and make decisions necessary to reach a peaceful conclusion" (House of Representatives 1996, 57). [4]

About the author

Catherine Wessinger is the Rev. H. James Yamauchi, S. J. Professor of the History of Religions at Loyola University New Orleans. She is editor of *The Oxford Handbook of Millennialism* (2011). Other publications include: "The FBI's 'Cult War' against the Branch Davidians" in *The FBI and Religion: Faith and National Security before and after 9/11*, edited by Sylvester A. Johnson and Steven Weitzman (2017); "Attempting to Educate Journalists about the Role of Cult Essentialism in the Branch Davidians-Federal Agents Conflict," in *"Cult" Rhetoric in the 21st Century: Deconstructing the Study of New Religious Movements*, edited by Aled Thomas and Edward Graham-Hyde (2024).

References

Arnold, J. Phillip. 2023. "Research Note: Did David Koresh Plagiarize Cyrus R. Teed?" *Nova Religio* 26(3): 101–115. https://doi.org/10.1525/nr.2023.26.3.101

Barker, Eileen. 1993a. "Charismatization. The Social Production of an Ethos Propitious to the Mobilisation of Sentiments." In *Secularization, Rationalism, and Sectarianianism: Essays in Honour of Bryan R. Wilson*, edited by Eileen Barker, James Beckford, and Karel Dobbelaere, 181–201. Oxford: Clarendon Press.

"Barricaded Cult Leader Wants Word Processor for Manuscript." 1993b. *Washington Post*. April 18. https://www.washingtonpost.com/archive/politics/1993/04/18/barricaded-cult-leader-wants-word-processor-for-manuscript/3f192634-5b3e-4d13-8325-ae0de6caebac/

Bartosh, Elizabeth G. 1971. *Koreshanity: The New Age Religion*. n.p: The Koreshan Foundation. Available in Internet Archive.

BBC Radio 5. 2018. *End of Days*. BBC Sounds. Podcast. Nine episodes.

Bernard, Stuart, dir. 2023. *Waco Untold: The British Stories*. Two episodes. MultiStory Media/ITVX. Documentary.

Bonano, Julian. 2023. Interview given to Catherine Wessinger in Waco, Texas. April 20. https://www.youtube.com/watch?v=BLj2BqbXMb0

Branch Davidians. 1993. "Inside Mount Carmel – Waco, TX." Parts 1–12. Videos on YouTube.

Bromley, David T. 2002. "Dramatic Denouements." In *Cults, Religion, and Violence*, edited by David G. Bromley and J. Gordon Melton, 11–41. Cambridge: Cambridge University Press. https://doi.org/10.1017/CBO9780511499326.003

---

4 I thank Dr. Nancy Ammerman for sending me a copy of Dr. Alan Stone's report to the Justice Department.

Bunds, David. 2023a. "David Koresh: The Adopted Son – Part One." Branch Davidian History. April 23. 46:59 mins. https://youtu.be/Lk3XL7DM1SU
———. 2023b. "David Koresh: The Adopted Son, Part Two, Isaiah 8." Branch Davidian History. April 30. 1:00:38 mins. https://youtu.be/WNfvj-NrF4k.
———. 2023c. "David Koresh: The Adopted Son, Part Three, The Affair with Lois." Branch Davidian History. May 8. 48:14 mins. https://youtu.be/UDw68cSVvHE
———. 2023d. "David Koresh and His One Brief Shining Moment." Branch Davidian History. May 23. 35:06 mins. https://youtu.be/PJIeTiHMyw8
———. 2023e. Email message to Catherine Wessinger. June 2.
———. 2023f. Telephone conversation with Catherine Wessinger. June 4.
———. 2023g. "David Koresh's Magnum Opus—'Our Foundation.'" Branch Davidian History. May 31. 1:00:35 mins. https://www.youtube.com/watch?v=aSAEqHNN4N4&t=198s
———. 2023h. "Escaping David Koresh: How Do You Get a Cult Out of Your Brain? Part 2." Branch Davidian History. 1:16:28 mins. https://www.youtube.com/watch?v=dYGQ-SNbF7E&t=2s
———. 2023i. "David Koresh Tried to Destroy My Marriage." Branch Davidian History. March 4. 57:50 mins. https://www.youtube.com/watch?v=2Vi0nM_cIUg&t=29s
———. 2023j. Telephone conversation with Catherine Wessinger. June 13.
Coney, Judith. 2013. *Sahaja Yoga: Socializing Processes in a South Asian New Religious Movement.* New York: Routledge. https://doi.org/10.4324/9781315027395
Craddock, Graeme. 1999. Deposition dated October 28, *Isabel G. Andrade, et al v. Phillip J. Chojnacki, et al*, United States District Court for the Western District of Texas, Waco Division, No. W-96-CA-139, vol. 1; Deposition dated October 29, vol. 2.
Craig, R. J. 1994. Testimony transcript dated February 8 and 9, 1994, in *United States of America v. Brad Eugene Branch, et al*, Criminal No. W-93-CR-046 in the United States District Court for the Western District of Texas, Waco Division.
Danforth, John C., Special Counsel. 2000. *Final Report to the Deputy Attorney General Concerning the 1993 Confrontation at the Mt. Carmel Complex, Waco, Texas.* November 8. Pursuant to Order No. 2256-99 of the Attorney General.
Dawson, Lorne L. 2006. "Psychopathologies and the Attribution of Charisma: A Critical Introduction to the Psychology of Charisma and the Explanation of Violence in New Religious Movements." *Nova Religio* 10(2): 3–28. https://doi.org/10.1525/nr.2006.10.2.3
———. 2011. "Charismatic Leadership in Millennial Movements." In *The Oxford Handbook of Millennialism*, edited by Catherine Wessinger, 113–132. Oxford: Oxford University Press. https://doi.org/10.1093/oxfordhb/9780195301052.003.0006

Doyle, Clive, with Catherine Wessinger and Matthew D. Wittmer. 2012. *A Journey to Waco: Autobiography of a Branch Davidian.* Lanham, MD: Rowman and Littlefield. https://doi.org/10.5771/9781442208872

England, Mark, and Darlene McCormick. 1993a. "The Sinful Messiah, Part One." *Waco Tribune Herald.* February 27.

———. 1993b. "The Sinful Messiah, Part Four: An Incident involving Vernon Howell and a Young Girl Sparks Marc Breault to Leave." *Waco Tribune Herald.* March 1.

Failure Analysis Associates. 1995. "Presentation by Failure Analysis Associates, Inc. of the Final Assault on Mt. Carmel." National Rifle Association of America. July 21. Video. 19:53 mins. Dick J. Reavis Collection, the Wittliff Collections, Texas State University. https://dc.library.txstate.edu/node-/6952?fbclid=IwAR1SjBm1sEjpWaM31x2U_2avGDP1eEtbzmXD1lpYLQp6U2ulFiq9sd2mTaM

FBI. 1993a. "FLIR Video of Tank Driving inside the Building to Gas Branch Davidian Mothers & Children." April 19. YouTube. https://www.youtube.com/watch?v=ddXU2FHdkXk

———. 1993b. "FLIR Video with Audio, Burning Building at Branch Davidians' Residence." April 19. https://www.youtube.com/watch?v=tPFrQOsGwac

———. 1993c. "Suicide References." March 27. In the Lee Hancock Collection, part of the Wittliff Collections Repository, Alkek Library,Texas State University, San Marcos, Texas.

———. 1993d. "Passover Analysis Addendum." April 18. In the Lee Hancock Collection, part of the Wittliff Collections Repository, Alkek Library,Texas State University, San Marcos, Texas.

———. 1993e. Transcript of Negotiation Audiotape #45. March 4. Available in the Dick J. Reavis Collection, Wittliff Collections, Texas State University, https://dc.library.txstate.edu/node/6834

———. 1993f. Transcript of Negotiation Audiotape #198. April 8. FBI Records: The Vault. Waco FBI Transcripts Tapes 197 – 199. https://vault.fbi.gov/waco-branch-davidian-compound/waco-fbi-transcripts-tapes-197-199/view

Gifford, Dan, William Gazecki, and Michael McNulty, prod. 1997. *Waco: The Rules of Engagement.* Film. Los Angeles: Fifth Estate Productions.

Grande, Todd. 2020a. "8 Signs of the Most Destructive Narcissistic Profile." January 30. 15:02 mins. https://youtu.be/DDqnT4FS8Oc

———. 2020b. "David Koresh / Mental Health & Personality." May 1. 23:24 mins. https://youtu.be/NOnvJV2MXvc

Grant, Barbara, prod. 2021. *When the Government Lied: Waco's Infrared Deception.* July 2021. Film. 39:16 mins. https://vimeo.com/ondemand/wacodeception

Haldeman, Bonnie. 2007. *Memories of the Branch Davidians: The Autobiography of David Koresh's Mother,* edited by Catherine Wessinger. Waco, TX: Baylor University Press.

Hall, John R. 1987. *Gone from the Promised Land: Jonestown in American Cultural History.* New Brunswick, NJ: Transaction Books.

Hall, Katie. 2018. "The Negotiators." *Austin Statesman.* February 28. http://specials.mystatesman.com/waco-negotiators/

Hinds, Michael Decourcy. 1993. "U.S. Pleads with Cult Leader to Let His Followers Go." *New York Times.* March 7. https://www.nytimes.com/1993/03/07/us/us-pleads-with-cult-leader-to-let-his-followers-go.html

HLN. 2018. *How It Really Happened with Hill Harper: Waco, Part 2, End of Days.* November 11.

Houteff, Victor. 2023. "Jezreel Letters." The Shepherd's Rod. https://www.shepherds-rod-message.org/Jezreel/

House of Representatives. 1995. *Activities of Federal Law Enforcement Agencies toward the Branch Davidians.* Transcripts of hearings, 3 vols. Washington, DC: U.S. Government Printing Office.

———. 1996. *Activities of Federal Law Enforcement Agencies toward the Branch Davidians.* Report 104-749. Washington, DC: U.S. Government Printing Office.

Jezreel, V. W. H. [Vernon Wayne Howell.] c. 1986. Palestine, Texas. Flyer. In Dick J. Reavis Collection, The Wittliff Collections, Texas State University, San Marcos, Texas. https://cdm15042.contentdm.oclc.org/digital/collection/p9010coll4/id/286/rec/1

Ji Zhe. 2008. "Expectation, Affection, and Responsibility: The Charismatic Journey of a New Buddhist Group in Taiwan." *Nova Religio* 12(2): 48–68. https://doi.org/10.1525/nr.2008.12.2.48

Kiyabu, Dana Okimoto. 2023a. Personal communication. April 17. Waco, Texas.

———. 2023b. Interview with Catherine Wessinger. Part 1. April 21. Waco, Texas. https://youtu.be/OB8EUkMr5vo

———. 2023c. Interview with Catherine Wessinger. Part 2. April 21. Waco, Texas. https://youtu.be/oeTtHrYjFVk

———. 2023d. Post in the Branch Davidian Survivors Group. May 29. Private group.

Koresh, David. 1993a. Telephone message left for Bonnie Haldeman. February 28. Audio recorded from *ABC Truth and Lies: Waco* (2018), at 38 mins.

Koresh, David. 1993b. CNN Interview. February 28. Video in author's possession.

Lewis, James R. 1994. *From the Ashes: Making Sense of Waco.* Edited by James R. Lewis. Lanham, MD: Rowman and Littlefield.

———. 2014b. "The Mount Carmel Holocaust: Suicide or Execution?" In *Sacred Suicide,* edited by James R. Lewis and Carole M. Cusack, 233–250. Farnham: Ashgate.

Lovelock, Derek. 2023a. "02 How Derek Lovelock Came into David Koresh's Message." June 1. Audio recording. 12:55 mins. https://www.youtube.com/watch?v=N5XalO8Ysmw&t=23s

———. 2023b. "03 Derek Lovelock Explains David Koresh's Teachings." June 6. Audio recording. 2:21:25 mins. https://youtu.be/bfbPyhW0G6o

———. 2023c. Post in Branch Davidian Beliefs Facebook Group. June 19.

Matteson, Catherine. 2004. Interview given to Catherine Wessinger in Waco, Texas. October 11. Transcript #2.

Moore, Rebecca. 2009. *Understanding Jonestown and Peoples Temple*. Westport, CN: Praeger. https://doi.org/10.5040/9798216183242

Nailling, Kathi. 2018. "Another Competency Hearing Set for Murder Defendant." *Athens Daily Review*. August 13. https://www.athensreview.com/news/another-competency-hearing-set-for-murder-defendant/article_4739951e-9f38-11e8-8b0c-d3e32293f485.html

Newport, Kenneth G. C. 2006. *The Branch Davidians of Waco*. Oxford: Oxford University Press. https://doi.org/10.1093/acprof:oso/9780199245741.001.0001

Noesner, Gary. 2010. *Stalling for Time: My Life as an FBI Hostage Negotiator*. New York: Random House.

Pitts, William L., Jr. 2009. "Women Leaders in the Davidian and Branch Davidian Traditions." *Nova Religio* 12(4): 50–71. https://doi.org/10.1525/nr.2009.12.4.50

Puko, Timothy. 2023. "EPA Proposes to Ban Most Uses of Methylene Chloride, a Toxic Solvent." *Washington Post*. April 20. https://www.washingtonpost.com/climate-environment/2023/04/20/epa-rule-toxic-methylene-chloride/

Richardson, James T. 2021. "Perspective: The Myth of the Omnipotent Leader: The Social Construction of a Misleading Account of Leadership in New Religious Movements." *Nova Religio* 24(4): 11–25. https://doi.org/10.1525/nr.2021.24.4.11

Samples, Kenneth R., Erwin M. de Castro, Richard Abanes, and Robert J. Lyle. 1994. *Prophets of the Apocalypse: David Koresh and Other American Messiahs*. Grand Rapids, MI: Baker Books.

Schechter, Dave. 2023. Interview with Catherine Wessinger in Bethesda, MD. March 17.

Schroeder, Kat. 2019a. "Kat Schroeder 05 15 19 Part 2." May 15. Interview in Tampa, Florida metropolitan area. https://www.youtube.com/watch?v=_JocbEKJLRI&t=28s

Stone, Alan A. 1993. "Report and Recommendations Concerning the Handling of Incidents Such as the Branch Davidian Standoff in Waco, Texas." November 10.

Tabor, James D., and Eugene V. Gallagher. 1995. *Why Waco? Cults and the Battle for Religious Freedom in America.* Berkeley: University of California Press.

Talty, Stephan. 2023. *Koresh: The True Story of David Koresh and the Tragedy at Waco.* New York: Mariner Books.

Thibodeau, David, with Leon Whiteson. 1999. *A Place Called Waco: A Survivor's Story.* New York: PublicAffairs.

Weber, Max. 1964. *The Theory of Economic and Social Organizations.* Edited and translated by A. M. Henderson and Talcott Parsons. New York: Free Press.

Wessinger, Catherine. 2006. "The Branch Davidians and Religion Reporting—A Ten-Year Retrospective." In *Expecting the End: Millennialism in Social and Historical Context*, edited by Kenneth G. C. Newport and Crawford Gribben, 147–172, 270–274. Waco, TX: Baylor University Press.

———. 2009. "Deaths in the Fire at the Branch Davidians' Mount Carmel: Who Bears Responsibility?" *Nova Religio* 13(2): 25–60. https://doi.org/10.1525/nr.2009.13.2.25

———. 2012. "Charismatic Leaders in New Religious Movements." In *Cambridge Companion to New Religious Movements*, edited by Olav Hammer and Mikael Rothstein, 80–96. Cambridge: Cambridge University Press. https://doi.org/10.1017/CCOL9780521196505.007

———. 2017. "The FBI's 'Cult War' against the Branch Davidians." In *The FBI and Religion: Faith and National Security before and after 9/11*, edited by Sylvester A. Johnson and Steven Weitzman, 203–331. Oakland, CA: University of California Press.

———. 2018. "Collective Martyrdom and Religious Suicide: The Branch Davidians and Heaven's Gate." In *Martyrdom, Self-Sacrifice, and Self-Immolation: Religious Perspectives on Suicide*, edited by Margo Kitts, 54–84. Oxford: Oxford University Press.

Wetherington, Walter. 2000. "Final Report concerning the Fire at the Branch Davidian Complex, Waco, Texas, April 19, 1993, Prepared for the Office of Special Counsel, Waco Investigation. Appendix D of *Final Report to the Deputy Attorney General Concerning the 1993 Confrontation at the Mt. Carmel Complex, Waco, Texas*, by John C. Danforth. November 8.

Wright, Stuart A. 1999. "Anatomy of a Government Massacre: Abuses of Hostage-Barricade Protocols during the Waco Standoff." *Terrorism and Political Violence* 11(2): 39–68. https://doi.org/10.1080/09546559908427503

———. 2009. "Revisiting the Branch Davidian Mass Suicide Debate." *Nova Religio* 13(2): 4–24. https://doi.org/10.1525/nr.2009.13.2.4

Zablocki, Benjamin. 1997. "The Blacklisting of a Concept: The Strange History of the Brainwashing Conjecture in the Sociology of Religion." *Nova Religio* 1(1): 96–121. https://doi.org/10.1525/nr.1997.1.1.96

III

MEDIA AND THE LAW

8

INVENTED RELIGIONS AND THE LAW: JEDIISM AND THE CHURCH OF THE FLYING SPAGHETTI MONSTER

CAROLE M. CUSACK

In 2018 a Dutch law student, Mienke de Wilde (Radboud University, Nijmegen) went to the highest court in the Netherlands to plead for her right to wear a colander on her head in official documents like her driver's license. This action was taken because she is a Pastafarian. The Church of the Flying Spaghetti Monster (Pastafarianism), a third millennium "invented religion" was founded by Bobby Henderson in 2005 (Henderson 2006a, 33–37). De Wilde's court case failed, and she filed an application in Strasbourg to the European Court of Human Rights, resulting in that court's first judgement on Pastafarianism (Wolff 2021). This chapter considers invented religions (or "fiction-based religions," "hyper-real religions," and "hypothetical religions"), examining their history, defining qualities, and legal status (Wolff 2022). Jediism and the Church of the Flying Spaghetti Monster are then discussed regarding ritual garb in public and official contexts (hoods for Jedis, colanders and pirate attire for Pastafarians). I argue that the distinction between Jedis and Pastafarians and traditional religions with mandated religious attire like Sikhs and Jews is not as clear-cut as non-religious studies scholars think (Cusack 2010, 32–34).

In 2018 a Dutch law student, Mienke de Wilde (Radboud University, Nijmegen) went to the highest court in the Netherlands to plead for her right to wear a colander (or in her case, a quite chic hat based on a pasta strainer) on her head in official documents (for example, her driver's license). This seemingly extraordinary action was because she is a member of the Church of the Flying Spaghetti Monster (or Pastafarianism), a third millennium "invented religion" founded by American physics graduate Bobby Henderson in 2005 (Henderson 2006a, 33–37). De Wilde's Netherlands court case failed, and she subsequently filed an application in Strasbourg to the European Court of Human Rights, resulting in that court's first judgement on Pastafarianism (Wolff 2021). This chapter opens with a discussion of invented religions (also known as "fiction-based religions," "'hyper-real religions," or "hypothetical religions"), examining their history, defining qualities, and legal status (Wolff 2022). A range of invented religions including Jediism and the Church of the Flying Spaghetti Monster are then analysed with regard to wearing ritual garb in public and official contexts (hoods in public for Jedis, colanders—and in some cases full pirate attire - for Pastafarians). I argue that the distinction between Jedis and Pastafarians, on the one hand, and traditional religions with mandated religious attire like Sikhs and Jews, on the other hand, is not as clear-cut as non-religious studies scholars think (Cusack 2010, 32–34).

From a religious studies perspective, which is methodologically agnostic and defers assessment of supernatural/ theological truth claims, there are few real distinctions that can be drawn between time-honoured traditional religions and "invented" new religions (Cusack 2013). This disciplinary stance sets religion scholars apart from non-specialist commentators, including legal practitioners. Given that significant concessions are made in many countries regarding traditional religious costume in legal contexts (yarmulkes, chadors, hijabs, turbans, "prairie clothes," crucifixes, and so on), members of new religious movements (NRMs), whether invented or following a more classic template, have precedents to invoke (Danchin 2008). When they are refused the right to wear mandated dress, this is religious discrimination that must be recognized as such and opposed, in the same way that hostility toward Muslim women who veil, for example, should be combatted (Madrazo 2014). Further, members of invented religions who have adopted ritual attire impact on the public sphere of the modern secular West and present challenges to conventional ideas of what is a religion and what religious freedom entails (Taira 2013). Indeed, egalitarian treatment of ALL religions is the aim of many public campaigns and high-profile legal cases pursued by new groups like the Satanic Temple, which has invoked the Religious Freedom Restoration Act to seek permission to erect statues of Baphomet in the vicinity of Christian monuments, for example, and to circumvent abortion bans by claiming abortion as a religious right (Laycock 2021). The focus of this chapter is costume, and a range of sources including news articles, legal judgements, and academic studies will be adduced to clarify the situation regarding such controversial garb in the twenty-first century.

Invented, Fiction-Based, and Hypothetical Religions: Fandoms and Tradition

The study of invented, fiction-based, or hypothetical religions was not considered a legitimate field of enquiry within religious studies until recently.

A methodological shift occurred around the turn of the third millennium: in 2005 David Chidester argued that indigenous, popular, and folk religions have always been required to demonstrate their religious legitimacy in comparison to the "recognized" religions of the World Religions Paradigm (Chidester 2005, 191; Owen 2011). His term for new religious phenomena emerging from popular culture, "authentic fakes," did not catch on, though Thomas Alberts used it to show the folk origins of such new religions:

> Fake religions can be usefully thought of as a kind of popular religion, a grouping of religious expressions and formations originating in the organic religious life of the ordinary people rather than the clergy, lower classes rather than the elite and the rural peasantry rather than the urban citizenry ... As a kind of popular religion, fake religions subvert the authentic religions of privileged elites, a transgressive act of resistance that gives further hints as to the wellspring of their power. Fake religions therefore stand not only at the intersection of religion with popular culture, but also at the intersection of religion with power ... Yet of all their imitations, fake religions' imitation of authentic religions' claim to being authentic is the most important. Whether as popular religion, a kind of indigenous religion of cyberspace, or an invented fakelore for late twenty- first-century techno-counterculture, fake religions deflect the burden of proof in the same instant that they question authentic religions' exemption from providing the same. (Alberts 2008, 128)

The second attempt at nomenclature for these newly recognised phenomena was Adam Possamai's use of the term "hyper-real" religions, loosely borrowed from Jean Baudrillard, in that Possamai argued that popular culture based religions were a simulacrum of religion constructed from popular culture (Possamai 2005), while Baudrillard argued *all* religions are hyper-real. In 2010 Carole M. Cusack published *Invented Religions: Imagination, Fiction and Faith* (Cusack 2010) and in 2014 Markus Altena Davidsen graduated with a doctorate from University of Leiden on "fiction-based religions," that is, new religions based on the *Legendarium* of J.R.R. Tolkien (Davidsen 2014). The final term in question, "hypothetical religion," was proposed by Alexander van der Haven as the opposite of fundamentalism. He suggested that if fundamentalism becomes the dominant form of religion in the twenty-first century, hypothetical religion will not be important, but "if fiction-based religiosity gains a wider and more committed audience, hypothetical religion can become a major form of religious epistemology in the future, be it near or far" (van der Haven 2017, 275).

The first noteworthy characteristic of these deliberately fictional religions is that they explicitly reject traditional means of establishing spiritual or historical lineage, and openly announce their fictional status (Cusack 2010, 1). Second, invented religions understand fictions, the ludic, and play as legitimate sources of ultimate meaning; in no sense inferior materials upon which to base a religion than factual accounts, attested experiences, or historical events (Cusack 2016). This attitudinal shift reflects the extent of secularisation in the West, and concomitant changes in both individuals wishing to belong to a religion, and scholars who study such groups. Ingvild Sælid Gilhus and Lisbeth Mikaelsson (2001) propose that the discipline of religious studies developed in three phases. The first relied on evolutionary models (and implicitly viewed Christianity as the apogee of religions), the second on the phenomenological method (and established the World Religions paradigm), and the third on cultural approaches (which opened the field to new religions, indigenous religions, and a fully naturalist view of religions as human cultural products).

In the mid-twentieth century, Christianity began to decline in popularity in the West, and Eastern religions were introduced by Hindu and Buddhist teachers, and scholars of religion, particularly sociologists, embraced NRMs and established method to study and understand them *as religions* in precisely the same ways that Buddhism and Christianity were religions. James R. Lewis argued the shift from the second to third phases involved sidelining the phenomenological respect for the believers position and enabling researchers to study religion like other cultural trends, with methodological naturalism as the default stance (Lewis 2014). Despite the fact that invention had been noted in cultural contexts in the 1980s (Hobsbawm and Ranger 1992 [1983]) and sociologists had identified NRM leaders as creatives in producing teachings, lifeways, and economies (Bainbridge and Stark 1979), the study of playful, self-consciously invented religions emerged, as noted above, only after 2000. The first religions of this kind that had endured were at that point roughly forty years old: Kerry Thornley and Greg Hill had created Discordianism, a "non-prophet irreligious disorganization" (Adler 1986, 332), dedicated to the worship of Eris (Greek goddess of strife and chaos, known as Discordia in Roman religion) in 1957, and Tim Zell and Lance Christie had instituted the Church of All Worlds (CAW) in April 1962, bringing to reality the church of the same name founded by Martian-born Valentine Michael Smith in Robert A. Heinlein's 1961 novel *Stranger in a Strange Land* (Cusack 2009). Discordianism was a classic invented religion, in that Hill (Malaclypse the Younger) wrote the sacred text *Principia Discordia*, whereas CAW was initially a fiction-based religion though it later incorporated elements of modern Paganism (Malaclypse the Younger 1994; Sulak 2014). A third significant invented religion, the Church of the SubGenius, was established by Ivan Stang (b. Douglass St. Clair Smith), Philo Drummond (b. Steve Wilcox), and the late Dr. X (b. Monte Dhooge) in Dallas, Texas in 1979 (Cusack 2010, 83–111).

Third millennium invented religions: Jediism and Pastafarianism

There was a hiatus between 1980 and the start of the third millennium, when a new group of invented religions, relying more on film and television, and with significant shared ground with popular culture fandoms, emerged. These included: Jediism (inspired by George Lucas' *Star Wars* films and dating to the 2001 census in Australia, the United Kingdom, New Zealand, and Canada); Matrixism (based on the Wachowskis' films and dating to 2004); and the Church of the Flying Spaghetti Monster (which parodied fundamentalist Christian Creationism, repackaged as Intelligent Design, and was founded by Bobby Henderson in 2005). This chapter focuses on Jediism and Pastafarianism, as of all the invented religions they have had the greatest struggles to gain approval to wear specific religious attire, an issue which did not ensue for Discordianism, the Church of All Worlds, the Church of the SubGenius, or Matrixism. The dominance of television in the 1960s contributed greatly to Jediism. In the 1960s a large and organized fandom focused on Gene Roddenberry's hit television series *Star Trek* (1966–1969) emerged. This was enhanced by the *Star Trek* film franchise from 1979 (Greenwald 1998). "Trekkies" re-enacted scenes from episodes, learned Klingon (a language devised for the series by Marc Okrand which enjoys some popularity), and attended science-fiction conventions costumed as their favourite characters (cosplay). In the 1990s Michael Jindra suggested that fandom behaviours were basically religious in nature (Jindra 1994), and the emergence of Jediism is at least partial confirmation of this.

The *Star Wars* films were a commercial success for George Lucas and attracted a signific fandom. However, the rise of Jediism is directly due to an internet campaign in 2001 urging Anglophone nations that were undergoing an official census that year to nominate "Jedi" as their religion. Censuses took place in Australia (7 August), New Zealand (6 March), Canada (15 May) and the United Kingdom (29 April). Such an email campaign was possible only because of the increase in online users since 1989 when Tim Berners-Lee's World Wide Web graphics interface was introduced. The number of those nominating Jedi or Jedi Knight in the 2001 Australian Census was 70,509 people. In the United Kingdom there were 390,000 self-identified Jedis (Levy 2010). Jedi groups often emphasise their religion's harmony with multiple faiths and Danielle Kirby suggested, in a brief discussion of the appeal of Jediism, that it lies in "adherence to the ideals espoused" rather than in a literal belief in the events or characters of *Star Wars* (Kirby 2009, 144). This is confirmed by Davidsen, who researched the real-world Temple of the Jedi Order (TotJO) and the Jedi Church. Both have taken steps to become institutionalized, such as gaining the right to perform legal marriages and, in the case of the Temple of the Jedi Order engaging in prison chaplaincy, and being recognised "as a non-profit religious and educational corporation under Texas law" since 14 December 2005 (Davidsen 2016, 384).

In the United Kingdom Jediism became a high-profile media test case, because the British definition of "religion" is considerably narrower than that of the United States, Australia or New Zealand (for example, the Church of Scientology does not have the status of a religion in Britain). The Labour member for Copeland (Cumbria), Jamie Reed, delivered his maiden speech in June 2005, identifying as the first elected Jedi parliamentarian (Singler 2014). This claim, which was untrue, was a pointed barb by Reed regarding the Racial and Religious Hatred Bill, which was being debated at the time. Dominic Grieve, the Conservative Party Shadow Justice Secretary argued for the exclusion of Jedi Knights (and others including Satanists) from the bill's protections. This was relevant, as twenty-three-year old Daniel Jones (Jedi name Morda Hehol), claimed religious discrimination when he was required to remove his hood or exit the Tesco supermarket in Bangor, North Wales. Jones and his brother Barney had founded the International Church of Jediism in 2008. Jones claimed Tesco's eviction was definitely religious discrimination, because he "walked past a Muslim lady in a veil. Surely the same rules should apply to everyone." The International Church of Jediism's rules state that "Jedis must wear a hood up in any public place." Jones had claimed to media representatives that the United Kingdom had recognised Jediism as a religion:

> [O]ur training is serious so we have to be taken seriously. With the 2001 Census, now everyone recognizes Jedi as a religion. If the government says to us "You can't do that because you're not a true religion," we can say "Yes we are" because there's more Jedi than Scientologists in Britain.
>
> (Carter 2009)

In 2010 Chris Jarvis refused to remove his hood at the job centre in Southend, and later received an apology from the manager for not respecting his "religion or beliefs" (Nevin 2010). His ire at this action reflected the (possibly anti-Muslim) sentiments of Jones: "I was just standing up for my beliefs. Muslims can walk around in whatever religious gear they like, so why can't I?" (Anon 2010). It must be acknowledged that such cases involving Jedis are rare.

In 2005 Bobby Henderson founded the Church of the Flying Spaghetti Monster (FSM), which was originally intended as a defence of science against Intelligent Design, a repackaged Creationism that Kansas high schools were going to teach as an explanation of equal merit to Charles Darwin's theory of evolution. Henderson wrote to the Kansas School Board that the intelligent designer of the universe was the FSM, a being formed of spaghetti pasta with meatball eyes. He then wrote *The Gospel of the Flying Spaghetti Monster* (2006a), a humorous best-seller. Henderson's ideas became popular, and the Church of the Flying Spaghetti Monster became a formal "real world" religion, something that was not Henderson's intention. The important doctrines of Pastafarianism include the FSM's initial creation of a mountain, trees, and a midget. Believers in the FSM assert that "global warming, earthquakes, hurricanes, and other natural disasters are a direct effect of the shrinking numbers of Pirates since the 1800s" and that for Pastafarians "it is disrespectful to teach our beliefs without wearing His chosen outfit, which of course is full pirate regalia" (Henderson 2006b). Scholars have noted Pastafarianism's mockery of Intelligent Design via doctrines: for example, in Heaven men "men [in the gendered use of the term] eternally live in a strip joint, to satisfy their visual sensuality and their natural tendency to sin" and "they enjoy the benefits of a permanently-erupting beer volcano" (Obadia 2015). Tim Wolff regards it as "uncontroversially a parody" (Wolff 2021, 262) and notes that "with parody belief systems, the motive is the making of a political point" (Wolff 2021, 263).

Pastafarianism, religious costume, and legal cases: Colanders and licenses, pirate garb and weddings

The Church of the Flying Spaghetti Monster became popular for three reasons: the popular culture appeal of pirates; the witty doctrines devised by Henderson (for example, the parodic image of a mass of spaghetti with meatballs for eyes replacing the Biblical God in Michelangelo's *The Creation of Adam*, with His "noodly appendage" reaching for the hand of Adam, is both hilarious and memorable); and because people who opposed Creationism liked it. It did not take long for the FSM to become a lightning rod for legal cases concerning "What is a religion?" Many of these cases involved ritual dress. An early example was Bryan Killian, a sixteen-year-old student at North Buncombe High School in North Carolina who was suspended from school for wearing pirate regalia (which included an eye-patch). He claimed this costume was religiously mandated by his membership of the Church of the Flying Spaghetti Monster. The school's Principal, Sarah Cooley, argued that Killian's Pirate regalia was "distracting" for other students and suspended him. Killian then stated, "I feel like my First Amendment was violated. Freedom of religion and freedom of expression. That's what I tried to do, and I got shot down" (Schrader 2007). More serious was the case of Stephen Cavanaugh, a prisoner in Nebraska State Penitentiary, Lincoln who in 2015 brought a civil rights lawsuit against prison administrators claiming religious discrimination.

Twenty religions are recognised by the institution, including Satanism and Rastafarianism, but not Pastafarianism. Law firm Fisher Phillips, in a review of the case, noted that:

> Cavanaugh was a bit vague in his lawsuit as to the specific accommodations he was seeking. He said he wanted to meet for worship services and classes, to receive communion, and to wear religious clothing. In examining the *FSM Gospel*, it appears that Cavanaugh wanted to be able to wear a pirate costume in prison, have the right to drink beer on Fridays, and to receive 'a large portion of spaghetti and meatballs' as communion. His lawsuit sought $5 million in pain and suffering. That particular lawsuit was (unsurprisingly) unsuccessful; more minor forms of legal recognition have had greater success. The most common instance is the right to wear a pasta strainer (colander) on the Pastafarian's head in official photographs, such as on a driver's license. (Anon 2016a)

The United States of America is notoriously pro-religion. It is arguably easier to register a new religion there than in any other country. It is also arguably far harder to be an atheist in America than it is to create your own religion (Edgell, Hartmann, Stewart and Gerteis 2016). A majority of the examples of early Pastafarians trying to get a pasta strainer recognized as religious headgear (like a Jewish yarmulke, Sikh turban, or Muslim hijab) were in the United States. For example: Asia Lemmon sought and received permission to wear her colander in Utah (The Associated Press 2014); Lindsey Miller was photographed in a strainer for her license in Massachusetts (Durando 2015); Shawna Hammond was allowed "unusual headgear" in Oklahoma (Reilly 2014); while Richard Steve Moser III of Ohio was pursuing the same right unsuccessfully in 2019 (Malongowski 2019). Pastafarians in Europe, though fewer, do exist, and their success is often surprising: for example, Austrian Niko Alm was an early applicant to win the right to wear a colander for his license photograph after three years of agitating (Peralta 2011); and Andrei Filin in the Russian Federation also secured the right to the pasta strainer license photograph, with a caveat.

> [D]eputy chief of Moscow's State Traffic inspectorate, Vladimir Kuzin, told Russian media that Mr Filin's victory for the satirical Church of the Flying Spaghetti Monster comes with a catch. "The next time he is stopped by the traffic police, if he doesn't have a pasta strainer on his head, his licence will be taken from him," Mr Kuzin said. (Brennan 2018)

In Australia, where the Jedi Census response was strong, there have been few high-profile Pastafarian headgear cases, but they are interesting because they have given rise to contradictory rulings (Brennan 2018). In 2016 Marcus Bowring, an IT professional, was granted a license in the state of Victoria featuring a photograph of him wearing a colander. This success was greeted with an official statement by Captain Tanya Watkins of the Church of the Flying Spaghetti Monster Australia, acknowledging legal permission to wear colander dating from 1 January 2016, and thanking the state government: "To the Victorian Government we would like to extend our thanks and appreciation for their non-discriminatory policies" (Cowie 2016). However, Simon Leadbetter, a Brisbane tradesman, was refused the right to wear a colander on his head and his license lapsed as a result, imperilling his livelihood. Mr Leadbetter argued that "I'm a devout member of the Church of the Flying Spaghetti Monster and I have a right to wear a colander just like Sikhs wear turbans" (Anon 2014), a familiar refrain like the British Jedis' analogy between their hoods and Muslim headgear. University of Sydney student Preshalin Moody received permission to wear his colander in New South Wales, yet South Australian Guy Ablon "had his legally obtained guns seized after he requested to wear a pasta strainer on his head for a firearms licence photo. He had his religion questioned and was forced to undergo a psychiatric evaluation before his weapons were returned" (Anon 2014). This points to an identical governmental situation to that of the United States, where federal law applies only to the federated nation, and states are able to pass varying and contradictory legislation.

Another aspect of recognition for Pastafarians has been permission to conduct legal marriages. Jedis in the United Kingdom were encouraged by the Marriage and Civil Partnership (Scotland) Bill (2014), which spoke of "celebrants of religious or belief bodies," where "'religious or belief body' means an organised group of people: a) which meets regularly for religious worship; or b) the principal object (or one of the principal objects) of which is to uphold or promote philosophical beliefs and which meets regularly for that purpose" (Scottish Parliament 2014). The first official Pastafarian wedding took place on a pirate ship in Akaroa Harbour, New Zealand in 2016 after the government approved the Church of the Flying Spaghetti Monster to conduct weddings the previous year. Journalist Eleanor Ainge Roy observed that,

> British man Toby Ricketts and New Zealander Marianna Fenn have been together for four years. Although they never considered marrying before, when the first Pastafarian marriage celebrant was sanctioned by the New Zealand government they decided the chance to hold a humorous and original wedding was too good to pass up. (Roy 2016)

In Australia, during the pandemic Pirate Priestess Angela Carter and her husband Captain Colin "Cupcakes" Carter filled in the 2021 Census and gave their affiliation as "no religion." They were, however, Pastafarians, having joined the Church of the Flying Spaghetti Monster in 2011 and lay claim to having had the first Pastafarian wedding in 2013, contradicting the information given above (the difference is that New Zealand had approved Pastafarian weddings whereas Australia had not, so their wedding was likely conducted by a Pastafarian who was a licensed civil celebrant). The Carters also own the Blue Church in Colac, south-western Victoria, which is their home, and also the first physical place of worship for Pastafarianism in Australia. It has become a tourist attraction (Neal 2022). It is also worth noting that in 2022 a Canadian couple had a Pastafarian wedding: "Dani Magnussen and Jaromir Pavlat were dressed in pirate outfits as they stood up in front of friends to tie the knot on Talk Like a Pirate Day" (Fenton 2022). Talk Like a Pirate Day pre-existed Pastafarianism but has been co-opted into its ritual calendar, rather like 4 May becoming a Jedi holy day (the salutation "May the 4th be With You" sounds like *Star Wars'* "May the Force be With You") (Hambrett 2018).

Pastafarianism and Jediism: Major legal cases and rulings

I met Mienke de Wilde, a law student and prominent Pastafarian in the Netherlands at Radboud University in Nijmegen in December 2016 while giving a public lecture on Harry Potter-themed religion. She introduced me to Derk Venema, a Law faculty member who was her legal counsel, and we discussed the right to wear a colander in all public identity documentation. In 2018 Mienke de Wilde went to the highest court in the Netherlands to plead for her right to wear a pasta strainer on her head in official documents (for example, her driver's license). Ms de Wilde argued that her membership of the Church of the Flying Spaghetti Monster required her to don religious headgear at all times. The action failed, as "the Dutch Council of State ruled that Pastafarianism was not a religion" (Henley 2018). Rather, it averred, the Church of the Flying Spaghetti Monster was a "satire" not a "religious faith." De Wilde then filed an application in Strasbourg to the European Court of Human Rights, resulting in that court's first judgement on Pastafarianism (Wolff 2021). The legal status of a range of invented religions including Discordianism, Jediism, and the Church of the Flying Spaghetti Monster differs in different countries. The wearing of ritual garb (hoods in public for Jedis, colanders and in some cases full pirate attire for Pastafarians) is generally tolerated for weddings and private events, but in Europe is often rejected on official documents, whereas in America it tends to be permitted, as discussed above.

The judgements in de Wilde's cases are more serious and far-reaching than state decisions to allow or disallow colanders on drivers' licenses, in various parts of the United States, Australia, and other Anglophone nations including Canada and South Africa. Derk Venema published a chapter titled, "Piety or ulterior motive," which drew on his work with de Wilde (Venema 2018). He compared Pastafarians desiring to wear colanders with asylum seekers who claimed to be a member of a religion that was persecuted in their country of origin. He argued that:

> In both cases, too, the authorities are suspicious and reluctant: the conversions and the FSM religion are often deemed not credible, because they are suspected of being devised as mere instruments to acquire a residence permit and to publicly express criticism of religion. These goals are viewed as the 'real' ulterior motives." (Venema 2018, 227)

This is an important argument. I noted at the beginning of this chapter that religious studies has a methodological commitment to not assessing the doctrinal content of religions as true or untrue, but rather as a cultural product that creates meaning for those who have built a community around it.

This understanding is enshrined in a minority judgment by Justice Lionel Murphy of the High Court of Australia, in The Church of the New Faith vs the Commissioner for Payroll Tax (1983), a controversial case brought by the Church of Scientology. All the judges were wary of attempting to formulate a definition of religion, but Murphy alone argued the evaluation of the content of a religion was improper. He suggested:

> [T]he following three examples of criteria that might be used to qualify a body as a religion:
> (i) Any body (i.e., organisation) which claims to be religious, whose beliefs or practices are a revival of, or resemble earlier cults, is religious.
> (ii) Any belief in a supernatural Being or Beings, whether physical and visible, such as the sun and the stars, or a physical invisible God or spirit, or an abstract God or entity, is religious belief.
> (iii) Any body which claims to be religious and offers a way to find meaning and purpose in life is religious (Mason *et al* 1983).

This judgment constructs a bridge between the beliefs of traditional and well-known religions, like Christianity, and newer, less familiar faiths such as that of the Church of Scientology (Cusack 2016–2017, 22). A vernacular remnant of this judgment (which is quite well-known in Australia) is discernible in the pronouncement of Peter Lee, the self-styled head of Jediism in Australia, on whether a nominated religion in the Census can be discounted: "You can never get that question wrong. If a person decides that their wheelie bin is their God, then we have absolutely no right to deny him, or to question it" (Hambrett 2018).

When the legal judgements regarding whether Jediism or Pastafarianism are "real" religions are examined, it is clear that the judges involved in de

Wilde's case in the Netherlands and in the European Court of Human Rights, for example, evaluated the content of Pastafarianism and found the doctrines (personally) unbelievable, as did the British Charities Commission which justified its denigration of Jediism as a satire, parody, fandom, or something that was not a "real" religion. Jediism sought registration in the United Kingdom with the British Charity Commission (as there is no formal process to register a religion) and was refused in 2016. The ruling of the Charity Commission asserted that Jediism "did not promote moral or ethical improvement," "lacked the necessary spiritual or non-secular element," and lacked the "cogency, coherence, or seriousness" to qualify as a religion or belief system (Somin 2016). After this ruling,

> Daniel Jones [Morda Hehol], leader of the Church of Jediism in the UK, said Jedi would continue to do charity work without any legal status and was convinced 'Jediism's status will change in the next five years'. Jediism has more adherents than Rastafarians and Jains, according to the 2011 census [177,000 members]. But the number of Jedi fell sharply from 2001, when 390,000 people said they were followers of The Force. (Anon 2016b)

Questions about the motivations of those who put their religion as Jedi in the Census have lingered since 2001, but in Australia, at least, the Australian Bureau of Statistics has instigated what are termed Category 7 religious groups: this includes groups inspired by popular culture, such as *Star Wars* and *Star Trek*; atheists; and those who have multiple religious affiliations (Bouma 2017).

With reference to de Wilde's case in the European Court of Human Rights, Paul Cliteur notes that her request to wear a colander exposed the fact that, despite passport photographs being theoretically free from "things that make the person's identification more complicated, such as sunglasses or headgear ... an exception is made for followers of religions. For example, the headscarf is allowed on the passport photo. So why not the colander as well?" (Cliteur 2023, 11). Tommy Cheung argued that the British Charity Commission rejected the application of TotJO in the United Kingdom on erroneous legal grounds. He acknowledged that differentiating religion from fandom is essential, and that religious Jedis were adamant that they

> [h]ave made a deliberate effort to separate their religious beliefs from Star Wars and George Lucas. Instead of trying to model their lives after the Jedi Knights, they view the Force as 'a valid term for a real, cosmic power existing in the real world'. However, because the general fandom of *Star Wars* shares some of these traits, it has often been difficult to distinguish a *Star Wars* fan from a Jediist who believes in the Force theology and practices Jedi ethics. (Cheung 2019, 351)

Interestingly, Cheung (a Hong Kong based academic) advocates the Australian Church of the New Faith vs Commissioner for Payroll Tax case as an exemplary way to deal with minority religions. Instead, as he demonstrates, the Charity Commission rejected Scientology's application for religious and charitable status in 1999, and continued to apply the same standards that are often not actually required under charity law, for example that religions and belief systems must be "characterised by a certain level of cogency, seriousness, cohesion and importance" (Cheung 2019, 366) to cases such as Jediism. Cheung also questions what "public benefit" means in the context of religion, and how a more liberal and flexible definition of religion might be arrived (though he ultimately agrees that TotJO does not meet the requisite criteria for a religion).

In contrast, Venema is interested in the question of how we might know what a person believes in the first place, and how this belief might then be assessed in crisis situations, such as the granting of asylum to religious refugees. He is very concerned that freedom of religion is clearly being violated when the content of a faith is being scrutinised in a legal context.

> Rational investigation by courts does not stop at the content of faith, where it should stop in order to respect freedom of religion. The principle of interpretative restraint is clearly violated in both cases: refugees are forced to be completely open about their religious opinions, doubts and changes and to justify their adherence to a certain religion. Pastafarianism is judged on the credibility of its content, and on the existence of explicit written commandments concerning certain rituals (holy headgear). (Venema 2018, 244)

Venema makes the excellent point that if a refugee from an Islamic country has converted to Christianity or Buddhism they are an apostate and will be liable to be executed if they are to be returned to their country of origin. He argues that the relatively unimportant outcomes of granting Pastafarians the right to wear religious garb in official photographs are not sufficient to justify widespread denial of religious freedom and parity in terms of the wearing of mandated attire by members of all religions (and not just Jews, Muslims, Christians, Buddhists, and Hindus, all members of the World Religions paradigm) (Venema 2018). This is not to argue that Muslim women, or any other group identified by religious dress, are treated humanely or reasonably (Singhi 2023); I merely state that they have the right to wear religious dress because they are members of a group that is unambiguously agreed to be a religion.

Conclusion

Invented religions are great test cases, in the sense that when they are rejected or calumniated it reveals cracks in the generally accepted definitions of religion, and the institutions we deem worthy of that title in society. Van der Haven acknowledges that hypothetical religion is "irrelevant" if fundamentalism becomes the dominant form of religion in the future; yet, if the rapidly changing, popular culture saturated, individualist Western culture comes to dominate the globe, he thinks "hypothetical religion can become a major form of religious epistemology in the future" (van der Haven 2017, 275). This article does not address the rise of "fake" news, celebrity culture, and consumerism, but these are the context in which fiction-based and invented religions acquire legitimacy and recruit members, and such phenomena also indicate the great importance of pop culture in the modern West, so much so that it is "spiritual" or "religious" to certain subcultures (including Jediists and Pastafarians). Twenty-first century life is provisional, flexible, consumerist, and the only constant is change (Rosa 2013). Thus, invented religions are important sites of the spiritual in the (overtly secular) West, and deserve greater scholarly attention, both as a particular type of new religion, and as a phenomenon that is linked to the everyday life of those who only enjoy pop culture, with organised fandom acting as the bridge between the two (Cusack 2010).

The type of religion that is most often in the news, and which has attracted the lion's share of research funding since September 11, 2001 is fundamentalism, particularly Islamic fundamentalism. Western nations view this type of religion as a threat, as it is illiberal; some of its adherents disregard the rule of law and reject the principles underpinning the secular, multi-faith state. Yet the same states are reluctant to authorise flexible, adaptable, creative religions generated by citizens. So, should we take invented religions seriously? Davidsen argues that fiction-based religions are separate from fandoms, because "fiction-based religion emerges when fictional narratives are used as authoritative texts for actual religious practice" (Davidsen 2013, 378). I would riposte that many different authorities are drawn upon by invented religions, and that the examples of Jedi hoods and Pastafarian colanders point to everyday life and shared experience as the context in which identity is constructed and expressed in the adoption of religious costume, and the scorn and ridicule that invites when the mandated ritual item is a colander are made sense of in the traditional understanding of religious persecution and exclusion.

Acknowledgements

This chapter was first delivered as an invited lecture on 19 February 2019, "Invented Religion and the Law: The Significance of Colanders, Hoods, and Pirate Costumes for Practitioners of 'Hypothetical Religion,'" at Mahidol University, Thailand. I thank Dr York Gunther for the invitation to address his students. I revised these ideas at the European Association for the Study of Religion (EASR) conference at the University of Turku, 25–29 June 2, 2019 in the paper "'Humorous' Ritual Costumes: The Significance of Colanders, Hoods and Pirate Costumes for Practitioners of 'Invented Religions'." My thanks are due to Essi Mäkelä (University of Helsinki), who chaired the session I participated in.

About the author

Carole M. Cusack is Professor of Religious Studies at the University of Sydney, Australia as well as Visiting Fellow at the Center for the Study of World Religions, Harvard Divinity School. She trained as a medievalist and her doctorate was published as *Conversion Among the Germanic Peoples* (Cassell, 1998). She now researches primarily in contemporary religious trends and Western esotericism. Her books include *Invented Religions: Imagination, Fiction and Faith* (Ashgate, 2010) and (with Katharine Buljan) *Anime, Religion and Spirituality: Profane and Sacred Worlds in Contemporary Japan* (Equinox, 2015). She edited (with Pavol Kosnáč), *Fiction, Invention and Hyper-reality: From Popular Culture to Religion* (Routledge, 2017).

References

Adler, Margot. 1986. *Drawing Down the Moon: Witches, Druids, Goddess-Worshippers, and Other Pagans in America Today*. 2nd edition. Boston, MA: Beacon Press.

Alberts, Thomas. 2008. "Virtually real: Fake religions and problems of authenticity in religion." *Culture and Religion* 9(2): 125–139. https://doi.org/10.1080/14755610802211510

Anon. 2010. "Jedi discrimination case highlights trend for 'bizarre' claims, experts say." *Personnel Today*, 18 March, retrieved from www.personneltoday.com/hr/jedi-discrimination-case-highlights-trend-for-bizarre-claims-experts-say/

———. 2014. "Tradie refused 'religious right' to wear pasta strainer on head in licence photo." *9News*, 3 October, retrieved from https://www.9news.com.au/9stories/tradie-refused-religious-right-to-wear-pasta-strainer-on-head-in-licence-photo/176815d8-f9fd-422e-b772-15d92ffe2f63

———. 2016a. "Insights: Do You Have To Accommodate An Employee Who Worships The Flying Spaghetti Monster?" *Fisher Phillips*, 19 April, retrieved from https://www.fisherphillips.com/en/news-insights/do-you-have-to-accommodate-an-employee-who-worships-the-flying-spaghetti-monster.html

———. 2016b. "Jedi is not a religion, Charity Commission rules." *BBC News*, 19 December. https://www.bbc.com/news/uk-38368526

Bainbridge, William Sims, and Rodney Stark. 1979. "Cult Formation: Three Compatible Models." *Sociological Analysis* 44(4): 283–295. https://doi.org/10.2307/3709958

Bouma, Gary D. 2017. "'No religion' and Jedi Knight find their place in Australian identity." *The Conversation*, 23 August, retrieved from https://theconversation.com/no-religion-and-jedi-knight-find-their-place-in-australian-identity-81392

Brennan, Ben. 2018. "'Pastafarian' will lose his licence if caught driving without a colander on his head." *Yahoo News Australia*, 30 March, retrieved from https://au.news.yahoo.com/pastafarian-lose-licence-caught-driving-063240550.html

Carter, Helen. 2009. "Jedi religion founder accuses Tesco of discrimination over rules on hoods." *The Guardian*, 18 September, retrieved from www.guardian.co.uk/world/2009/sep/18/jedi-religion-tesco-hood-jones

Chidester, David. 2005. *Authentic Fakes: Religion and American Popular Culture*. Berkeley: University of California Press. https://doi.org/10.1525/9780520938243

Cliteur, Paul. 2023. "Atheists, Agnostics, Skeptics, and the Unconcerned: Why the European Court is Inconsistent in its Case Law and Violates Article 9 ECHR." *Journal of Religion & Society* 25. Retrieved from: https://cdr.creighton.edu/server/api/core/bitstreams/e9e87365-fd68-414c-8572-e10c7731c510/content

Cowie, Tom. 2016. "This guy got a Victorian driver's licence with a pasta strainer on his head." *The Age*, 29 November, retrieved from https://www.theage.com.au/national/victoria/this-guy-got-a-victorian-drivers-licence-with-a-pasta-strainer-on-his-head-20161129-gszuu7.html

Cusack, Carole M. 2009. "Science Fiction as Scripture: Robert A. Heinlein's Stranger in a Strange Land and the Church of All Worlds." *Literature & Aesthetics* 19(2): 72–91.

———. 2010. *Invented Religions: Imagination, Fiction and Faith*. Farnham and Burlington, VT: Ashgate.

———. 2013. "Play, narrative and the creation of religion: Extending the theoretical base of 'invented religions'." *Culture and Religion: An Interdisciplinary Journal* 14(4): 362–377. https://doi.org/10.1080/14755610.2013.838797

———. 2016. "Invention in 'New New' Religions." In *The Oxford Handbook of New Religious Movements*, edited by James R. Lewis and Inga Bårdsen Tollefsen, 2nd edition, 237–247. Oxford: Oxford University Press.

———. 2016–2017. "Vestigial States: Secular Space and the Churches in Contemporary Australia." *Modern Greek Studies* 18: 8–31.

Danchin, Peter. 2008. "Suspect Symbols: Value Pluralism as a Theory of Religious Freedom in International Law." *The Yale Journal of International Law* 33(1): 1–61.

Davidsen, Markus Altena. 2013. "Fiction-based religion: Conceptualising a new category against history-based religion and fandom." *Culture and Religion* 14(4): 378–395. https://doi.org/10.1080/14755610.2013.838798

———. 2014. "The Spiritual Tolkien Milieu: A Study of Fiction-Based Religions," Unpublished PhD thesis. Leiden University.

———. 2016. "From Star Wars to Jediism: The Emergence of a Fiction-Based

Religion." In *Words: Religious Language Matters*, edited by Ernst van den Hemel and Asja Szafraniec, 376–389. New York: Fordham University Press. https://doi.org/10.2307/j.ctt1bmzp8v.23

Durando, Jessica. 2015. "Pastafarian can wear a strainer on head in license photo." *USA Today*, 16 November, retrieved from https://www.usatoday.com/story/news/nation-now/2015/11/16/church-flying-spaghetti-monster-massachusetts-religion/75862946/

Edgell, Penny, Douglas Hartmann, Evan Stewart, and Joseph Gerteis. 2016. "Atheists and Other Cultural Outsiders: Moral Boundaries and the Non-Religious in the United States." *Social Forces* 95(2): 607–638. https://doi.org/10.1093/sf/sow063

Fenton, Claire. 2022. "'Til sauce do us part: Canadian couple married under Church of Flying Spaghetti Monster" (VIDEO). *Daily Hive*, 24 September, retrieved from https://dailyhive.com/vancouver/flying-spaghetti-monster-wedding

Gilhus, Ingvild Sælid and Lisbeth Mikaelsson. 2001. *Nytt blikk pa religion: Studiet av religion i dag*. Oslo: Pax.

Greenwald, Jeff. 1998. *Future Perfect: How Star Trek Conquered Planet Earth*. London: Penguin Books.

Hambrett, Micaela. 2018. "May the 4th: Australian Jedi 'head of the faith' calls for peace and formal recognition." *ABC Central West*, 27 June, retrieved from https://www.abc.net.au/news/2018-05-04/jedi-faith-leader-speaks-out-on-may-4th/9724758#

Henderson, Bobby. 2006a. *The Gospel of the Flying Spaghetti Monster*. New York: Villard.

———. 2006b. "Open Letter to Kansas School Board." *Church of the Flying Spaghetti Monster*, retrieved from https://www.spaghettimonster.org/pages/about/open-letter/

Henley, Jon. 2018. "Spaghetti injunction: Pastafarianism is not a religion, Dutch court rules." *The Guardian*, 16 August, retrieved from https://www.theguardian.com/world/2018/aug/16/pastafarianism-is-not-a-religion-dutch-court-rules

Hobsbawm, Eric J. and Terence Ranger, eds. 1992 [1983]. *The Invention of Tradition*. Cambridge: Cambridge University Press.

Jindra, Michael. 1994. "*Star Trek* Fandom as a Religious Phenomenon." *Sociology of Religion* 55(1): 27–51. https://doi.org/10.2307/3712174

Danielle Kirby. 2009. "From Pulp Fiction to Revealed Text: A Study of the Role of the Text in the Otherkin Community." In *Exploring Religion and the Sacred in a Media Age*, edited by Christopher Deacy and Elisabeth Arweck, 141-154. Farnham and Burlington, VT: Ashgate.

Laycock, Joseph P. 2021. "How the Satanic Temple is using 'abortion rituals' to claim religious liberty against the Texas 'heartbeat bill'." *The Conversation* 22 September. Retrieved from: https://theconversation.com/how-the-satanic-temple-is-using-abortion-rituals-to-claim-religious-liberty-against-the-texas-heartbeat-bill-167755

Levy, Andrew. 2010. "Political correctness strikes back: Jedi believer wins apology after being kicked out of Jobcentre for wearing a hood." *Daily Mail*, 17 March retrieved from www.dailymail.co.uk/news/article-1258365/Jedi-believer-wins-apology-Jobcentre-kicked-wearing-hood.html

Lewis, James R. 2014. "Using the 'F-Word' in Religious Studies: Toward a General Model of Sacred Forgeries." *Alternative Spirituality and Religion Review* 5(2): 188–204. https://doi.org/10.5840/asrr2015221

Madrazo, Alejandro. 2014. "Gender and (Religious) Attire: A Matter of (Free) Speech." *Journal of Law and Policy* 22(2). Retrieved from: https://brooklynworks.brooklaw.edu/jlp/vol22/iss2/3

Malaclypse the Younger. 1994. *Principia Discordia: How I Found Goddess and What I Did to Her When I Found Her.* Austin TX: Steve Jackson Games.

Malongowski, Kate. 2019. "Man fighting to wear pasta strainer in driver's license photo claims religious discrimination." *KMBC News*, 31 October, retrieved from https://www.kmbc.com/article/man-fighting-to-wear-pasta-strainer-in-drivers-license-photo-claims-religious-discrimination/29658801

Mason, Anthony (Chief Justice), Lionel Murphy, Ronald Wilson, F. Gerard Brennan, and William Deane. 1983. *Church of the New Faith vs Commissioner For Payroll Tax (Judgement).* Canberra: High Court of Australia.

Neal, Matt. 2022. "Australia's only Church of the Flying Spaghetti Monster brings visitors to new Pastafarian 'religion'." *ABC News*, 28 June, retrieved from https://www.abc.net.au/news/2022-06-28/church-of-the-flying-spaghetti-monster-attracts-more-pastafarian/101189332

Nevin, Charles. 2010. "Jedis stand up for religious rights." *The Guardian*, 19 March, retrieved from https://www.theguardian.com/commentisfree/belief/2010/mar/18/jedis-religious-rights-star-wars

Obadia, Lionel. 2015. "When Virtuality Shapes Social Reality—Fake Cults and the Church of the Flying Spaghetti Monster." *Online: Heidelberg Journal of Religions on the Internet* 8: 115-128.

Owen, Suzanne. 2011. "The World Religions Paradigm: Time for a Change." *Arts and Humanities in Higher Education* 10(3): 253–268. https://doi.org/10.1177/1474022211408038

Peralta, Eyder. 2011. "Austrian Man Wins Right To Wear Pasta Strainer In License Photo." *NPR: The Two-Way*, 13 July, retrieved from https://www.npr.org/sections/thetwo-way/2011/07/15/137824732/austrian-man-wins-right-to-wear-pasta-strainer-in-license-photo

Possamai, Adam. 2005. *Religion and Popular Culture: A Hyperreal Testament.* Bern: Peter Lang Publishing. https://doi.org/10.3726/978-3-0352-6259-9

Reilly, Jill. 2014. "'Pastafarian' allowed to wear spaghetti strainer on her head in driving licence photo because it is classed as 'religious headgear'." *MailOnline*, 8 September, retrieved from https://www.dailymail.co.uk/news/article-2747880/Pastafarian-allowed-wear-spaghetti-strainer-head-driving-licence-photo-classed-religious-headgear.html

Rosa, Hartmut. 2016. *Social Acceleration: A New Theory of Modernity.* Translated by Jonathan Trejo-Mathys. New York: Columbia University Press.

Roy, Eleanor Ainge. 2016. "World's first Pastafarian wedding takes place in New Zealand." *The Guardian*, 18 April, retrieved from https://www.theguardian.com/world/2016/apr/18/worlds-first-pastafarian-wedding-takes-place-in-new-zealand

Schrader, Jordan. 2007. "School: Pirates are not welcome." *Asheville Citizen-Times*, 29 March, retrieved from www.citizen-times.com/apps/pbcs.dll/article?AID=200770328123&template=printart

Singhi, Yash. 2023. "The Treatment of Religious Attire by Courts and International Fora reveals the need for new justifications for Religious Freedom beyond Personal Autonomy." *Research Blog Jindal Global Law School, India*, retrieved from https://research.jgu.edu.in/the-treatment-of-religious-attire-by-courts-and-international-fora-reveals-the-need-for-new-justifications-for-religious-freedom-beyond-personal-autonomy/

Somin, Ilya. 2016. "Opinion: Their lack of faith is disturbing—British Charity Commission rules that the Jedi are not a religion." *The Washington Post*, 21 December, retrieved from https://www.washingtonpost.com/news/volokh-conspiracy/wp/2016/12/21/their-lack-of-faith-is-disturbing-british-charity-commission-rules-that-the-jedi-are-not-a-religion/

Sulak, John C. 2014. *The Wizard and the Witch: An Oral History of Oberon Zell and Morning Glory.* Woodbury, MN: Llewellyn Publications.

Scottish Parliament. 2014. *Marriage and Civil Partnership (Scotland) Act 2014.* Edinburgh: Scottish Parliament.

Taira, Teemu. 2013. "The category of 'invented religion': A new opportunity for studying discourses on 'religion'." *Culture and Religion: An Interdisciplinary Journal* 14(4): 477–493. https://doi.org/10.1080/14755610.2013.838799

The Associated Press. 2014. "Utah woman wears colander for license photo in honor of Flying Spaghetti Monster." *The Salt Lake Tribune*, 18 November, retrieved from https://www.sltrib.com/news/2014/11/18/utah-woman-wears-colander-for-license-photo-in-honor-of-flying-spaghetti-monster/

Van der Haven, Alexander. 2017. "Hypothetical Religion: The Supernatural as an Experience and Experiment." In *Super Religion: From the Supernatural to the Paranormal*, edited by Jeffrey J. Kripal, 263–276. Farmington Hills, MI: Macmillan Reference.

Venema, Derk. 2018. "Piety or Ulterior Motive." In *Migration and Religious Freedom: Essays on the Interaction between Religious Duty and Migration Law*, edited by Carolus Grütters and Dario Dzananovic, 227–248. Nijmegen: Wolf Legal.

Wolff, Tim. 2021. "True Believers?—Sincerity and Article 9 of the European Convention on Human Rights." *European Constitutional Law Review* 17: 259–286. https://doi.org/10.1017/S1574019621000171

———. 2022. "Cogency, Seriousness, Cohesion, and Importance: Assessing the Strasbourg Case-Law on Religion or Belief." *Oxford Journal of Law and Religion* 11: 177–196. https://doi.org/10.1093/ojlr/rwad006

9

DIRECTOR'S CU(L)TS, REEL RESEARCHERS:
EXPLORING SECTS IN THE MOVIES

STEFANO BIGLIARDI, ABDELMOJIB CHOUHBI, MOHAMED AMINE GHAFIL, AMINE NAKARI, DANYA TAZI MOKHA AND SALMA ZAHIDI

Since Fall 2016, Stefano Bigliardi has served as Associate Professor of Philosophy at Al Akhawayn University in Ifrane, a liberal-arts, English-speaking college in Morocco. In Fall 2022, for the first time at this university, he offered, under the general title of History of Ideas, undergraduate courses (in two parallel sections: PHI 2302 01 and PHI 2302 02) focusing on the history and beliefs of NRMs (their full title read: "Starships, Shamans, Skeletons, and Satan: Exploring New Religious Movements").[1] Final course evaluations indicated that the topic and pedagogy were enthusiastically received by students. This essay was co-authored by Stefano and five of the most dynamic and curious participants in said courses, who decided to join the writing project after an internal call was circulated; they conducted their research and wrote under the instructor's coordination but based on equitable work distribution and intense exchanges of ideas. It is worth specifying that all five students major in Computer Science at AUI's School of Science and Engineering. We are convinced that focusing on the representation of NRMs in pop-culture products such as mainstream fictional films, while engaging in research and intellectual conversation involving older and younger generations, is an ideal way of preserving Professor Jim Lewis's spirit and ideals.

The present pages examine the plots, dialogues, and visual elements of twenty-two movies depicting "cults" or "sects." To be sure, we are well aware that such terms are far from being scholarly, in that they carry strongly derogatory tones; however, we employ them in our analysis since they are used in the very films we survey and analyze. In other words, the idea guiding our research is that not many people are knowledgeable about New Religious Movements (henceforth: NRMs). The public tends to view them as "cults" or "sects" and to imagine such "cults" and "sects" as they are typically represented by mainstream cinema. For this reason,

---

1. A sample syllabus is available here: https://tinyurl.com/43cb66zh.

an investigation and discussion of such cinematic production is scholarly worthwhile.

Obviously, we needed to narrow down the scope of our research. Countless films include the representation of cults and sects of different kinds, not to mention secret societies without strong religious connotations. Most readers may be familiar with Stanley Kubrick's (1928–1999) *Eyes Wide Shut* (1999), depicting the orgiastic, masked gatherings of frightening and powerful aristocrats in present-day New York. Cinephiles may be familiar with Robin Hardy's (1929–2016) *The Wicker Man* (1973), in which a police sergeant comes across a disturbing if cheerful pagan community on a Hebridean island. And perhaps a few will have heard of Aldo Lado's (1934–2023) *The Short Night of Glass Dolls* (1971), set in Communist Prague, where an eerie society of seniors is intent on sacrificing young victims in sexualized and cruel rituals.

For our survey and analysis, we have selected films that deal with *fictional* groups (although possibly inspired by real ones), and that represent their investigation, or at least some kind of systematic approach, on behalf of characters who are equipped with scientific/structured knowledge, information, or expertise (or who build and develop it throughout the movie), including academics, students, psychiatrists/psychologists, journalists, and even "deprogrammers."[2] We refer to such characters with the term "expert" or "researcher." We are interested in how movie creators imagine and depict the religious groups, the relationship and interaction between the sect and their researchers, as well as how sects and experts are represented as to their respective cultures, ethnicities, motives, and genders.

In Mark Robson's (1913–1978) *The Seventh Victim* (1943), Mary Gibson, a girl enrolled at a prestigious boarding school, travels to New York City in the hope of finding her older sister Jacqueline, who has mysteriously disappeared, and failed to pay her tuition fees. Mary is anxious and naive, yet she also shows great determination. She soon teams up with three male characters: Gregory, a lawyer (and Jacqueline's estranged husband), Jason, a charismatic bohemian poet who constantly speaks in riddles, and Dr. Judd, Jacqueline's psychiatrist, who together with Jason can be considered this film's "experts"—since they educate themselves about the group they come across by reading books.

Through their teamwork, the improvised investigative gang quickly makes an unsettling discovery: Jacqueline was a member of the Palladists,

---

2. In the films we selected, police members may be involved in the investigations; however, they are always assisted by "experts" as we define them—this explains why Hardy's and Lado's aforementioned films, as well as others, are not included. We are aware that our choice may seem arbitrary, but we regard our research as the first step of a project that could potentially be broadened.

a Satanist group that is now set on punishing her for breaking one of their rules: whoever talks about the group to a non-member must die (Jacqueline is the seventh case, hence the title). The woman had resorted to Dr. Judd's services due to the depression she had developed while in the group.

In reality, the Palladists were members of a Masonic-*cum*-Satanic society that French writer Léo Taxil (1854-1907) claimed to have discovered, as part of the hoax that he famously conceived in the 1890s, intending to mock both Freemasonry and the Catholic church. In the film, given its focus on the relations among the main characters, the Palladists remain largely mysterious, and their beliefs are only hinted at. However, it is clear that the group is not very large, with no more than a dozen members: men and women who, judging by their attire, must be fairly wealthy. They seem to rely on scripture written by a deceased founder, Johann Rozenquartz.[3] However, their current leader is Mr. Brun, a charismatic, distinguished and imposing middle-aged man who seems to speak for the group and is well versed in their scripture. The Palladists are seen gathering in the apartment of Natalie Cortez (a lady with one arm); however, no specific rituals are shown.

Remarkably, one scene shows the Palladists debating their scripture regarding Jacqueline's punishment. On this occasion, they are represented in a surprisingly human way. One female member, Mrs. Swift, states: "But it can be such a horrible decision because we are all pledged to non-violence." Another female member, Miss Rowan, responds: "Our founder must have known when he wrote these seemingly contradictory rules—the rule of non-violence and the law that whoever betrays us must die—he must have known." The fact that the group seems conflicted gives the impression that it has been a long time since someone last betrayed the group, and that the Palladists' activities are rarely violent. In fact, in the original script Mrs. Swift stated: "But it can be such a horrible decision. *I found peace here. I know that a large portion of that peace came* because we are all pledged to non-violence."[4] Perhaps, the statement about peace (italics mine) was cut from the film because that would have portrayed the movement as too human and relatable to be appropriate in America in the 1940s.

In another remarkable scene near the movie's end, Jason engages with the Palladists, sharing with them his views about the group, that he regards as a bunch of "lost souls." Mr. Brun retorts to him that "right" and "wrong" are subjective terms, so that there is no way to prove to him what is fundamentally wrong about the group. Judd then replies by reciting the Lord's Prayer,

---

3. Possibly reminiscent of Christian Rosenkreuz, the mythical founder of Rosicrucianism.
4. Available here: https://sfy.ru/?script=seventh_victim

which leaves the Palladists speechless and embarrassed (for some unspecified reason—once again, this may be a clumsy attempt at creating a strong contrast between the group and mainstream Christian morals, since the Palladists may have been perceived as all too likable throughout the film[5]).

In Jacques Tourneur's (1904–1977) *Night of the Demon* (1957; US title *Curse of the Demon*), US-American psychologist Dr. John Holden arrives in London for a scientific convention on the paranormal. Shortly earlier, a colleague of his, Professor Henry Harrington, was fatally electrocuted under mysterious circumstances. Harrington had publicly promised to expose at the symposium a "devil cult" led by Julian Karswell, an expert in black magic who resides in a country mansion with his mother and possesses a large collection of rare books about "witchcraft and the black arts." Holden, a hard-boiled skeptic, does not give credit to speculations about Harrington's death involving paranormal and demonic elements, and thinks that Karswell is "a harmless faker." Later on, however, with the help of Joanna, Harrington's niece (a kindergarten teacher), Holden surrenders to the evidence: Karswell is indeed assisted by the devil and can therefore count on supernatural powers.

Holden is a relatively young, handsome, self-assured and dynamic white man, who, as an academic, enjoys international fame (his trip to London is reported by the press; additionally, he is interviewed by reporters awaiting his arrival at the airport) and can afford an affluent lifestyle (he flies overseas and occupies a spacious suite). He has a rather empiricist/rationalist outlook; he states, for instance: "But logic... the reality of the seeable and the touchable... that's what convinces me finally. Certainly not rumor or intuition or funny feelings." In London, Holden connects with international colleagues including an Indian professor, K. T. Kumar from Bombay, whose attire and accent are depicted quite stereotypically. Another colleague of Holden's, middle-aged Irish professor O'Brien, is shown as being rather open-minded towards the possibility of paranormal events actually occurring—and so is Kumar.

In his investigations, Holden resorts to chemical analyses, as well as to hypnotism. Holden performs the latter (with the aid of medical drug injections), for an audience of colleagues, on Rand Hobart, an individual connected to Karswell's cult. Interestingly, however, hypnosis is also used by Karswell on Joanna. In a highly ironic scene, Karswell is represented performing sleights of hand for a crowd of children he is hosting on the premises of his mansion, in a clown's attire and makeup. His actual sorcery involves the use of parchments ornate with runic writing that Holden also

---

5 Also, the camera angles and the music in this scene convey the impression that Jason and Judd are in heaven looking down at the Palladists in hell.

finds at Stonehenge. Karswell's cult is never shown, but its existence is suggested, including the representation of a family of peasants (the relatives of Hobart), who are reticent to the point of being hostile towards Holden, and who self-identify as "believers."

In John Llewellyn Moxey's (1925–2019) *The City of the Dead* (1960; US title *Horror Hotel*), university professor of history Alan Driscoll, after delivering a passionate lecture about witchcraft, encourages enthusiastic (and naive) student Nan Barlow to conduct research on the subject at Whitewood, a (fictional) village in New England, where a supposed witch by the name of Elizabeth Selwyn had been burned at the stake in 1692. Driscoll isn't taken very seriously by Nan's boyfriend, Bill, who sarcastically states that he is going "bring the matches" to the next lecture—and whom the professor bitterly rebukes stating he had hoped that Bill had joined the lectures "in a spirit of scientific curiosity." Driscoll is also challenged by Dick Barlow, Nan's brother, also an academic, and a scientist with a rather empiricist worldview, who finds that witchcraft and sorcery is "nothing but fairytale mumbo-jumbo"—a statement to which Driscoll responds that "the basis of fairy tales is reality, the basis of reality is fairy tales."

Once in Whitewood, Nan finds accommodation at The Raven's Inn and gets acquainted with several villagers: the inn's owner, Mrs. Newless,[6] her mute housekeeper Lottie, a blind pastor, and Patricia, an antiques dealer, from whom Nan borrows a book about witchcraft. On Candlemas Eve, the girl is lured to a basement and sacrificed to Satan by Mrs. Newless, who is in fact Elizabeth Selwyn, and her coven's members, all dressed in black capes. Nan's fiancé Bill, her brother, and Patricia, eventually investigate the student's disappearance; they find out about Mrs. Newless's identity; Professor Driscoll is also discovered to be a member of the coven.

Terence Fisher's (1904–1980) *The Devil Rides Out* (1968; US title *The Devil's Bride*) is set in London in 1929. Nicholas, Duc de Richleau and his friend Rex Van Ryn discover that Simon Aron, son of a late friend of theirs, has fallen into the clutches of a satanic cult. Duc de Richleau is an occult expert who has extensively studied esoteric doctrines related to satanic cults, and throughout the movie we see him engage in black magic and hypnosis to combat the cult. He also has connections to people in the British Museum and is granted full access to occult volumes that are safely guarded under lock and key. It can be presumed that Rex Van Ryn is a pilot, as he is seen flying in in the opening scene, and Duc de Richleau mentions later on that they, along with Simon's father, were companions in the Escadrille Lafayette. Almost nothing is known about Simon's background; he initially

---

6   Almost an anagram of Selwyn.

mentions that he is part of an astronomical society, but it is soon discovered that the society is just a cover for his involvement in the satanic group.

The cult is led by Mocata, an "Ipsissimus"[7] or "master of the highest grade"—as de Richleau describes him. He is a well-built white man in his 40s with very peculiar bright eyes that he uses, along with his psychic abilities, to control some of his followers and, to a certain extent, outsiders too. Mocata plans to baptize Simon and his female friend, Tanith, to the service of evil at the Grand Sabbath of the year. The ceremony takes place in an isolated spot in the woods. The setting is dimly lit by scattered candles and fire pits; one can discern bones and what appears to be animal skin hanging throughout the place. Mocata initiates the ritual by reciting some sort of incantations; he and four of his subordinates are dressed in purple gowns, while the rest of the followers are dressed in white robes. He then sacrifices a white goat, and the members scream with delight at the sight of blood (that is collected in a receptacle by Mocata's subordinates), then proceed to celebrate by dancing, kissing, drinking, and crying with joy. They soon after start reciting some sort of invocations and summon the devil, in the shape of the Goat of Mendes,[8] and bow before him. Later, Mocata is also seen summoning the Angel of Death, depicted as a figure fully dressed in black, except for its purple cape, and riding a black winged horse. It is also wearing a helmet, which it removes at the very end when it wants to make its attack and reveals a skull underneath.

Sergio Martino's (1938) *Tutti i colori del buio* (*All the Colors of the Dark*, 1972) is the story of Jane Harrison, a young woman tormented by nightmares in which she witnesses her mother's grotesque murder, and who has suffered a miscarriage. Barbara, her sister, recommends that she sees Dr. Burton, a therapist, against the wishes of her boyfriend Richard. Dr. Burton adopts a rather classical psychoanalytical approach to the woman's obsessions. Returning from the first session with him, Jane meets her new neighbor Mary, who suggests that Jane should participate in a sabbath, that is more likely to cure her than ordinary medicine. The ceremony, taking place at a rural castle-like mansion, turns out to be a fully-fledged satanic ritual, including the sacrifice of a puppy; its throat is slit by the leader of the ceremony, a young, white, long-haired, bearded man who wears long fake nails of metal and a pendant representing an eye inscribed in a triangle. Eventually, the participants in the ceremony drink the animal's blood and engage in sexual intercourse with the newcomer.

---

7   Latin for "own very self."

8   The Goat of Mendes, or Baphomet, is an esoteric winged figure with the head and legs of a goat and the body of a human. It is often associated with Satanism, though its origins are rather obscure (it may have originated in Ancient Egypt or Greece).

Upon her return, Jane notices a blue-eyed man following her; we had seen him earlier in the movie as her mother's killer. He stalks Jane almost everywhere, and she becomes increasingly paranoid. Mary proposes they attend another ceremony to ease her mind, but on this occasion, things take a disastrous turn. Jane is handed a dagger which Mary then throws herself on, all for the sake of "freeing herself." Jane manages to run away, just to be caught by the leader and his aides who disclose a terrible revelation: her mother was murdered for wanting to leave the group.

The sect is portrayed as a powerful, influential, and sinister organization, with at least one woman in a prominent role (in fact, it is mentioned in passing that she was manipulating the group beyond its original mission). It is suggested that notable members of the group, while having a criminal or psychiatric background, hold respectable jobs, including in the police, conveying the idea that this organization has a vast network and is capable of manipulating the wider community. Their rituals are overtly sexual and involve the use of inverted crosses and pentagrams, stereotypically known as satanic symbols. While members express their devotion through hypnotic chanting, they noticeably lose their sense of reality, morality, and restraints, experiencing an altered state of consciousness.

Properly, it is Jane and Richard who investigate the group; the former, however, is assisted by Dr. Burton, who can be defined as the film's "expert" according to the definition adopted in this paper. Dr. Burton plays a marginal but symbolically relevant role; although his field is psychiatry, he is able to recognize the sect's symbol, that is initially seen in the leader's pendant and that at some point Jane finds on her body, as "a cabbalistic sign...like the one that the Jews used to indicate God, also used in the Middle Ages by witches and charlatans for their black magic practices." However, the doctor's approach is very skeptical and materialistic: he interprets Jane's experience as a nightmare and prescribes her some pills, claiming that she just needs to sleep "possibly without dreaming." His approach soon turns out to be wrong, with extreme consequences for him.

In Francesco Barilli's (1943) *Il profumo della signora in nero* (*The Perfume of the Lady in Black*, 1974), Silvia Hacherman, the young, hard-working, and ambitious director of a chemical laboratory, is obsessed with sinister memories and hallucinations of her mother, who died when she was a child. One evening Silvia visits with her boyfriend and some African friends. Andy, a young professor of sociology, tells her how black witchcraft is still widespread and powerful in his native country, in rural and urban locations alike, and how sects resort to "demonic practices" and human sacrifice. Andy is represented as respectable by Western, bourgeois standards; while he is slightly "exoticized" through his accent (in addition to his looks), he manifestly is upper class, he is eloquent, and always elegantly dressed. Silvia seems deeply upset by his words, but the professor withdraws what he has just said stating: "Did I scare you? I was just joking, Ms. Hacherman. I hope you don't want to believe this, we no longer do these things."

Later, during a tennis match, Silvia pinches her hand with a nail protruding from her racket, and Andy shocks her by intensely sucking the blood. Eventually, the two participate in a séance during which a blind clairvoyant makes disturbing revelations about Silvia's past. Eventually, Andy turns out to be, together with multiple acquaintances of Silvia's, part of a cannibalistic sect. Their rituals are not represented, but it is obvious that they have the power to alter the mind of their victims. They are seen gathering at a subterranean, dimly lit location, all dressed in gray coats, to eviscerate and devour a corpse.

In Ralph L. Thomas' (1939) *Ticket to Heaven* (1981), David Kappel, a young Canadian school teacher, joins a religious community in San Francisco after breaking up with his girlfriend. The group is called Heavenly Children and resides at a rural location called Liberty City. Its doctrines draw upon Christianity, yet its founder (a messianic "Father") is Asian. The "Father" is worshiped by the community, but he is not present on the camp, where leadership is exerted by strong, charismatic, and young figures including Patrick, a motivational speaker, and Ingrid, who, among other things, presides over worshiping ceremonies. During such ceremonies the Children sit on the floor; men and women are separated, the former dress in long white tunics and the latter in formal suits complete with a tie; under Ingrid's guidance they bow in front of a portrait of the founder and his spouse.[9]

All tasks on the camp are performed communally; activities include chanting ("bomb with love!" is one of the Children's favorite slogans), dancing, outdoor games, storytelling, and campfires. The lifestyle participants are vigorously encouraged to embrace includes a special diet (in fact bordering with starvation), as well as sleep deprivation; the group raises funds by selling flowers on the streets of San Francisco.

In a revealing scene, David realizes that one of his comrades, Patrick, doesn't hesitate to lie to a passerby regarding the group's activities in order to collect money, claiming that it is for a drug rehabilitation center. Patrick thus justifies himself: "It's only Satan's money we're taking, all right? And since Satan cheated to get it, it's our mission to get it back. …

---

9 The "Father's" Asian origin, his attire, and the fact that he is represented with his wife are all reminiscent of Sun Myung Moon (1920–2012), founder of the Unification Church; the film was inspired by Josh Freed's 1980 book *Moonwebs: Journey into the Mind of a Cult*.

Say that man was dying in a fire—wouldn't you do anything you had to, to save him? Even lie? Well, he is dying, spiritually he is dying. But we just sold him a ticket to heaven."

Despite initial reluctance, David ends up assimilating into the group; his hair is cut short, and he starts wearing white clothes like the rest of the members. The process is facilitated by the company (and surveillance) of a flirtatious good-looking girl who is tasked with overseeing him. David ends up being conditioned to the point of vomiting a hamburger he has eaten during an escape attempt transgressing the cult's rules.

David's best friend Larry joins the camp, realizing the manipulation followers are subjected to. Larry works as an accountant, but he is also an amateur stand-up comedian, and he takes advantage of his skills to communicate with the Heavenly Children; one evening he even resorts to humor to tell them publicly how he really feels about the group, and eventually he uses his gab to pretend he has an interest in their doctrines. He is helped by another young man who eventually reveals to be undercover and has infiltrated this community and similar ones in search of his sister.

Larry teams up with David's ex-girlfriend and his family to kidnap him. David's parents end up being placed under arrest for this. Additionally, they hire Linc Strunk, a deprogrammer around David's age, to make David realize that the group has deceitfully conditioned him. The deprogrammer, abrasive, charismatic, and energetic, appears twenty minutes before the film's end. His credentials and methodology aren't illustrated with precision, but the latter can be inferred from his actions; he coerces David to behave in a way that runs contrary to all the ways implemented in the group, and he vigorously debates with him both the movement's scriptures (the "Father" authored a voluminous book called *Divine Imperative*) and the founder's integrity (he is extremely affluent and leads a luxurious lifestyle).

This is a film with a message, and that obviously conveys a negative representation of the religious group; however, it also clearly displays how the "deprogrammer" resorts to means similar to those that characterize the group.

In Ted Kotcheff's (1931) *Split Image* (1982), Danny Stetson, a talented gymnast, is lured to a cult by a beautiful young woman named Rebecca. The community, known as Homeland, resides on an isolated green land complete with a futuristic, white communal building with golden domes;[10] the community is made up of about 200 white men and women around their 20s, except for their leader, Neil Kirklander, who is also white and seems to be in his early 40s. The people of Homeland are self-sufficient; they rely on renew-

---

10 Religiously symbolic items that can be spotted at Homeland's premises include at least one Buddha effigy and relatively small, pyramid-shaped structures.

able energy, grow their own food, and have dedicated units for producing everything they need, from utensils and clothes to furniture and housing. At first, Danny is skeptical and wary of Homelands's beliefs and activities despite their cheerful and warm welcome. However, upon witnessing how affectionately Neil treats the members, Danny becomes intrigued.

Neil is like a father figure to the cult. He is portrayed as a loving and caring individual, a savior of lost souls, and for that, all the members look up to him. The ultimate purpose of Homeland is to create a better world by rescuing people from "death in life," that is, the torture brought upon the soul by seeking pleasure. To achieve this, members need to first work on their inner selves, hearts and minds, becoming "Olympic Champions with [their] lives" as Neil puts it. They gather in groups and talk about Neil's teachings, as well as the positive impact the cult has had on their lives. Upon Neil's command, they also speak in tongues—or, as Neil himself says, "the language of angels."

Eventually, Danny ends up joining Homeland's commune and becomes fully immersed in it, abandoning his previous life, including his name (he elects the new name of Joshua) and his family, during a special ceremony in which his hair is cut short and he burns his old clothes and belongings including his wallet (that contains his family pictures and his university ID), and stands naked surrounded by the community members, who chant and cheer ecstatically "Danny is dead, Joshua is born!"

Danny's parents hire Charles Pratt, a deprogrammer, who subjects Danny to psychological abuse to have him abandon Homeland. Charles considers Neil to be his arch-enemy. He is a man in his late 30s/early 40s, and based on his account, has already succeeded in deprogramming a number of people, including Homeland members. He is formally dressed, and though he is depicted as a charismatic individual dedicated to his cause (saving people from cults), he seems to be doing so single-mindedly, resorting to abusive and unethical behavior.

The film elaborates on the impact of cults on vulnerable individuals. From the beginning, one can sense that Danny is not completely satisfied with his life, lacking a sense of purpose. Homeland appears to promise and deliver a sense of belonging, making up for all the love and affection Danny is missing. Although Homeland is not portrayed in a completely negative light, it still imposes restrictions on its members' lifestyle, including severe rules on relationships, which Danny and Rebecca find repressive as they cannot openly express their feelings. Even after leaving Homeland, Danny still feels some sort of connection to it. He refuses to label his experience as brainwashing, stating that everything he felt back in the movement was genuine. As soon as he reconnects with Rebecca, he realizes that she was the primary reason why he joined the cult, and that they do not need Homeland to spend their life together.[11]

Steven Spielberg's (1946) *Indiana Jones and the Temple of Doom* (1984) is set in the mid-1930s and follows the adventures of the titular protagonist, a renowned archaeologist, his sidekick Short Round (a Chinese boy), and showgirl Willie Scott who, running away from a criminal gang in Shanghai, get stranded in northern India. Coming across a poor village, the three are welcomed reverentially, since the villagers believe that they were sent by God to help them. A sacred stone, that has the power to keep evil at bay, has been stolen from the village, and most, if not all, of the village children were abducted.

Upon reaching the nearby (fictional) Palace of Pankot, Jones and his friends discover a cult that has secretly taken over Pankot's young maharaja's government. The cult worships the Hindu goddess Kali, honoring her in the shape of a sinister, giant effigy located in the palace's dungeons, through human sacrifices that are carried out by the cult's leader, while members (seemingly, only Indian men) assist and chant ecstatically. The leader is Mola Ram, a ruthless, imposing middle-aged Indian man, willing to do whatever it takes to achieve his goals with no regard to human life. The children were abducted to use them as slaves in the palace's dungeons, in the attempt at digging out other sacred stones.

While the movie is undeniably entertaining, it also has strongly racist (and sexist[12]) undertones and does not excel in accuracy and logic. In particular, the cult's representation draws upon the thuggees, bands of bandits and murderers that allegedly operated in India in the 1800's and that were suppressed by British colonizers by the 1870s; however, the thuggees' actual existence as a monolithic entity as well as the connection with Kali by individuals described as thuggees has been severely questioned by contemporary scholars. The movie's cultists are shown to make use of a hallucinogenic concoction that individuals about to be sacrificed are forced to drink. Additionally, Kali's cult is hybridized with voodoo, since its members are able to harm their adversaries at a distance by sticking pins into dolls that represent them. The cult's depiction includes a supernatural element (although one may even interpret some scenes as hallucinatory rather than real), and Mola Ram is represented as entertaining some kind of imperialistic ambition (he states: "The Hebrew God will fall, the Christian God will be forgotten, and Kali will rule the world!").

---

11 The film, like *Ticket to Heaven*, may have also been inspired by Josh Freed's work (see note 9), which explains the strong similarities between the two.

12 This is particularly clear in the depiction of Willie Scott, the only female protagonist, as an anxious, clueless, mawkish individual.

Kali's worshippers are highly racialized, although racist motives are somewhat diluted by the filmmakers by showing that other Indians fall victim to their crimes, and that the cult ultimately stems from a "betrayal" of Hindu god Shiva (as Indiana Jones tells Mola Ram during their final showdown).

While being (mildly) characterized as a (stereotypical) academic, for instance, through the title of "doctor," the knowledge he displays, his stereotypical glasses, and occasional references to academic life including controversies, Indiana Jones, a white man in his early 40s, is in fact a superhero of sorts. He masters (and effortlessly shifts across) difficult languages including Hindi and Chinese (in fact, a few variants of it), he can fly a plane, he can count on almost inexhaustible physical strength and extraordinary courage, and he is even ready to kill. In the end, Jones leaves the stones with the people they belong to, thus suggesting that he is ultimately not as cynical as his words and deeds throughout the movie had suggested.

In Gianfranco Giagni's (1952) *Il nido del ragno* (*The Spider Labyrinth*, 1988), young professor of oriental languages Alan Whitmore (serving at a fictional university in Dallas) is sent by his superiors, including chancellor Hubbard and a clergyman, to Budapest, in order to check on senior colleague Professor Roth. The Hungarian professor participates in an international project coordinated by Whitmore, called Intextus; the project involves academic participants in India, Egypt, and Germany. Such research, that seems to be extremely important for Whitmore's university, is aimed at studying what seems to be a religion dating back to 3000 BCE. It turns out that such religion is still alive, and counts on a widespread, indeed global, network (a "cobweb," as stated in the film) of affiliates as well as on supernatural powers.

Professor Whitmore fails to detect the signals given by other characters who try hard to steer him away from danger, and ends up being coerced into the sect, with catastrophic results for his superiors as well (who in fact, it turns out, had failed to inform him about the risk). He is, supposedly, a brilliant academic, considering his young age (he is, apparently, in his early 30s). However, Whitmore doesn't appear to be particularly "street-smart"; besides his academic background he shows no other special qualities if one doesn't consider his good looks (however, he is the one who ends up being seduced by a female character).

The sect, whose symbol is a spider, also in the form of a scar that all affiliates have on an arm, is depicted as sinister, cruel, and all-powerful: it has massacred an entire district in Budapest and turned its underground into a graveyard. Its exact beliefs are never made explicit, but it seems to worship a monstrous baby that possesses the affiliates.

In Jeff Kwitny's (1951) *Il treno*[13] (*Beyond the Door III*,[14] 1989), a horror B-movie (with plenty of supernatural elements), a group of students from Los Angeles visits a rural community in Yugoslavia in order to witness an "ancient Balkan rite," a "passion play" whose central character is a virgin female; the play dates back two thousand years, is only celebrated every hundred years, and is attended by thousands of pilgrims from around the world. The group includes Beverly Putnic,[15] a shy girl of Serbian origins. The students are welcomed by professor Andromolek, a local scholar. The middle-aged professor speaks English fluently but with a strong local accent; he wears classy attire including an elegant hat and a red scarf and walks with a cane ornate with an elaborate knob. From the beginning, Andromolek seems to have a special connection (beyond the obvious linguistic and cultural one) with local villagers, who are represented as destitute, primitive, incommunicative, ghoulish, and cruel.

The "passion play" is in fact a Satanic rite, for which Beverly has been designated as its "princess," that is, Satan's bride, to be possessed by him during the ritual. The eerie professor, unsurprisingly, turns out to be affiliated with the Satanic sect and plays an important role in the ceremony—indeed, he is Lucifer's servant. The ritual is represented in great detail; it takes place at night. Beverly, wearing a black veil, is expected to meet Lucifer on a raised altar provided with a bed and a red cushion. Locals attend silently, dressed in black capes and holding candles; an elderly, grotesque lady (whose name is, ironically, Vesna, that is, "spring") is tasked with inspecting whether the girl is a virgin; and Lucifer appears in monstrous shape.

In Roman Polański's (1933) *The Ninth Gate* (1999), Dean Corso, a New York rare-book dealer, is hired by Boris Balkan, a wealthy book collector, to authenticate one of his books called *The Nine Gates of the Kingdom of Shadows*. The book is believed to have been written by Aristide Torchia, a 17th century author, in collaboration with Satan. Eventually Torchia was burned at the stake. There only exist two other copies of *The Nine Gates*. Each one contains three special engravings signed L.C.F. instead of Torchia's initials: the three letters stand for Lucifer, who created the engravings in question, and all nine engravings must be combined to unlock the book's power. Corso soon finds out that a cult, led by Tiana Telfer, the widow of a bil-

---

13 Italian for "the train."

14 The English title is unrelated with the movie's actual content; it was chosen by the production to capitalize on the success of the film *Beyond the Door* (1974, original title is *Chi sei?*—i.e., "Who are you?") and its sequel (*Shock*—original title *Schock*-, or *Beyond the Door II*, 1977, also without real connection with the former).

15 Serbo-Croatian word for "passenger" or "traveler."

lionaire who used to possess one of the copies, is also after *The Nine Gates*, intending to use it in order to conjure up and worship Lucifer. The cult is called the Order of the Silver Serpent; it was founded after Torchia's death to perpetuate the memory and preserve the secrets of his book.

Telfer and her group go as far as to use deception, violence, and even murder to retrieve the book; however, one elderly female character in the movie, Baroness Kessler, in fact describes it as a degeneration of the original Order, now used by "bored millionaires and celebrities... as an excuse to indulge their jaded sexual appetites"—she adds that she used to be a member, but her "orgy days are over."[16] Only one ritual is shown. The group's representation is the standard/stereotypical one for Hollywood-like Satanists. Members are, seemingly, only white, except for one person of color who accompanies and helps Tiana Telfer throughout the movie. Their ceremony takes place at a luxurious mansion, in a room ornate with red drapery, effigies of dragons, and an elaborate altar complete with figures of snakes. Both Telfer, who leads the ritual, and the followers, wear black capes and golden necklaces with pentacles; the members hold lit candles. The woman reads from *The Nine Gates* (in Latin), and the followers reply like in a responsorial psalmody.

Corso[17] is young (in his mid-30s), dynamic, cynical and profit-driven; he sports a certain negligence in his work—since he smokes cigarettes while he is leafing through rare manuscripts. While he cannot be described as a proper cult expert, he does approach Telfer's sect and understands their plans through his quest as an expert of ancient manuscripts, and therefore he does conduct an investigation aided by a scholarship of sorts. That being said, it is not specified whether Corso has any academic credentials, and he only succeeds in overcoming the threats posed by Telfer and her followers with the help of a mysterious young lady with seemingly supernatural powers.

In Jane Campion's (1954) *Holy Smoke* (1999, also known as *Holy Smoke!*), 18-year-old Australian Ruth Barron joins an Indian cult led by a guru named (somewhat predictably) Baba. Based on his physical appearance, the charismatic leader is of South Asian descent, and he wears traditional Indian clothing. Baba is said to be "spiritually married" to female affiliates; on one occasion, he taps on Ruth's forehead, sending her into a trance-like state.

---

16 In fact, the Order of the Silver Serpent is only mentioned once, by the Baroness; Telfer and her followers are never heard stating their cult's name. However, we assume that Order and Telfer's cult are one and the same, considering the presence of the snakes in their altar and the analogies between the description given by the Baroness and the group whose ceremony is represented.

17 His name, as mentioned in the movie, is related to the Italian word for "running."

Ruth's family, by subterfuge, has her travel back to Australia (where she had no intention of returning) and entrusts her to PJ Waters, a famous deprogrammer from California. In order to make a strong case for the usefulness of his services, Waters screens the family for an overview of misdemeanors and atrocities committed by actual NRMs including the Rajneesh Movement, the Manson Family, the Branch Davidians, and Heaven's Gate.

Eventually, PJ begins his "treatment" on Ruth[18] in an austere cabin at a remote location. The two initially argue, then, following Ruth's loss of faith in the cult, engage in sexual intercourse after she seduces him (previously, he had engaged in sexual intercourse with one of her relatives). One of the arguments used by PJ to convince Ruth of the inanity of her Indian experience is the female condition in India—to which she retorts that, at least, Indian men are less hypocritical than he is. Later on, she induces him into wearing lipstick and a dress, and calls him a "lezzo" (lesbian). The girl ends up leaving the cabin, and PJ, infatuated with her, chases her and confronts her physically, to the point of making her bleed and putting her in the car trunk. Upon finding out how things have unfolded between the deprogrammer and Ruth, her family decides to chase the man away. Ruth returns to the ashram, accompanied by her mother, and PJ moves on to a career as a novelist.

The film depicts Baba's movement neither extensively nor in detail. Like its leader, it has a generic, stereotypical "Indian patina" to it. The people in Ruth's life, the deprogrammer and even her family, are notable for their duplicity and arrogance towards the girl, and, significantly, the former ends up defeated, after having adopted, in order to obtain the "deprogramming," means and behavior of the kind that he reproaches to the sect. It is also shown that Ruth's family has a Christian background and resorts to reciting prayers in times of despair. In addition to the idea that deprogrammers end up turning into a mirror image of the cults they purport to fight, the film suggests that natural, erotic instincts end up having the upper hand of humans, no matter the side they stay on.

Les Rivières pourpres II: Les Anges de l'apocalypse (*The Crimson Rivers 2: Angels of the Apocalypse*, 2004) is a film by Olivier Dahan (1967). The protagonist Pierre Niemans[19] is a French inspector, sent to a monastery at the German

---

18　The name evokes a well-known Biblical character, a convert to Judaism and an ancestor of Jesus, who is also a symbol of kindness and altruism, as well as of loyalty and obedience.

19　Although indisputably a French surname, Niemans is also reminiscent of the German word *niemand*, "nobody"—that is, in its turn, reminiscent of Odysseus's famous trick to the Cyclops. The name Pierre (Peter) also strongly ties into the film's symbology.

border to investigate a peculiar homicide. He joins forces with captain Reda, once his student at the police academy, and agent Marie, a religious specialist. The three find themselves thrown in a conspiracy and try to prevent a series of assassinations that are part of a plan for a Nazi uprising.

The killers appear to be sinister monks that seemingly count on inexhaustible strength and near-invincibility. The victims are part of a community of men whose names and occupations are the same as those of Jesus and his apostles. The exact reasons for their obsession with the apostles (and whether they changed their names and jobs or if it just was a coincidence) are not specified. Marie, whose role is rather marginal, defines them as "true believers." It turns out that the "apostles" are being chased by a group of Nazis led by an elderly German minister, in cahoots with friars known as Montanists (in reality, they were the followers of Montanus, a rather obscure early Christian preacher, prophet and schismatic). The Montanists, who have their own monastery, are led by Father Vincent, a middle-aged man who is rather reserved about the activity of the monastery and irritated by the investigation of the police; they collaborate with the Nazis since both groups are after a treasure that the monks seek for religious purposes and the Nazis to increase their power. The "apostles," who used to work at the monastery, just happened to stumble across a key that is crucial to reach the treasure. However, the monk-killers, dressed in brown capes with hoods that fully hide their face, do not identify with the Montanists; they are actually Nazi militants in disguise; they are depicted as dark, sinister, and mischievous but in a rather cartoonish way, including the fact that they make use of a drug that is described as a chemical created during the war, but that, as a matter of fact, allows them quasi-supernatural deeds.

The police force is represented as powerful, high-tech and muscular in its approach, and it is obviously an institution embodying patriotic ideals; analogous observations hold specifically valid for Niemans, who is depicted as being cold but who also bonds with an elderly man upon hearing he served in the same regiment as his father. However, the film also characterizes the police and the inspector as being almost overwhelmed by their adversaries. This is achieved by showing the Montanists and the Nazis as also being powerful, structured, and institutional forces (the Nazi in fact include prominent political figures).

The way in which the film's two religious groups are represented responds to this very logic. When Niemans interrogates the wife of Jesus, he describes the "apostles" as "real Christians." Later, he expresses contempt towards Father Vincent, scolding his order for "peddling fake relics for 2,000 years." At first sight, therefore, he seems to carry a mixed message as to his disposition towards religion; although it is ultimately unclear whether he talked to Jesus' wife in a somewhat flattering way so to elicit more information from her of if he was expressing his true opinion, he seems to appreciate one Christian group and to despise the other one. However, the fact that Niemans sympathizes with a weak group ultimately contributes to the depiction of the police and of the inspector as an "underdog" of sorts in relation to the forces they are fighting; and Nieman's vilification of the monks turns out to be fully meaningful once it is discovered that they work with the Nazis.

In Ron Howard's (1954) *The Da Vinci Code* (2006), Robert Langdon, a Harvard professor of Art History and "symbology" (a fictional field) teams up with French police cryptologist Sophie Neveu[20] to investigate the murder of her grandfather Jacques Saunière,[21] curator of the Louvre Museum, who left a series of clues to discover and decrypt. Things are made complicated by the fact that Langdon is accused of being the murderer and is forced to go on the run while trying to solve the mystery. The protagonists end up being pursued both by the French police and by the Opus Dei. While in reality it was founded in Spain in 1928 by priest Josemaría Escrivá de Balaguer (1902–1975) with the goal of spreading Christian values, Opus Dei is portrayed in the movie as a sinister and powerful organization that is willing to use any means to protect the secrets of the Catholic church.[22]

It turns out that Saunière was the grand master of a secret Christian society, the Priory of Sion. In reality, the Priory was a neo-chivalric order allegedly created in France in 1956 by Pierre Plantard (1920–2000): in fact is largely recognized to have been a hoax based on Plantard's outlandish and exaggerated claims. However, it is portrayed in the movie as a real organization intent on protecting the descendants of Jesus Christ as well as on secrets (including the very existence of Christ's offspring) that would gravely upset Catholic theology and hierarchy. Robert and Sophie also seek help from elderly, aristocratic historian Sir Leigh Teabing, in fact a rival of the Harvard "symbologist."

The male protagonist, a man in his early 40s, is an academic celebrity. At the beginning of the movie, he holds a brilliant conference and holds a book signing; he also seems to be quite affluent. Additionally, the

---

20 Her names evoke, respectively, "wisdom" (in Greek) and "nephew" (in French)—the latter a concept reminiscent of the more general one of "progeny" that plays an important part in the story.

21 Also the surname of a nineteenth (and early twentieth) century French Catholic priest who was popularly believed to have found a treasure.

22 For the real organization's response to Dan Brown's (1964) book *The Da Vinci Code* (2003) the film is based on, see Opus Dei 2004.

"symbologist" is very analytical and resourceful, and has a nearly supernatural talent for the interpretation of symbols. He tries to stay impartial and objective: he approaches religion through a scientific perspective rather than a spiritual one, yet he is mindful not to offend believers while still trying to uncover the truth. Notably, he suffers from claustrophobia due to past trauma.[23] Sophie, a woman in her early 30s, doesn't bother hiding her skepticism while investigating the Priory of Sion and the existence of the Holy Grail. She is agnostic, which proves to be a key part of her character since, as she starts discovering the truth about her grandfather, she becomes more conflicted about her beliefs. Teabing is portrayed as crippled, egocentric, and extremely wealthy (he even owns an airplane). Sir Leigh is, like his younger counterpart, extremely learned, and a man of action as well despite his handicap; he is discovered to have been part of the conspiracy on the side of Langdon's adversaries.

In Gregory J. Read's *Like Minds* (2006, retitled *Murderous Intent* for US distribution), forensic psychologist Sally Rowe and police detective Martin McKenzie investigate the case of 17-year-old Alex, charged with the murder of his schoolmate Nigel, and implicated in two other violent deaths. Alex and Nigel were class- and roommates at the prestigious boarding school run by Alex's father. Nigel stood out for his sharp intelligence, wide knowledge, and antagonizing attitude—in addition to his passion for taxidermy. After initial friction, the two youngsters had become friends, with Nigel in fact exerting a strong fascination on Alex.

When Alex is detained and first meets with Sally, he mentions to her the story of the Cathars (a medieval heretical movement) and of their extermination by the Pope, as well as the concept of *Gestalt*, that he defines as "an organized whole in which each individual part affects every other, but the whole being more important than the sum of its parts."

The boarding school is confessional; the schoolers congregate and sing "Onward Christian soldiers!" The history teacher is a clergyman, Reverend Donaldson; Alex engages in a heated in-class confrontation with him, stating that the murder of medieval Catholic archbishop and saint Thomas à Becket (1118–1170), that Donaldson has just defined as a "sacrilegious act of gross profanity," was simply political, like other atrocities committed by the church. Nigel is also obsessed with the story of the Templar Knights.

To make things even more complicated, McKenzie turns out to be a member in a secret order, or brotherhood, that also Alex's father is affiliated with. Once Sally finds out, the detective downplays it, calling it

---

23 This seems to be a variation on the trope of "Achilles' heel"—notably, also the nearly invincible and extremely valiant Indiana Jones in Spielberg's movie cannot stand snakes.

"a business network" and pointing out that he inherited the affiliation from his father. Viewers are led to suspect that the "order" may in fact be some sort of contemporary version or continuation of the Templars, and that it may have had a hand in the different murders (and even in the death of Alex's mother). The "brotherhood," however, is extremely elusive, and quite tangential to the narrative—no gathering or ceremony is ever seen— only its symbol, a pike harnessed by interlinking loops, is occasionally shown, including one engraved on a lighter owned by McKenzie, that in fact he gives back to Alex's father, thus symbolizing his disaffiliation.[24]

The detective and the psychologist are represented as having a troubled interaction (there are several hints at a past relationship) due to the difference in their respective personalities and approaches. McKenzie is impulsive and muscular; Sally, a woman in her 30s, is composed and intellectual. The psychologist tries her best to keep a poker face during her first meeting with Alex, dismissing his mention of Gestalt by replying that she is "familiar with first-year psychology theory." She is, in fact, fully thrown off by the young man's reference, that she wrongly sees as an allusion to a troubled parental relationship. In fact, her whole interpretation of the events is based on such an idea, and before the end of the movie she is seen lecturing on the concept of Gestalt at an academic venue. However, it is the detective who turns out to have been right in his initial intuitions about Alex.

In Zal Batmanglij's (1981) *Sound of My Voice* (2011), Lorna and Peter, a couple in their twenties, investigate a small group that gathers around Maggie, a beautiful, soft-spoken, charismatic and elusive girl (approximately the age of Peter and Lorna) who claims to come from the future and who apparently needs constant specialized medical care due to her vulnerability to present-day diseases. Maggie describes the future as a troubled time and claims to be training her followers for the challenges that await them.

Both protagonists have a difficult background. Peter's mother was "a longtime member of a New Age cult" that induced her to neglect proper cancer therapy, so she died while he was still a child. He is thus full of resentment and wants to expose Maggie as a fraud—he sees himself as engaged in investigative journalism, but it's also clear that his motives are personal. Lorna, the daughter of a Hollywood producer and of a model-actress, has a story of abandonment and addiction, and seems slightly less

---

24 The skull and bones that the protagonists are obsessed with may be an allusion to the "Skull and Bones" secret society of Yale University, a student society composed of strong and influential alumni who are referred to as "Bones." A lot of conspiracy theories surround it, including claims according to which they plot to control the world.

invested in the project. Peter works as a primary school teacher, and Lorna is an aspiring writer. The outcome of their investigation should be a documentary. In order to meet Maggie at a secret basement location, they have to clean themselves thoroughly, put on blindfolds, and wear surgical gowns. Maggie is taken care of by two middle-aged characters, Klaus and Joanne, but most other followers are as young as Lorna and Peter, and ethnically diverse, including an Asian couple and another person of color.

The activities Maggie's followers engage in, prompted by her, and the group's characteristics in general, are strongly reminiscent of several NRMs: the Rajneesh movement (meditation, singing, dancing); Heaven's Gate (Maggie makes reference to the followers' new condition as "graduation"); Scientology (the very location, California; the psychological exercises; Maggie's smoking habits); the Raëlians (white clothing). Also, the fact that Lorna gets instructed by Joanne on how to use firearms and that the movement is suspected by the Justice Department of arming and being fashioned into a militia may remind one of the Branch Davidians.[25]

Maggie encourages her followers to let go of their inhibitions and constraints, and they give plenty of time, work and energy to the movement (in fact, they even donate blood to Maggie). As far as the protagonists are concerned, an analogy is strongly suggested between their dedication to their investigative project and their activities in the movement: in both cases, Peter and Lorna force themselves to engage in body-related activities they would normally be reluctant towards. In particular, Peter swallows a transmitter in order to secretly film the gathering through a camera encapsulated in his glasses. In the same session, Maggie encourages the followers to vomit an apple they just have eaten and later, she requires them to fast and eventually prompts them to eat worms. It is suggested as well that, ultimately, the reasons that motivate the protagonists to expose the cult and the reasons that motivate other characters to follow Maggie are deeply similar: they do so following a strong moral imperative but also in the hopes of turning their life into something extraordinary.

Peter and Lorna end up being deeply psychologically impacted, and indeed disrupted as a couple, by their investigation and the interaction with Maggie and the group. Lorna, paradoxically, turns out to be the most critical of the two towards Maggie, and Peter, while operating over the claim and belief that he is exposing the cult, ends up being highly involved in its activities. He has a major argument with Lorna after choosing to continue committing to the work even after weeks of fruitless effort to gather

---

25 Additionally, Klaus' looks bear resemblance to Steve Jobs (1955–2011) who, famously, held strong beliefs about "alternative medicine" to the point of neglecting standard cancer therapy; also, apples are conceptualized in the film as a symbol of logic.

evidence and goes as far as to willingly bring a schoolgirl from his class, Abigail Pritchett, to Maggie, upon Maggie's own (mysterious) request—thus essentially betraying his mission as an educator and teacher. Lorna recognizes the danger of the situation and helps the Justice Department to thwart Maggie's plans. In the end, however, both characters fail, although in different ways. Significantly, the location where the last, surprising segment of the story takes place is a museum, a place that symbolizes that very linearity of history, and reliance on tangible evidence, that Maggie so dramatically challenges.

In Ti West's (1980) *The Sacrament* (2013), VICE reporter Sam and cameraman Jake accompany their friend and colleague, photographer Patrick, to a community called Eden Parish, where his sister Caroline, a recovering drug addict, resides. The three are white men in their early to mid-30s. The community is situated outside of the US, in a remote agricultural settlement in the forests only accessible by helicopter, and it is protected by armed guards. Sam and Jake take the visit as an opportunity to explore and document Eden Parish, including filmed interviews with its members and leader.

The community is fairly diverse in terms of age, gender, and ethnicity (perhaps with a prevalence of people of color). The members live in spartan bungalows and gather at a communal pavilion; Eden Parish can also count on a medical center and day care. All the interviewees state that they found new hope, and they fondly refer to the founder and leader as the "Father." The journalists learn from a nurse that members have sold all their belongings to create the community and that the Father is also a skilled businessman. In a welcome note, they are informed that "Father wants only to create a community where peace and love are cherished, where the needs of one another are met on equal levels as we're all God's children and it is how He Himself intended us to live. We do not seek to isolate ourselves from the outside world, but we do seek a distance from imperialism, violence, poverty, racism and all other unacceptable attacks on basic human rights."

During a filmed interview in public, the Father proves able to disorient Sam with his eloquence and charisma, taking him by surprise with a reference to Sam's pregnant wife. It eventually turns out that multiple members are utterly unhappy with their life in the community; their passports have been confiscated, and they are being abused by the leader and his most devoted followers. The journalists' visit, in fact, sparks an upheaval. The Father, however, summons all members and, claiming that the community is under severe threat from outside, encourages them to "lay down" their lives as a "last sacrament." The events that follow are a re-elaboration of the real-life ones that notoriously unfolded at Jonestown in 1978.

The Father, a stocky white man in his sixties, is strongly reminiscent of Jonestown's founder and leader Jim Jones (1931–1978), in particular in that he constantly wears sunglasses. His real name is Charles Anderson Reed. He speaks with a strong southern accent, he is fond of citing the Bible (and several crosses can be spotted at the settlement) and calls American society "cancerous," claiming to have saved his "Children" from "poverty, violence, greed and racism." He states that "America is coming apart at the seams because of the way it's being run, and the values it instills" and reminds his followers that leaders like Malcom X and Martin Luther King were "struck down and killed."

In Riley Stearns' (1986) *Faults* (2014), cult expert Ansel Roth (a white man in his mid-50s) is approached by a married couple to deprogram their daughter Claire from a cult known as Faults. Initially, he brushes their pleas aside, but he ends up accepting their request the next morning because they offer to pay for his breakfast. Roth comes up with a plan to deprogram Claire, that involves forcibly taking her to an unfamiliar place with the help of two men around their 30s (one of whom is portly, black, and compliant, while the other one is white and somewhat insubordinate) and breaking her down by making her question her beliefs and the group's influence over her.

Upon being kidnapped, Claire feels disconcerted; however, she only attempts once to escape, and stops trying later on even when presented with the opportunity. Throughout the rest of the movie, she maintains a nonchalant demeanor. Claire is in her mid-20s; she is dressed in loose and billowy garments, showing little to no concern for her looks. When Ansel announces that he specializes in helping "lost souls" who are under the control of others, Claire (who in fact does not like to be called by this -highly symbolic- name as she feels dissociated with her pre-Faults self[26]) tries to make him understand that she is not lost, and that she has found God and did so by her own free will. The girl talks about Faults' practices, which involve finding God through meditation. Then she goes on to mention that people are weighed down by their physical form and that, to take full control, one has to move on, going through different levels. It is later hinted that moving on means leaving one's physical body in order to reach a higher level of existence – this, by committing suicide (in such beliefs, the group's depiction seems to be inspired by Scientology and Heaven's Gate).

From the opening scene, Roth is portrayed as helpless. Once a best-selling author, he has lost everything, from his financial stability to respect from his manager. He desperately tries to sell a new book titled *Follower: Inside the Mind of the Controlled* during a presentation to a scarce

---

26 She doesn't specify her preferred name; however, by the end her parents call her Ira.

and bored audience. In his talk he labels cults as mind controlling entities that "exploit your weaknesses and remove you from those who care about you. They create emotional and physical barriers distancing you from everyone and everything you once knew, including yourself." Deeply dissatisfied with his current situation, and wounded in his self-esteem, Roth even tries to kill himself by inhaling gasoline vapor after he is dropped by his manager and asked to pay his debt within a week. The irony is clear: one who is supposed to be liberating others is still struggling to liberate himself from his own misfortunes. Additionally, he does not hesitate to resort to dishonest means—like in the scene in which, at a restaurant, he tries using an expired voucher to pay for a meal.

Initially, Ansel views Claire as a victim of the cult and believes he can help her break free from it. However, the more he spends time with her, the more he realizes that she is far from being vulnerable, and that with her complex persona and firm beliefs, she may in fact be his last and only hope to find peace of mind and salvation, which eventually leads him to put into question all of his assumptions about cults and religion. Bit by bit the two protagonists start to display affection and care for one another, and as the story progresses, one witnesses a shift in each of them. As Claire gets stronger, Ansel gets more and more weighed down with his debt to his previous manager. The film's climax comes in a sort of improvised meditation session where Claire convinces Ansel that he owes nothing to anyone but himself and persuades him to stay with her. He finally states that he feels clear and liberated and mentions that he trusts Claire unquestionably: wherever she goes, he is willing to follow.

Faults presents a complex picture of cults and their followers, one that has the potential to shake the viewers' possible assumptions and preconceptions, and their notion of freedom, similarly to what happens to Ansel. Instead of portraying the cult as vile or its followers as brainwashed, the film suggests that Faults' members, Claire included, joined it for various reasons, and that some of their ideas and rituals may hold some validity. This doesn't mean that the film conveys an entirely positive message about cults. In fact, it does suggest that cult members may well be "controlled" (and therefore prone to committing harmful and questionable actions)— yet in ways similar to how people can be influenced by mainstream consumerist society through advertising.

Regression (2015), by Alejandro Amenábar (1972), is set in Minnesota, in 1990. As the opening captions explain, the US has been experiencing the "Satanic Panic" for a decade. Detective Bruce Kenner,[27] a white man in his

---

27 The name means "knower" in German.

mid-40s, is investigating the case of Angela Gray,[28] a 17-year-old who is accusing her father, John, of sexual abuse. Strangely, the man does admit to the abuse, but he is unable to remember the details. John is also examined by the reverend of the church he joined after his wife's death, and by Professor Kenneth Raines, an expert in regressive hypnosis (a white man in his early 50s), that implements such "therapy" (as he calls it) also on Angela's brother who has left the family and lives in Pittsburgh.

Initially, Kenner seems to discover that the girl was abused in the context of Satanic rituals in which even a colleague was involved, who is promptly incarcerated. According to the girl's testimony and in the hallucinatory nightmares that the detective starts experiencing, the Satanists wear black hooded capes and white makeup, and their "black masses" include fornication, torture, and child sacrifice. The detective starts getting involved with Angela also romantically and experiences paranoid bouts. Eventually, however, he realizes that memories and hallucinations are scraped up from other elements, such as the print on a common soup pouch, and that Angela's case has to do with her tragic familiar background rather than with Satan's worshipers.

This is a film inspired by Satanic panic-related real events, and it conveys a clear message warning from regressive hypnosis in particular and from moral panic in general. The final captions specify that "no proof was ever found of organized satanic cults practicing ritual abuse" and "today regression therapies have been discredited for generating false memories." The movie represents plenty of Satanic panic-related tropes: an alleged victim of "satanic abuse" being interviewed on TV, her face in the shadow, recalling how she has attended ceremonies for 15 years and having authored a national bestseller (also purchased by the police) by the title of *In the Name of Satan*;[29] a journalist stating on TV that nobody is safe since the Satanists are invisible and branching out; an expert in "demonology," also on TV, pointing out that the devil would do anything to make people believe that he does not exist.

Interestingly, both the reverend and the professor are ultimately shown to be wrong in their assumptions about, and approach to, the whole case of Angela and John. Rather than representing a contrast of religion and science, the film shows how the latter can turn into pseudoscience and

---

28 Name and surname obviously (and paradoxically) conjure up the concepts of innocence and of ambiguity, respectively.

29 The fictional author's name is S. Cooper. A book by the same title (subtitle: *How The Forces Of Evil Work And What You Can Do To Defeat Them*) was published in 1996 by Rev. Bob Larson (1944), a radio and television evangelist who was quite active and visible during the Satanic panic.

create a noxious alliance with religiously-nourished delusion (the reverend at some point claims he has heard the voice of God; the professor, while substantially agreeing with him, responds that he prefers calling that "intuition"). The story teaches that only accurate consideration of empirical evidence can discriminate between the real facts and paranoia fueled by calumny. The professor at some point invokes science responding to the detective's doubts; however, it is eventually made clear that his method, rather than investigating reality, makes it up.

Luca Guadagnino's (1971) *Suspiria* (2018) is a multifaceted and multilayered film that can be variously classified, including as a horror one with supernatural elements.[30] It features a coven of witches living under cover in West Berlin in the late 1970s. The dance school they run, live and work at isn't, in fact, just a disguise, since dancing is an activity that features prominently in the witches' rituals, and conjures up powerful supernatural forces. The character investigating the school-*cum*-coven is not an academic, but a psychoanalyst, Dr. Josef Klemperer, a man in his eighties whose curiosity is piqued by a pupil of the school who discovered its real nature and resorts to Dr. Klemperer's assistance.

Initially, Dr. Klemperer is skeptical and convinced that the girl is delusional, obsessed with a "constructed mythology" (as he writes in his notebook). The witches' activities, he guesses, may well be criminal, but their rituals and customs may be symbolic elements as opposed to genuinely supernatural ones. In Klemperer's study, one can spot a book on Freemasonry,[31] as well as, significantly, a book by Carl Gustav Jung (1875–1961). The Swiss psychiatrist and psychotherapist famously elaborated on *archetypes*, universal ideas or patterns of thought forming what he called the "collective unconscious" and variously symbolized across different cultures. The film also features a reference to the psychoanalyst and psychiatrist Jacques Lacan (1901–1981), whose conference at the Freie Universität Berlin is mentioned in passing by a character and that Klemperer does not seem too enthusiastic about.

Eventually, Klemperer finds himself compelled to acknowledge not only that the coven's powers are as much supernatural as they are real, but also that the witches' activities may explain a series of sinister and violent global-historical events, including extreme-left terrorism and the rise of National Socialism, the latter being also responsible for the greatest tragedy in Klemperer's life, the disappearance of his wife.

---

30 The film is a remake of Dario Argento's (1940) one with the same title (1977).

31 This may be a visual pretext to introduce the motif of the eye (printed on the book cover).

Interestingly, the coven is not represented as monolithic: overall, it is intent on operating evil, but it is internally divided in factions and its leaders are chosen somewhat democratically (by voting openly). Additionally, the witches and their pupils are diverse in terms of age and ethnicity. Whereas their schemes and actions tend towards the preservation of power, and usually run contrary to humanitarian ideals, the witches occasionally display mercy towards each other, as well as towards ordinary human beings.

Dr. Klemperer's main fault is shown to be his rationalism; he is represented as someone who is overcome by events whose real nature and magnitude he barely manages to grasp. It is significant that the character is elderly (and suffers from hearing impairment) as well that the supreme revelation for him comes while he is forcibly involved in a sabbath, stripped naked.

In Ari Aster's (1986) *Midsommar* (2019), the protagonist Dani is a US-American undergraduate student who recently suffered through the murder of her parents by her sister, who eventually committed suicide. In the hopes of getting away, she joins her boyfriend Christian, along with his friends Mark, Josh and Pelle,[32] on a trip to Sweden. Pelle has invited them to visit the rural commune he was raised in, called Hårga,[33] and attend their midsummer festival, which is of great interest to Josh who is an anthropology student writing his thesis on European midsummer festivities.

Located in a rural part of Sweden, the Hårga is a group of people who live communally, and essentially worship the sun. They see life as a cycle, a journey not marked by death—or in which individual death is regarded as untroubling. In fact, at least one important ceremony of theirs involves the suicide of elderly members who are believed to have completed their respective, individual cycles—with nobody seeming too upset about this fact, but in fact rejoicing in the ritual, that appears shocking and cruel to the outsiders.

The members of the community also seem to hold pan(en)theistic beliefs including in gods and spirits, often conducting rituals or ceremonies to communicate with them. They love visual symbols, which can be seen, for instance, in their murals and tapestry. Their approach to sexuality is also communal and ritualistic, and they do not seem to have the same inhibitions as their visitors towards the performance of sexual intercourse in public.

---

32 Both Christian and Mark are White American, Josh is African American, and Pelle is Swedish.

33 The name Hårga comes from the Swedish folk song *Hårgalåten*, which is about the legend of a fiddler who comes to a village called Hårga and bewitches the villagers to dance until they die.

Hårga community's beliefs are mostly passed down orally, from generation to generation; however, records are also being kept in scrolls or manuscripts placed in a sacred library. They contain teachings from the "oracles," community members that seemingly suffer from special physical conditions due to the fact that they are (intentionally) inbred; however, they are seen by the community as "unclouded by normal cognition" and therefore "closer to the source. "The representation of the group is heavily inspired by Nordic myths and Swedish folklore. Midsummer is an actual festival in Sweden celebrating the summer solstice, with the central figure being the May Queen, a symbol for fertility and renewal. Multiple Hårga ceremonies require the consumption of some sort of psychedelic substance, similar to what happens in Santo Daime with ayahuasca (and analogously to shamanic practices the world over). However, while in the Brazilian NRM the decoction helps one to access superior realities, increase their wisdom, strengthen their ethics, and discover their true self, in the Hårga psychedelics are ultimately used to manipulate and control members.

Josh and Christian can be considered as researchers, due to their background as students in cultural anthropology and the fact that they are studying the group. Their role is functional to the exploration of the community's traditions, practices, and beliefs—that are often illustrated by Pelle and other members, although somewhat elusively. However, Josh's curiosity almost turns into obsession, making him disregard the strict rules of the commune. Also Christian, while trying to be respectful and keep an open mind, ends up offending the members. Almost all visitors face tragic consequences. For Dani, however, the interaction with the group plays out quite differently; and in fact, her motive for joining the community is to get away from the recent tragedies in her life while immersing herself in a new and unusual context rather than to learn about Hårga. She grows to appreciate and find comfort within the community as she is invited to take part in many of their rituals, and she ends up finding exactly what she lost: a family who values and appreciates her, thus resulting in a positive depiction of the group, despite what an outsider can regard as outlandish beliefs and cruel practices.

Comparative and concluding remarks

It did not come as a surprise that most, if not all, of the films we examined portray cults and sects in a highly simplified way in comparison with the complexities of real-life NRMs, although they are often inspired by them. Among the elements of actual groups' dynamics that receive little to no coverage in fictional films, we can list the financial dynamics (and struggles), but also theoretical beliefs and theological debates, and the groups' relationship with major religions. However, admittedly, not all such elements easily lend themselves to cinematic representation, let alone spectacularization.

Oversimplification often goes hand in hand with distortion. We cannot fail to note that cinematic sects and cults are, almost invariably, represented in an utterly negative light. A special, and especially telling case, is Satanism, that is overrepresented in the movies we have selected (it features in *The Seventh Victim*, *Night of the Demon*, *The Devil Rides Out*, *Tutti i colori del buio*, *Il treno*, *The Ninth Gate*[34]), and that is exclusively represented as intent on worshiping a real Satan and/or on carrying out evil deeds including murders and human sacrifices. Filmmakers show little or no awareness of cultural or atheistic Satanists, and seem inclined to conflate Satanism, magic, witchcraft, and paganism.

Racist/orientalist stereotypes are also present in the depiction of cinematic sects, but they can't be said to be prevalent. We have mentioned *Indiana Jones and the Temple of Doom* and its representation of Indians; similar observations may hold valid for Baba's group in *Holy Smoke*. However, not all evil groups are depicted as non-Western or non-white. In *Il treno* it is the Yugoslavian villagers and professor who are represented as cruel and sinister (interestingly, the film was created shortly before the Fall of Communism, which may explain the exoticization of, and fear towards, East Europeans). More generally, multiple films can even be said to represent their respective sects, although in different ways, as "deviant" forms of Western society/Christianity and, very often, as white-only (for instance, *Ticket to Heaven*,[35] *Split Image*, *Les Rivières pourpres II*, *The Da Vinci Code*, and *Like Minds*). A special case is that of *Midsommar*'s Hårga: in this film, the threatening and outlandish group embodies the epitome of *Scandinavian* paganism. In other words, filmmakers, while definitely "otherizing" and depicting as evil the sects that they represent, do not always and necessarily resort to racist/orientalist stereotypes.

Academic experts approaching cults and sects are usually represented through oversimplifications of actual scholarly life, and with an emphasis on their most spectacular traits. In this regard, Indiana Jones and Robert Langdon are a case in point, since, with their extraordinary skills and capacities, they are both reminiscent of superheroes (and it's perhaps no accident that, of all cinematic professors who fight against a sect, they secure a neat triumph against the groups that they confront). Whenever films represent university professors, one may see the occasional learned

---

34 Also, *Regression* represents Satanists, and quite stereotypically at that; however, the group turns out to never have existed.

35 To be sure, as we already have explained (note 9), the "Father" is Asian—however, he is not physically present in the community, which is led by white figures.

dispute among colleagues, a conference, and the unfolding of the academics' research (that, in fact, is usually more of an adventurous quest). However, such movies hardly show elements that likewise mark an actual academic scholar's life, such as long reading and writing sessions, interaction with students in- and outside classrooms, faculty meetings, grant writing, struggles with publishers, friction with university administrators, and so on. Such elements may be unknown to filmmakers, or perhaps they simply do not make for cinematic spectacularization.

Most of the experts, academic or otherwise, are white males, with the exception of female characters in *The City of the Dead*, *Les Rivières pourpres II*, *The Da Vinci Code*, *Like Minds*, and *Sound of My Voice*.[36] The depiction of sects in terms of gender is more varied. Multiple groups feature a female leader or female characters in a prominent role. *Suspiria* presents an extreme case of a female-only group, but we can also mention Nathalie, the (disabled) female Palladist in *The Seventh Victim*, Selwyn/Newles in *The City of the Dead*, Barbara in *Tutti i colori del buio*, Ingrid in *Ticket to Heaven*, Telfer in *The Ninth Gate*, Maggie in *Sound of My Voice*, and Claire/Ira in *Faults*. It is, however, debatable whether the representation of such female characters defeats sexist stereotypes, or it is ultimately marked by misogynistic nuances and tones, given the negative portrayal of sects.

It is also interesting that, in various movies, academic experts end up defeated, or absorbed by the sect, or even turn out to have been involved in it since the beginning (*The City of the Dead*, *The Spider Labyrinth*, *Il treno*, *Sound of My Voice* [Peter], *Suspiria*, *Midsommar* [Josh and Christian]). Remarkably, all films that focus on the work of a "deprogrammer" either show their duplicity, that is, how they need to resort to manipulation and coercion in order to achieve their goals (*Ticket to Heaven*, *Split Image*), or they represent them as sorely defeated in the end (*Holy Smoke*, *Faults*).

Very often, the movies in question include a supernatural element, especially in those sects that are represented as evil, sinister, and conspiratorial in character. Some experts end up defeated as to their skeptical/empiricist outlook. In other words, they have to acknowledge the existence of the supernatural: such is the case of *Night of the Demon* and *The City of the Dead* (in both films, however, the experts triumph over the sects they confront), and of *Suspiria* (in which the expert is vanquished by the sect).[37] And those experts who, one way or another, end up being defeated (either

---

36 In fact, in *The City of the Dead* Nan is just a student, and in *Sound of My Voice* Lorna qualifies as an "expert" only in a rather broad sense.

37 In some cases, the existence of the supernatural is just hinted at, for instance in the ending of *Sound of My Voice*. Other characters who can be said to give up on their initial skepticism include Rex (in *The Devil Rides Out*—although he does not qualify

because they have to give up on their approach, or because they are murdered), are, in several cases, psychologists and psychotherapists (*Night of the Demon, Tutti i colori del buio, Like Minds, Regression, Suspiria*).

Occasionally, but significantly, spectators' preconceptions about cults and sects are shaken; this happens not only in regard to the actual existence of the supernatural, but rather as to the sects' very evil character. We have already elaborated on the representation of the Palladists in *The Seventh Victim*, which subtly includes positive elements in a group that is otherwise depicted as Satanic. Similar observations hold valid for the titular movement in *Faults*. *Midsommar*'s Hårga, while engaging in activities and actions that most viewers may find outlandish at best and ethically repulsive at worst, ends up offering a comfortable environment to the female protagonist. Finally, a special case is *Regression*, a veritable cinematic caveat against Satanic panic.

In conclusion, it seems safe to state that fictional films depicting cults and sects create powerful "filters" through which the public ends up perceiving, reacting to, and interacting with real NRMs including their leaders and members. It is our hope, in the interest of the diffusion of a more fine-tuned approach towards such movements, but also of mere entertainment, that filmmakers, while proposing fictional NMRs, will prove increasingly able to move away from stereotypical and monolithic stories and depictions, to novel and complex ones, of the kind exemplified by at least some of the films we examined.

About the authors

Stefano Bigliardi serves as Associate Professor of Philosophy at Al Akhawayn University in Ifrane, a liberal-arts college in Morocco that he joined in 2016. He is the author of the Cambridge University Press *Islam and Science: Past, Present, and Future Debates* (with Nidhal Guessoum; 2023) and *New Religious Movements and Science* (2023).

Abdelmojib Chouhbi, Mohamed Amine Ghafil, Amine Nakari, Danya Tazi Mokha, and Salma Zahidi are majoring in Computer Science at AUI's School of Science and Engineering. In Fall 2022 they participated in Stefano's undergraduate course in History of Ideas focusing on the history and beliefs of NRMs.

---

as an "expert") and Langdon (in *The Da Vinci Code*—who is more skeptical about the whole story than just the supernatural elements of it).

References

Amenábar, Alejandro. *Regression*. 2015. Mod Producciones, First Generation Films, FilmNation Entertainment.
Argento, Dario. *Suspiria*. 1977. Seda Spettacoli.
Assonitis, Ovidio Gabriel and Roberto D'Ettorre Piazzoli. 1974. *Chi sei?* [*Beyond the Door*]. A Erre Cinematografica, Montoro Productions.
Aster, Ari. 2019. *Midsommar*. A24B, Reel Films, Nordisk Film.
Barilli, Francesco. 1974. *Il profumo della signora in nero* [English title: *The Perfume of the Lady in Black*]. Euro International Films.
Batmanglij, Zal. 2011. *Sound of My Voice*. Skyscraper Films.
Bava, Mario. 1977. *Schock* [English title: *Shock*, also released as *Beyond the Door II*]. Laser Films.
Brown, Dan. 2003. *The Da Vinci Code*. New York: Doubleday.
Campion, Jane. 1999. *Holy Smoke*. India Take One Productions, Miramax.
Dahan, Olivier. 2004. *Les Rivières pourpres II: Les Anges de l'apocalypse* [*The Crimson Rivers 2: Angels of the Apocalypse*]. Studio Légende, EuropaCorp, TF1 Films Production.
Fisher, Terence. 1968. *The Devil Rides Out* [US title: *The Devil's Bride*]. Associated British-Pathé Hammer Films.
Freed, Josh. 1980. *Moonwebs: Journey into the Mind of a Cult*. Toronto: Dorset Publishing.
Giagni, Gianfranco. 1988. *Il nido del ragno* [*The Spider Labyrinth*]. Reteitalia, Splendida Film.
Guadagnino, Luca. 2018. *Suspiria*. Frenesy Film Company, Videa, First Sun.
Hardy, Robin. 1973. *The Wicker Man*. British Lion Film Corporation.
Howard, Ron. 2006. *The Da Vinci Code*. Columbia Pictures, Imagine Entertainment, Skylark Productions.
Kotcheff, Ted. 1982. *Split Image*. PolyGram Filmed Entertainment.
Kubrick, Stanley. 1999. *Eyes Wide Shut*. Warner Bros.
Kwitny, Jeff. 1989. *Il treno* [English title: *Beyond the Door III*]. Avala Film, C.F.S. Kosutnjak, Epic Entertainment.
Lado, Aldo. 1971. *La corta notte delle bambole di vetro* [English title: *Short Night of Glass Dolls*]. Production companies, Dieter Geissler Filmproduktion, Doria G. Film, Dunhill Cinematografica.
Larson, Bob. 1996. *In the Name of Satan. How The Forces Of Evil Work And What You Can Do To Defeat Them*. Nashville, TN: Thomas Nelson.
Martino, Sergio. 1972. *Tutti i colori del buio* [*All the Colors of the Dark*]. Lea Film, National Cinematografica, Astro C.C.
Moxley, John Llewellyn. 1960. *The City of the Dead* [US title: *Horror Hotel*]. Vulcan Films.
Opus Dei. 2004. "The Da Vinci Code, the Catholic Church and Opus Dei. A Response to the The Da Vinci Code from the Prelature of Opus Dei in the United States," November 12: https://opusdei.org/en/article/the-da-vinci-code-the-catholic-church-and-opus-dei/

Polański, Roman. 1999. *The Ninth Gate*. Artisan Entertainment, R.P. Productions, Orly Films.
Read, Gregory. 2006. *Like Minds* [US title: *Murderous Intent*]. Australian Film Finance Corporation (AFFC), Lumina Films, Bluewater Pictures.
Robson, Mark. 1943. *The Seventh Victim*. RKO Radio Pictures.
Spielberg, Steven. 1984. *Indiana Jones and the Temple of Doom*. Paramount Pictures, Lucasfilm.
Stearns, Riley. 2014. *Faults*. Snoot Entertainment.
Thomas, Ralph L. 1981. *Ticket to Heaven*. Canadian Film Development Corporation (CFDC), Famous Players, Ronald Cohen Productions.
Tourneur, Jacques. 1957. *Night of the Demon* [US title: *Curse of the Demon*]. Sabre Film Production.
West, Ti. 2013. *The Sacrament*. Worldwide Entertainment, Arcade Pictures.

10

THE COMPLICATED RELATIONSHIP BETWEEN XIE JIAO AND CULT IN THE PRC

ZHANG XINZHANG AND XU WEIWEI

The People's Republic of China ("PRC") maintains a systematic and consistent set of policies toward Xie Jiao (邪教), often mistranslated as "destructive cults." Due to the sensitiveness of the topic and for certain other reasons, international academic scholars often lack appreciation of the concept according to PRC's own understanding. When James R. Lewis visited Zhejiang University in 2018, he asked this author to write an objective and detailed introduction of the PRC's own view toward Xie Jiao. China is a big country with a long history of experiences and lessons relating to this issue, so the topic is worth critical exploration. The main purpose of this chapter is to offer a critical exploration of the Chinese official viewpoint and policies. Thus, this article will analyze the logic behind the whole system in order to render this system comprehensible for western scholars. This article consists of three main parts: The first part introduces the PRC's definition of Xie Jiao and the PRC perspective on how and why Xie Jiao may be considered destructive. The second part illustrates Falun Gong as a typical Xie Jiao, acknowledging its transformation from Qi Gong to Exceptional Function to Buddhism to apocalyptic cult. The third part is the analysis of the PRC's treatment of Xie Jiao from the perspective of religious policy, including criteria of identification, the policy principles, and its potential difficulties.

We have noticed that scholars studying new religions in the international academic community have a strong interest in the PRC's definition, criteria, prevention and treatment policies of *Xie Jiao* (邪教), and there are also some serious misunderstandings of this topic (Introvigne 2019). This paper will describe the policy documents issued by Chinese authorities related to *Xie Jiao*, in order to explore the thinking behind the policy measures as well as the protective intentions of Chinese authorities toward *Xie Jiao* members. It also will explore the potential difficulties in fulfilling PRC policy principles. The case of Falun Gong will be used as an example for analysis.

The Western versus Chinese understanding of the notion of cult

China's *Xie Jiao* (邪教) is not identical to what the West considers as "cult." Literally, "Xie" means crooked (邪), the opposite of "upright" ("Zheng" 正), Jiao (教) means firstly doctrine or teaching, and means secondly a religious organization. *Xie Jiao* as the combination of these two words has also two senses, one is heterodoxy, the other is deviant religious organization. *Xie Jiao* in the first sense is evaluated in the context of accepted religions within the PRC. *Xie Jiao* in the second sense is a political judgment by government or society. These two senses of *Xie Jiao* are intertwined with each other. In this paper we use it mainly in the second sense, from the perspective of government. While cult in the west tends to be a religious category, referring to special kinds of religious groups which meet certain characteristics, *Xie Jiao* in China is mainly a political category, referring to the relationship between certain religious groups, the government and the social order. Whether it is upright or crooked depends on its good or bad relationship with government and society. While the concept of cult in West tends to be pejorative, the Chinese perspective approaches every religion equally. All religions are equally good and permitted by government if they are harmless or even beneficial to social stability, and all religions are equally bad and are prohibited by government if they threaten the safety of the society. Thus, in one sense, China may be argued to extend wide freedoms to all religions, while at the same time China is very strict toward all religions.

To gauge Chinese sensitivity to *Xie Jiao*, it first should be noted that over the course of China's long history, there have been many subversions of the social order by *Xie Jiao*, resulting in catastrophes. For instance, as early as the Eastern Han Dynasty (CE 25–220), a Daoist healer Zhang Jue (张角) in 184 initiated the "Way of Supreme Peace" (太平道, Taiping dao), which came to be known as the Yellow Turban rebellion (黄巾起义). It mobilized tens of thousands of fighters in a bloody revolt against what was perceived as a corrupt administration. The Eastern Han dynasty was seriously weakened and collapsed a few decades later (Seidel 1969). Other examples include rebellions known as the White Lotus (白莲教 1796), the Eight Trigrams (八卦教 1813), and the Taiping (太平天国 1851–1864), all resulting in huge casualties. From the Chinese perspective, warding off *Xie Jiao* is a way to prevent a time when, as the traditional saying goes, "people devour one another, white bones scattered everywhere, no smoke from cooking for a thousand miles, people were all displaced without cloth, the cities were all ruined, everywhere were thieves and robbers in groups." Historically speaking, then, Chinese *Xie Jiao* have a record of destruction. Broadly speaking, in Chinese perspective there are three outstanding problems in the field of religions that affect national security and social stability: the utilization of religion by foreign forces, religious extremism, and *Xie Jiao*. Religious organizations in China can be divided into three categories. The first category is registered, open, legal, law-abiding organizations which are beneficial to society; the second category is unregistered, secret, illegal, non-compliant groups with respect to the law, but harmless to the society; the third category is unregistered, secret and illegal problematic religious organizations that do not abide by the law and are harmful to society. The third category of problematic religious organizations can be further divided into three situations: the first one is that they follow an exclusive and extremist path because of their secrecy; the second one is that they are controlled and infiltrated by foreign forces and do not comply with the principle of independence and autonomy; the third one is that the one or two of these first two situations are utilized by some person with ulterior motives. The organization formed with ulterior motives is considered *Xie Jiao*.

In keeping with the protectionist orientation of the PRC, China's main legal provision dealing with *Xie Jiao* is Article 300 of the Criminal Law, which describes the crime of organizing and using *Xie Jiao* in Section 1. Crimes of Disrupting Public Order:

> Article 300. Whoever organizes or utilizes any superstitious sect, secret society, or cult organization or uses superstition to sabotage the implementation of any law or administrative regulation of the state shall be sentenced to imprisonment of not less than three years but not more than seven years in addition to a fine; if the circumstances are especially serious, [he can] be sentenced to imprisonment of not less than seven years or life imprisonment in addition to a fine or forfeiture of property; or if the circumstances are minor, [he might] be sentenced to imprisonment of not more than three years, criminal detention, surveillance or deprivation of political rights in addition to a fine or be sentenced to a fine only.
>
> Whoever organizes or utilizes any superstitious[1] sect, secret society, or cult organization or uses superstition to cheat any other person, which leads to the person's serious injury or death shall be punished in accordance with the provisions of the preceding paragraph.

---

1. The concept "Superstition" (迷信) is a term already outdated in Western scholarship since nineteenth century. But it is still used in Chinese official documents. I use this term as it is in the official document. This concept here means folk beliefs without support of established religions.

Whoever also commits the crime of raping a woman or swindling any person of his or her property while committing a crime as mentioned in paragraph 1 shall be punished according to the provisions on the joinder of penalties for plural crimes.[2]

On January 4, 2017, China's Supreme People's Court and Supreme People 's Procuratorate issued "Interpretation on Several Issues concerning the Application of Law in the Handling of Criminal Cases involving Sabotaging the Enforcement of Laws by Organizing and Utilizing Cult Organizations" [法 释 [2017] No. 3] (关于办理组织、利用邪教组织破坏法律实施等刑事案件适用法律若干问题的解释) (CLI.3.289471(EN)).[3] The first sentence is the definition of a *Xie Jiao* organization:

> Article 1. Illegal organizations that are set up by using religions, Qi Gong, or other things as a camouflage, [that] deify their leading members, and confuse and deceive people, recruit and control their members, and endanger the society by fabricating and spreading superstitious heresies shall be determined as cult organizations as prescribed in Article 300 of the Criminal Law. 冒用宗教、气功或者以其他名义建立、神化、鼓吹首要分子，利用制造、散布迷信邪说等手段蛊惑、蒙骗他人，发展、控制成员，危害社会的非法组织，应当认定为刑法第三百条规定的"邪教组织."

In this definition of *Xie Jiao*, we can notice some terms such as "set up," "using," "camouflage," which aim to distinguish the organizer from the organized, the user from the used, the camouflage from the essence beneath camouflage. If a cult group, or a Qi Gong group, or a religious sect, is used by someone to sabotage the implementation of law and administration or to commit other crimes, then the person or group who used this cult for this purpose could be judged as having committed the crime of *Xie Jiao*. So, *Xie Jiao* is a wider category than cult, and a cult itself is not necessarily *Xie Jiao*. Only when it is used by someone to commit crimes is

---

2. This official English version is not totally identical to the Chinese version due to the difficulty of translation. "Superstitious sect, secret society" in this version corresponds to "会道门" (Hui Dao Men)in Chinese version. "会道门" is secret societies in the camouflage of religious organizations, which are named after 会 (Hui)，道 (Tao) and 门 (Men), which were common end names used by Chinese traditional religious groups to mean association, practice method and gate way to truth. "Cult organization" in this version corresponds to "邪教组织" (*Xie Jiao* Zuzhi) in Chinese Version. All Chinese relevant official documents mistranslate *Xie Jiao* as cult organization. Actually "*Xie Jiao*" could not be translated accurately into cult. We will discuss it later in this article. https://www.ilo.org/dyn/natlex/docs/ELECTRONIC/5375/108071/F-78796243/CHN5375%20Eng3.pdf

3. Interpretation of the Supreme People's Court and the Supreme People's Procuratorate on Several Issues concerning the Application of Law in the Handling of Criminal Cases involving Sabotaging the Enforcement of Laws by Organizing and Utilizing Cult Organizations, Interpretation No. 3 [2017] of the Supreme People's Court [CLI Code].

it named *Xie Jiao*. What is particularly important here is the distinction between the organizer and the organized, the user and the used. This is the principle which is consistently adhered to when the PRC judges crimes of *Xie Jiao*.

In this strict sense, *Xie Jiao* is not religion or sect or cult or Qi Gong. It is an organization that exploits problematic religions or Qi Gong, etc., to take control of followers (附体). To use a metaphor, *Xie Jiao* is like a piece of rat excrement that falls into the porridge pot of religious groups. It is very difficult to separate the polluted *Xie Jiao* from pot of porridge. *Xie Jiao* thus is the result of criminal forces using religious groups as tool, and dressing sinister aims with a religious veneer.[4]

Falun Gong: Transformation from Qi Gong to exceptional function to Buddhism to apocalyptic cult

David Palmer observed that Falun Gong (hereinafter FLG) has transformed itself step by step from Qi Gong (气功) to Exceptional Function (特异功能) to Buddhism and finally apocalyptic cult (Palmer 2003). When Qi Gong was prevalent in China, FLG modeled itself on Qi Gong and appeared as a Qi Gong group. When the pursuit of Exceptional Functions prevailed in China, FLG presented itself as a technique to acquire extraordinary bodily powers. When Buddhism prevailed in China, FLG rendered itself as a Buddhist group. FLG thus proved itself adaptable to popular tastes and continuously changed its self-representation. Qi Gong (气功) has a long history in China. It began as a technique for bodily cultivation in different religious traditions, Chinese Medicine traditions and Traditional Martial Arts traditions. Qi (气) means a kind of invisible energy like breath or moving air. Gong (功) means technique, as in the ways one pursues this energy and the power one achieves when one obtains it. It was under the impulsion of Chinese Communist Party in the 1940s that Chinese national medical institutions began to extract these kind of beneficial body cultivation methods from their religious and cultural backgrounds and to put them together under the title of "Qi Gong," in order to form standardized, secularized, and modernized techniques of bodily healing and spiritual cultivation. In the 1950s, Qi Gong was listed as a technical specialty alongside acupuncture, herbalism, moxibustion and massage within the Traditional Chinese Medicine system. In 1953, a party cadre Liu Guizhen (刘贵珍 1920–1983), who cured his cancer with the Standing Posture (站桩) under the guidance of a master of body cultivation, founded the world's first Qi Gong clinic in Tangshan,

---

4. In order to clarify the difference of the category of *Xie Jiao* and Cult, China tries to translate *Xie Jiao* into Evil Cults or Destructive Cults. But this translation is enough to distinguish these two concepts.

Hebei province. Two years later, he founded another Qi Gong sanatorium at Beidaihe (北戴河), an exclusive seaside resort for high-ranking PRC cadres.

By the end of the 1970s, an artist and self-healed cancer victim Guo Lin (郭林) taught Qi Gong in Beijing parks, turning the institutional Qi Gong of the 1950s into a mass activity practiced in public spaces. His "New Qi Gong Therapy" (郭林新气功疗法), hailed as a cure for cancer, quickly spread to all parts of China.

In the 1980s, with the support of laboratory research, mass media, and the popularity of Hong Kong kung fu (功夫)movies, Qi Gong developed into a popular movement. About one hundred million people practiced Qi Gong. David Palmer called it Qi Gong Fever. In that period, Qi Gong was seen no longer as a mere branch of Chinese medicine, but as a scientific discipline in its own right, with a focus on the research of how the mind could control Qi. The original medical and bodily cultivation of Qi Gong was regarded as low level Qi Gong. People began to believe in and pursue advanced, high level Qi Gong, which could help people attain Exceptional Functions (特异功能), such as penetrating vision, distant vision, distant sensation, the ability to immobilize one's body, to fly miraculously, to penetrate walls, to soar spiritually, to call the wind and bring the rain, to know the past and the future. By this time, Qi Gong had become an "art of the immortals" for which nothing was impossible. As David Palmer observed, throughout the 1980s Qi Gong became a legitimate outlet for the resurgence, reconfiguration and "modernization" of religious beliefs and practices. It had shifted gradually from a medical and secular practice toward religious practices and beliefs that adhered to Chinese sectarian traditions, culminating in the emergence of Falun Gong (Palmer 2003).

Falun Gong represented itself as a high-level Qi Gong method starting in 1992. From 1992 to 1994, Li Hongzhi was active in Qi Gong circles. Semi-official Qi Gong associations helped him in organizing highly profitable lecture tours. He claimed to have attained all the exceptional functions of high level Qi Gong. He could cure sick people with his thoughts, see the future, see people's interior thoughts, know the end of time and the various historical ages that have come and gone. He appeared at that time as a successful Qi Gong master, and by mid-1990s, Falun Gong had acquired tens of millions of adherents (Farley 2014a, 244).

In the 1990s, a number of experts from scientific, educational, journalistic and political circles began to expose some deceits played by the self-proclaimed "Qi Gong masters"—such as moving objects with thoughts, stopping an electric fan with one finger, and taking pills out of concealed bottles. People started realizing the contrast between traditional Qi Gong and pseudo-Qi Gong. The so-called advanced Qi Gong beliefs and practices came to be recognized by people as superstition or pseudo-Qi Gong.

Then, around the end of 1994 and beginning of 1995, Li Hongzhi began to shift the FLG focus from Qi Gong to Buddhism. He claimed that Falun Gong was not a form of Qi Gong but a higher universal Dharma. In his book Turning the Dharma Wheel (转法轮) (LiHonzhi 1998), first published in 1995, Exceptional Functions were relegated to lower forms of Qi Gong, whereas the focus of Falun Gong practice was instead one's "spiritual nature" (心性 xinxing) and salvation from the demonic world of "ordinary people"(常人 changren). Li Hongzhi insisted that the goal of Falun Gong was not therapy but spiritual accomplishment (圆满 yuanman), detachment from the world of ordinary people and personal elevation into the mystical hierarchy of the arhats, bodhisattvas, Buddhas and gods. The earlier concern of Qi Gong with illness and healing gave way to the Buddhist concern of suffering and salvation. The focus of the FLG adepts then shifted from health and therapy to "propagating the Dharma" (hongfa 弘法) and "defending the Dharma" (hufa 护法).

Thus, at a time when the promise of Qi Gong was increasingly in doubt, Li Hongzhi shifted the emphasis of FLG from Qi Gong to Buddhism. He used the explanatory framework of Buddhism to avoid questions Qi Gong faced. Now, when one was sick, one was to pay off karmic debts; when one was ostracized by society, one was to move closer to spiritual accomplishment; when one was facing physical or social failure, one was spiritually to gain a source of Force against demonic power in order to obtain victory. Many people who were disappointed with Qi Gong now became attracted by FLG's Buddhist rhetoric.

Buddhism was not the last face of FLG. On May 24, 2015, Li Hongzhi rewrote the preface "Lunyu"(论语) of his scripture, Turning the Dharma Wheel (转法轮), referring to Falun Gong as Dafa.[5]: "Dafa is the wisdom of the Creator. It is the bedrock of creation, what the heavens, earth, and universe are built upon." Not only is Dafa the bedrock of creation, but LiHongzhi now presented himself as superior to any Buddha or gods, having brought the whole Buddha Law to human beings (Lu 2005, 178), and having averted the destruction of the earth by a comet and by world War III (Østergaard 2004, 223). This was the moment when FLG took off the cloak of Buddhism publicly and began to appear as an apocalyptic cult, emphasizing the pressing end of time as a turning point in cosmic history and a cosmic war between FLG and ordinary people, as well as between

---

5. http://www.minghui.org/mh/articles/2015/5/24/论语-309965.html. "In this context, both 'Dafa' and 'Fa' are rough translations of the Sanskrit term 'Dharma,' a complex term that can mean 'religion,' 'teaching,' the 'truth,' the spiritual order of the universe etc." Lewis 2018, 172–190.

FLG and the demonized evil government. There was an urgent mission for FLG members to martyr themselves for the cause, as seen in the 1.23 incident in 2001, discussed ahead. This pressing urgency may be heard in the increasingly militant tone of in Li Hongzhi's thinking in that same year:

> We must expose and eliminate the evil. Chinese people have been the biggest victims amidst the evil's damage. All the methods employed by the evil political gang of scoundrels in the Chinese government are the most despicable, the most evil, and unknown to history—they have reached the extreme, they couldn't possibly be worse. Never before has a government been used to do these scoundrel things. All the things our Dafa disciples have done with good thoughts have moved the world's people and have moved the beings at every level, while the evil that has reared its head in Mainland China has infuriated beings at every level. The contrast between these evil beings and our goodness (shan) is dramatic. You know, when this evil sees that it's going to be eliminated it runs totally rampant. It is bad, it is venomous, and it is evil. And just like poison, if you want it not to poison people it can't do that—that's just how it is. So, in the process of eliminating it don't be lenient at all—just clean it out! (Li Hongzhi 2001)

Who is to initiate this war against evil? While Falun Gong refers to all its followers as "students," in practice its members are divided into three categories. The first is ordinary practitioners. These are primarily attracted to the practices and meditation of Falun Gong as advanced Qi Gong or popular Buddhism or traditional Chinese Culture. The second category is dedicated practitioners who are attracted by apocalyptic teachings of FLG. They worship Li Hongzhi as Creator, and actively participate in spiritual and political warfare against a demonized enemy. They would personally sacrifice themselves for the cause of Da Fa and have done so. The innermost group consists of the leaders of FLG and Li Hongzhi himself. They manipulate the organization and the former two categories of students, while they themselves don't appear to believe in the FLG doctrines (Fraser 2019). While they instigate the second group of students to be sanctioned, to be imprisoned and to endure public martyrdom inside China, they themselves enjoy safe haven in foreign countries.

PRC's treatment of *Xie Jiao* and its potential difficulties

China lists FLG as *Xie Jiao* and fights against it not because it is Pseudo Qi Gong, or false Buddhism or cult, but rather because the FLG takes advantage of Pseudo Qi Gong, false Buddhism and cult as a way to manipulate followers and to mobilize them to challenge the Communist Party and Government. It thus endangers social order. It is not because of its strange doctrines, but because of its actual political crimes and the sufferings it has brought to its followers (Lewis and Chao 2020).As the number of Falun

Gong practitioners grew into the tens of millions at the end of the 20th century, Li Hongzhi did not hesitate to challenge his adversaries and show that FLG's social power could rival that of the Communist Party. After Li Hongzhi and his family emigrated to the United States, he directed his Chinese followers to become increasingly confrontational, which they did, eventually staging a mass demonstration in front of government offices in Beijing on 25 April 1999. Up to 15,000 Falun Gong adherents surrounded Communist Party Headquarters at Zhongnanhai (中南海). This was the largest protest in China since the student democracy protests in 1989 and came as something of a shock to Chinese authorities. This action was the direct reason that Falun Gong was deemed *Xie Jiao* (Ownby 2005).

While outside observers perceive FLG as a pacifist group because individual members appear to engage in passive resistance tactics rather than taking up arms against the PRC, Li Hongzhi's apocalyptic teachings do instruct his followers to engage in spiritual warfare with the government and to hurt themselves in the act, including by martyrdom and self-immolation. Li teaches that the "Ending Period of Catastrophe" is almost here, that contemporary society is degenerate and will be purged. The only ones who will be saved are those who are genuine Falun Gong practitioners. Li Hongzhi called Jiang Zemin, president of the Communist Party from 1989 to 2002, "the highest representative of the evil force in the human world, who was being manipulated by higher beings to persecute the Falun Gong." According to Li Hongzhi, only when the evil is eliminated can practitioners return home through Consummation to the Falun Dafa paradise (Farley 2014a, 222–223). He instructed his followers that they should not continue to simply passively forebear the advance of evil beings (especially those who persecute Falun Gong), but rather should actively resist:

> Forbearance (忍ren) is not cowardice, much less is it resigning oneself to adversity. ... [But] Forbearance is absolutely not the limitless giving of free rein, which allows those evil beings who no longer have any human nature or righteous thoughts to do evil without limit. ... If the evil has already reached the point where it is unsaveable and unkeepable, then various measures at different levels can be used to stop it and eradicate it. ... the way the evil beings are currently performing shows that they are now completely without human nature and without righteous thoughts. Such evil's persecution of the Fa can thus no longer be tolerated. Li Hongzhi 2001.

With this kind of call to action, FLG adherents inside China protested bravely against the Chinese government, without thought of personal danger. On January 23, 2001, the first New Year's Eve of the new century, while the whole nation was celebrating and reuniting with their families, seven FLG members self-immolated themselves as a dramatic way of protesting the suppression of their movement by the People's Republic of China. They set themselves on fire at Tiananmen Square.⁶ Five practitioners out of the group–which included a talented young music student as well as a 12-year-old girl–succeeded in setting themselves afire. One practitioner died in the square and four were seriously burnt, one of whom subsequently died. This event was later referred to as the "1.23 Incident." Subsequent to the incident, Falun Gong quickly distanced itself from the self-immolations, denying all responsibility for the tragedy. Within 24 hours of the event, FLG issued a press release asserting that the Chinese government had staged the self-immolations as a tactic for defaming the organization. Falun Gong eventually created a video documentary, False Fire, designed to bolster the movement's assertion that the event was faked.

At around the same time as the Tiananmen Square event, there was a series of FLG related suicides or attempted suicides in the PRC. On 16 February 2001, another member of Falun Gong member, Tan Yihui, a shoe shiner from Hunan province, committed suicide by setting himself on fire. He poured gasoline over his head, lit it, and burst into flames. Officials said they discovered a six-page suicide note nearby that identified him as a member of Falun Gong and that said he wished to "forget about life and death and achieve perfection in Paradise." There were also numerous cases of practitioners committing suicide by throwing themselves off buildings (Lewis and Chao 2020). The teaching of Li Hongzhi about virtue or merit (德) could explain the willingness of practitioners to challenge the power of the Chinese state. Virtue or merit (de), according to Li Hongzhi, is a form of white matter which enters our body each time we do a good deed or are victimized by others. Bad karma, on the other hand, is a kind of black matter which penetrates us when we commit an evil deed. Thus, if someone insults you, the aggressor's white matter will pass from his body into yours, while your black matter will be absorbed by his body. Therefore, even though you may appear humiliated, the real loser is the aggressor, because he took your black matter and gave you his white matter (Palmer 2001). This esoteric view of the karmic process motivates practitioners to actively seek oppression. At the unseen spiritual level, what is actually happening is that practitioners are attacking policemen–not vice versa. This is the covert meaning of Falun Gong's "Forbearance." As for followers who die while forbearing, Li Hongzhi assured those "who suffered or died for their beliefs" with "the promise of instant 'consummation'" (or enlightenment), "the goal toward which every adherent struggles" (Farley 2014b:211).So, FLG meets the definition of *Xie Jiao* in the Article 300 of the Criminal Law, and meets the criteria listed in the "Notice of the Ministry

---

6. https://www.chinafxj.cn/n184/c837722/content.html

of Public Security on Several Issues of Identifying and Prohibiting *Xie Jiao* Organizations" (公安部关于认定和取缔邪教组织若干问题的通知)(公通字 [2000] 39号).[7]

According to the Notice, the most important features of a *Xie Jiao* organization are that it is secret, illegal, unregistered, or hidden behind a legal facade. The most important characteristic of behavior is manipulation. The use of religion or Qi Gong, the deification of the leader, and the creating and spreading of malicious teaching all serve the purpose of manipulation. The most serious harms are two kinds of organizational crimes: one is political, as in disturbing the social order; the second is aimed at individuals, who try to accumulate wealth by unfair means and to urge adherents to risk their lives.

We can see more clearly now that China's *Xie Jiao* is not identical to what in the West is considered a "cult," but refers to an organization hidden behind the cult which manipulates and uses the cult to achieve criminal purposes. Both cult doctrine and cult organization are only the means or instruments of crime, and the identification of *Xie Jiao* is mainly based on the crimes committed instead of on the falsehood of their doctrine.[8]

While dealing with FLG issues, the State Council Office of the State Council of China issued a notice[9] in 1999 on further improving the education, transformation, and release of Falun Gong practitioners, requiring strict control of policy boundaries in order to release the vast majority through transformative education.[10] The notice pointed out that the vast majority of Falun Gong practitioners who participate in the exercise are deceived victims. Therefore, sincere, patient, in-depth and meticulous rehabilitation should be carried out toward them. The behind-the-scenes propagators of the chaos should be selected out. Through this notice issued by high authority, it can be seen clearly that the law punishes only "behind the scenes" personnel who hide behind the organization. As long as the members of the cult organization are willing to sever ties with the organization, they can be exempted from punishment, they are actually the aim

---

7. http://www.china21.org/docs/CONFI-MPS-CHINESE.htm)

8. This opinion is similar to that of Massimo Introvigne. According to Introvigne, the concept of "*Xie Jiao*" in Chinese corresponds to "criminal religion movements," which refers to religious groups that either (or both) consistently practice and justify common crimes such as terrorism, child abuse, rape, physical violence, homicide, and serious economic crimes. But he didn't notice that the activities of "worship" or "brainwashing" are means of criminal (2018:13-32).

9. http://www.people.com.cn/rmrb/199908/25/newfiles/wzb_19990825001026_4.html; https://rmrb.online/read-htm-tid-1182522.html

10. http://www.people.com.cn/rmrb/199908/25/newfiles/wzb_19990825001026_4; html; https://rmrb.online/read-htm-tid-1182522.html

of protection through education. There is thus a clear distinction between the agent who deceives and the subject who inadvertently is deceived. From this perspective, the so called Chinese persecution of *Xie Jiao* believers actually does not exist. If there were persecution against individuals in practice, that is not the original intention of the law, and it needs to be corrected.

Since *Xie Jiao* have the ability to change their positions on religious issues and tend to be secretive, it is very tricky to combat them. It is easy to accidentally harm followers and normal religious organizations while cracking down on *Xie Jiao*. If the crackdown is too broad and lacks precision, it may lead to human rights issues and do harm to many beneficial cultural resources such as Qi Gong. On the other hand, if the measures are not strict enough, it could give room to Xie Jiao to endanger political stability and social harmony. The government should use "support the good and remove the evil (扶正祛邪)" and use a "guiding" technique, to form a harmonious mutual help relationship with religions and religious groups. The authority knows well that the Article 300 of criminal laws should be used in caution.[11] Education and transformation and fostering a scientific spirit are fundamental strategies for addressing the root issues.

About the authors

Zhang Xinzhang is Associate Professor and Deputy Director of the Institute for Marxist Religious Studies in New Era, at Hangzhou City University, Hang Zhou, Zhejiang Province, China. His research Interests are Gnosticism, Patristics, Taoist Culture, and Marxist Religious Studies.

Xu Weiwei is a special research fellow at the Institute for Marxist Religious Studies in New Era, Hangzhou City University, Hang Zhou, Zhejiang Province, China, and expert in Chinese local folk religions and spiritual movements, religious policies, and Chinese literature.

References

Farley, Helen. 2014a. "Death by Whose Hand? Falun Gong and Suicide." In *Sacred Suicide*, edited by James R. Lewis and Carole Cusack, 222–223. London: Routledge.

———. 2014b. "Falun Gong: A narrative of pending apocalypse, shape-shifting aliens, and relentless, persecution." In *Controversial New Religions*, edited by James R. Lewis and J.A. Petersen, 241–254. Oxford: Oxford University Press. https://doi.org/10.1093/acprof:osobl/9780199315314.003.0014

---

11. In an interview with local officers who engaged in the work of prevention and treatment of *Xie Jiao*, it is known that to apply Article 300 of criminal law very carefully is a consensus among them.

Fraser, Campbell. 2019. "The Falun Gong Political narrative: Creating the illusion of so-called 'forced organ harvesting.'" In *Enlightened Martyrdom*, edited by James R. Lewis and Huang Chao, 230–243. Sheffield: Equinox Press. https://doi.org/10.1558/equinox.34323

Introvigne, Massimo. 2019. "Article 300: CCP's secret weapon of religious persecution." *Bitter Winter* https://bitterwinter.org/article-300-ccps-secret-weapon-of-religious-persecution/?fbclid=IwAR1A3gScRqA8mEuO_oYkMOy6omoQh83aIpIiiDC5c.

Lewis, James R. 2018. *Falun Gong: Martyrdom and Spiritual Warfare*. Cambridge: Cambridge University Press. https://doi.org/10.1017/CBO9781108564557

Lewis, James and Huang Chao. 2020. "Falun Gong: Origins, growth, and conflict." *Oxford Research Encyclopedia of Religion*. https://doi.org/10.1093/acrefore/9780199340378.013.677

Li Hongzhi. 1998. "Zhuan Falun" [转法轮Turning the dharma-wheel], in *Falun Dafa"* [法轮大法The great law of the Dharma wheel]. Hailaer : Neimenggu Wenhua Chubanshe.

———. 2001. "Teaching the Fa at the 2001 Canada Fa Conference" (May 19). https://falundafa.org/eng/eng/daohang_3.htm [Accessed 17 February 2017].

———. 2001. "Beyond the limits of forbearance" (2 January 2001). https://falundafa.org/eng/eng/jjyz2_19.htm [Accessed 13 June 2015].

Østergaard, Clemens Stubble. 2004. "Governance and the political challenge of Falun Gong." In *Governance in China*, edited by Jude Howell, 207–225. Lanham, MD: Rowman & Littlefield.

Ownby, D. 2005. "Falun Gong." In *Encyclopedia of Religion*, 2nd edition, vol. 5, edited by L. Jones, 2978. Detroit, MI: Macmillan Reference.

Palmer, David A. 2001. "Falun Gong: Between sectarianism and universal salvation." *China Perspectives* 35: 17. https://doi.org/10.1558/equinox.30552

———. 2003. "Modernity and millenialism in China: Qi Gong and the birth of Falun Gong." *Asian Anthropology* 2(1): 79–109. https://doi.org/10.1080/1683478X.2003.10552531

———. 2004. "Body at the junction of religion and Scientism: Modernisation of meditative traditions in contemporary China." *Chinese Cross Currents* 1(1): 54–87. Reprinted *Religion and Culture: Past Approaches, Present Globalisation, Future Challenges*, 313–333. Macau: Macau Ricci Institute.

Seidel, Anna K. 1970. "The image of the perfect ruler in early Taoist messianism: Lao-tzu and Li Hung." *History of Religions* 9(2–3): 216–247. https://doi.org/10.1086/462605

Ter Haar, Barend. 2023. "The demonological framework of the Heavenly Kingdom of Great Peace." In *Cambridge Companion to Religion and War*, edited by M. Kitts, 428–442. Cambridge: Cambridge University Press. https://doi.org/10.1093/acrefore/9780199340378.013.733

Electronic sources

http://www.china21.org/docs/CONFI-MPS-CHINESE.htm
https://www.chinafxj.cn/n184/c837722/content.html
https://www.ilo.org/dyn/natlex/docs/ELECTRONIC/5375/108071/F-78796243/CHN5375%20Eng3.pdf
http://www.minghui.org/mh/articles/2015/5/24/论语-309965.html.
http://www.people.com.cn/rmrb/199908/25/newfiles/wzb_19990825001026_4.html; https://rmrb.online/read-htm-tid-1182522.html
http://www.people.com.cn/rmrb/199908/25/newfiles/wzb_19990825001026_4.html; https://rmrb.online/read-htm-tid-1182522.html
http://www.minghui.org/mh/articles/2015/5/24/论语-309965.html
https://www.ilo.org/dyn/natlex/docs/ELECTRONIC/5375/108071/F-78796243/CHN5375%20Eng3.pdf

INDEX

A

Ablon, Guy 137
Abouhalima, Mahmud 18–19, 23–24, 24–25
Abrams, Stacey 51
Åkesson, Jimmie 74
Alberts, Thomas 131
Alm, Niko 136
Almansor (Heine, 1823) 62
Alternative for Sweden 68, 69
American Civil War Museum 51
Andersson, Magdalena 71–72
Andersson, Tobias 70
anti-Catholic conspiracy theories 28, 29
anti-Semitism
  book burnings 61–62
  conspiracy theories 28, 29
apocalyptic cults 187–188
apocalyptic outlook 87
Applewhite, Marshall 88
areas of exteriority 67, 68, 73
Arnold, J. Phillip 110–111, 119
Aum Shinrikyo 7, 19, 86, 89
Australia
  Category 7 religious groups 140
  definition of a religion 139
  Jediism 133
  Pastafarianism 136–137, 137–138
  Sovereign Citizens Movement 34
Australian Sovereign Council 34
Awan, Akil N. 66

B

Barker, Eileen 104
Barruel, Abbe 28
Bartosh, Elizabeth G., *Koreshanity: The New Age Religion* 110–111
Baudrillard, Jean 131
Bertho, Alain 73
bibliocaust 5–6, 59–76
  Easter/Qur'an Riots 69–73, 74
  economic and social background of Sweden 67–68
  elections in Sweden (2022) 74–76
  history of book burnings 60–64, 75–76
  Qur'an burnings in Sweden 59–60, 64, 66, 68, 69–70
Black Lives Matter 50
blasphemy, rights to 72
bombers *see* Abouhalima, Mahmud
bombings 25
Bonano, Julian 115–116
book burning *see* bibliocaust
Bowring, Marcus 136–137
Branch Davidians 7, 92–93, 99–100, 100–103, 108, 109–110, 111–112, 113
Bray, Michael 23
Breault, Marc 92, 117
Breivik, Anders 4, 27, 35–37, 39, 66
Bromley, David T. 120
Brown, Michael, Jr. 50
Brown University 52

Index

Buddhism 21–22, 185, 187
Bunds, David 108, 109, 110, 111, 114, 115, 117
Busch, Ebba 74, 75

C

Canada 34, 88, 138
Carter, Angela & Colin 137–138
Catholic Church 28, 29
Cavanaugh, Stephen 135–136
censuses 133, 140
charisma of the cadre 90
charismatic leaders 103–105
  David Koresh 103, 115–116, 117, 118–119, 120
Charity Commission 140, 141
Chauvin, Derek 50
Cheung, Tommy 140–141
Chidester, David 131
children
  additional wives of David Koresh 114–115
  book burnings and 61, 65
  of David Koresh 114
  at Jonestown 90, 91
  sex with 68, 69
  at Waco, Texas 101, 102, 103
China see People's Republic of China
Chinese medicine 185–186
Christian militants 23
Christie, Lance 132
Church of All Worlds (CAW) 132
Church of Saint James, the Muslim Slayer 66
Church of Scientology 134, 139
Church of the Flying Spaghetti Monster see Pastafarianism
Church of the SubGenius 132
churches and the Lost Cause Movement 48, 51
cinema see sects in the movies
Cisneros, Ximénes de 62
Civil Rights Movement 50
Civil War 5
  background to 44–45
  history, control of by the Lost Cause Movement 49
  post-war impacts 45–46
Cliteur, Paul 140
colanders 136–137, 138, 140
colleges and universities 52
Coney, Judith 104
Confino, Alon 61
conspiracy theories
  about Jonestown 91
  about "Skull and Bones" society 167n24
  see also transnational conspiracy theories
Constitution of the United States, 14th Amendment 33
constructed conspiracies 36–37
Cooley, Sarah 135
costume see religious costume
cotton-based economy 44
Covid-19 38
Craddock, Graeme 100
critical race theory 53
crusades 35, 37, 66
  see also Lost Cause Movement
CS gas 102–103
cultural transformations 44
Cusack, Carole M. 131
Cyrus the Great, king 110

D

The Da Vinci Code (Howard, 2006) 165–166
Davenport, Andrew 48
Davidsen, Markus Altena 131, 133, 142
Dawson, Lorne L. 104–105
de-memorialization 50–52
deaths of African Americans 50
decolonization of museums 51
Delgado, Richard 86–87
DeLucia, Christine 48
Denmark 65
destructuration/restructuration 44
Di Mambro, Joseph 88
Discordianism 132
Doyle, Clive 110, 111
Dr. X 132
Drummond, Philo 132

E

Easter/Qur'an Riots (Sweden, 2022) 69–73, 74
economy of the United States 44–45
Episcopal Church 48, 51
epistemic worldview analysis *see* religious terrorism research interviews
Erdoğan, Recep Tayyip 76
European Court of Human Rights 138, 140
Exceptional Functions 185, 186
executions 99–100
exit costs 117–118

F

fake religions 131
Falun Gong 11
    demonstrations 189
    development of 185–188
    membership categories 188
    self-immolation protests 189–190
    suicides and attempted suicides 190
    as *Xie Jiao* 188–190
Faye, Guillaume 66
Federal Bureau of Investigation (FBI) 99–100, 101, 102, 119, 120–121
Fenn, Marianna 137
fiction-based religions *see* invented religions
Filin, Andrei 136
films *see* sects in the movies
fire 102–103
Fisher Phillips 136
Floyd, George 50
Fonseca, Damián 63–64
Freed, Josh 156n9, 159n11
freedom of expression 71–73, 76
freedom of religion 130, 141
fundamentalism 142

G

Gardell, Mattias 37
Garner, Eric 50
Garry, Charles 89
genocide 63–64
Germany, book burnings 5, 60–62

Gilhus, Ingvild Sælid 132
Godwin's Law 93
Goebbels, Joseph 61
gold standard 33
Goodlett, Carlton 88, 89
Grande, Todd L. 119
Great Replacement 64, 67
Grieve, Dominic 134
Guo Lin 186
Guyana *see* Jonestown studies, James R. Lewis and
Gyarfas, Aisha 114

H

Haldeman, Bonnie 105, 106, 107, 110
Hammond, Shawna 136
Hard Line Sweden 69
Harvard University 52
Hassan, Steven 7, 87
hate crime 72–73
headgear 134, 136–137, 138, 140
Heavens Gate 7, 88
Hebrew Bible 61
Heine, Henrich 5–6, 62
Heinlein, Robert A., *Stranger in a Strange Land* (1961) 132
Henderson, Bobby 129, 134–135
Hill, Greg 132
Hinduism 159–160
history, control of by the Lost Cause Movement 49
holocaust 5, 63–64
hoods 134
Horswell, Mike 66
hot dogs 75
Howell, Vernon *see* Koresh, David
hyper-real religions *see* invented religions
hypothetical religions *see* invented religions

I

illiberal societies 9, 142
Illuminati conspiracism 28, 29
incitement of hatred/hate speech 72–73
India 20–21

Index

Indiana Jones and the Temple of Doom (Spielberg, 1984) 159–160
individual citizens 33
Intelligent Design 134–135
interviews *see* religious terrorism research interviews
Introvigne, Massimo 86, 93, 191n8
invented religions 8–9, 129–143
  fundamentalism and 142
  legal status of religions 139–141
  marriages and 137–138
  religious costume and 130, 135–139
  religious freedom and 130, 141
  study of 130–135
  third millennium invented religions 133–135
Islam *see* Abouhalima, Mahmud; Muslim associations; Muslim extremists; Muslims
Israeli activists 22–23

J

James the Great, saint 66
Japan 7, 19, 86, 89
Jarvis, Chris 134
Jediism 9, 133–134, 137, 138, 140
Jewell, Kiri 114
Jewell, Sherri 114
Jews
  book burnings and 5, 61–62
  conspiracy theories about 28, 29
  expulsion from Spain 62
  public humiliation of 61
Jiang Zemin 189
jihadi activists *see* Abouhalima, Mahmud
Jim Crow era 46
Jindra, Michael 133
Jobs, Steve 168n25
Johansson, Morgan 72
John Birch Society 29
Jones, Constance 87
Jones, Daniel 134, 140
Jones, Jim 6, 7, 87, 88–89, 170
Jones, Michele 114
Jones, Perry 111
Jones, Rachel 111, 112
Jones' Corollary 93, 94
Jonestown studies, James R. Lewis and 6–7, 85–95
  diversity and uniqueness of new religious movements 94–95
  monolithic inferences 89–91
  pathology of leaders 86–89
  study of new religious movements 91–94

K

Kahane, Meir 22–23
Kali 159–160
karma 190
Kendrick, Debbie 110
Killian, Bryan 135
King, Martin Luther 73
Kirby, Danielle 133
Kiyabu, Dana Okimoto 114, 115, 119
Knights Templar 35, 36, 37
Koresh, David 7–8, 99–121
  biblical interpretations 110–111, 115, 116
  charisma of 103, 115–116, 117, 118–119, 120
  conflict at Mount Carmel Center 101–103, 118–121
  death of 103
  exit plan 101, 118, 119
  fear of 117, 118
  God's Voice, hears 107
  hubris of 120
  James R. Lewis on 93, 99, 100
  learning disability 106, 110
  life before Mount Carmel 105–108
  Mount Carmel Center, arrival at 108, 109–110
  psychopathologies of 119, 120
  sacrifices, did not make 118
  Satan, battle with 107
  Son of God, claims to be 112–114
  Spirit of Prophecy and 112
  women and 107–108, 111, 114–115
Kristallnacht pogroms 61
Kristersson, Ulf 76
Kwiecien, Brunon 36

L

Lambertz, Göran 72
Lane, David 4
Lapshyn, Pavlo 36
Larsson, Peppe 74
Leadbetter, Simon 137
leaders 6–7, 86–89, 103–105
  David Koresh 103, 115–116, 117, 118–119, 120
leadership cadre 90, 91
Lee, Peter 139
Lee, Robert E. 47–48, 49, 51
legal definitions of religion 9, 139–141, 183–184
Lemmon, Asia 136
Lewis, James R. 1–2, 3, 4, 6–7, 132
  and Jonestown studies 85–95
Li Hongzhi 11, 186, 187–188, 189, 190
liberal societies 6, 9, 67
Lincoln, Abraham 45
Liu Guizhen 185–186
lone wolf attacks 4, 36–37, 39
Lost Cause Movement 5, 43–54
  emergence of the movement 44–46
  fall of the movement 49–53
  indicators of success and influence 53–54
  opposition to the movement 50–51
  resistance to de-memorialization 52–53
  rise of the movement 46–49
Lost Cause Narrative 47–48
Lovelock, Derek 110, 117

M

Mangs, Peter 36
marriages
  of David Koresh 114
  in new religious movements 137–138
Martin, Trayvon 50
martyrdom 90–91, 100
Masonic movement 28, 29
massacres 99–100
Matrixism 133
Matteson, Catherine 112
May the 4th be With You 138

McCrary, Gregg O. 101, 118
McVeigh, Timothy 25
members of cults 87, 89, 90, 93–94
memorialization and the Lost Cause Movement 49, 50–52, 54
messiahs 104
Midsommar (Aster, 2019) 10, 174–175, 176, 178
migrants in Sweden 67–68
Mikaelsson, Lisbeth 132
military bases 52
millenarian beliefs 7, 8, 36, 39, 87, 88
Miller, David Wynn 34
Miller, Edith Starr 29
Miller, Lindsey 136
Mlynek, Vojtech 36
monolithic inferences 2, 7, 86, 89–91
Monument Avenue, Richmond, Virginia 49, 50–51
Moody, Preshalin 137
Moon, Sun Myung 156n9
Moriscos 63–64
Moser, Richard Steve, III 136
movies *see* sects in the movies
Murphy, Lionel 139
museums 48, 51
Muslim associations 71
Muslim extremists 21–22
  see also Abouhalima, Mahmud
Muslims 6
  in Myanmar 23
  in Spain 62–64
Myanmar *see* Wirathu, Ashin

N

National Socialists 5, 60–62
naval vessels 52
neo-liberal societies 67
Netherlands 138, 139–140
New World Order 4, 27, 30, 31
New Zealand 4, 137
Newton, Huey P. 91
no-go zones 67, 68, 73
Noesner, Gary 120
Norway 4, 35–37
nostalgia 74–75

Index

O

Oklahoma City Federal Building 25
Omega Kingdom Ministries 38
Opus Dei 165
Östlund, Michael 70

P

Palestinians 23
Palladism 9–10, 151–152
Palmer, Brian 49
Palmer, David 185, 186
Paludan, Rasmus 6, 59, 64–67, 68, 76
Park, Dan 66
Parke, Jo Anne 86
Pastafarianism 8, 129, 133, 134–139
Patrick, Ted 86
People's Republic of China 10–11, 181–192
  definitions of *Xie Jiao* and cults 182, 184–185, 191
  Falun Gong 185–188
  Falun Gong as *Xie Jiao* 188–192
  legal provisions dealing with *Xie Jiao* 183–184
  religious organizations 183
Peoples Temple 6–7, 87, 88, 90–91, 93–94
pirate costume 135, 137, 138
pogroms 61
police 70, 74
Possamai, Adam 131
Posse Comitatus 32
Priory of Sion 165
prophets 104, 108, 109–110
protestors 70–71
The Protocols of the Elders of Zion 29
public space, appropriation of 47–48, 49, 51, 54
  see also memorialization and the Lost Cause Movement

Q

QAnon movement 4, 27, 37–38, 54
Qi Gong 185–187
Qur'an burnings 6
  in Spain 62–64
  in Sweden 59–60, 64, 66, 68, 69–70, 76
  in Turkey 76

R

racial cleansing 63–64
racial injustice 73
racial segregation 46–47
Racist Spectacles 65, 68–70
radical localism 32–33
Reconquista 6, 66
Reed, Jamie 134
refugees 141
relational reasoning 22
religious costume 8, 130, 134, 136–137, 138, 140
religious freedom 130, 141
religious terrorism research interviews 3, 17–26
  assumptions of the interviewer 22–24
  background preparations 24, 25
  definition of 17
  informative encounters 20–21
  interview approaches 19–20
  mindset of activists 18–19
  motivations of activists 17–18
  relational knowledge 21–22
  worldviews or versions? 24–25
reparations 52
representative democracy, exclusion from 73
Republican Party 45
restorative justice initiatives 52
revolutionary suicide 91
Richardson, James T. 103
Ricketts, Toby 137
rightwing political parties 74–75
rioters 70–71
riots
  Easter/Qur'an Riots (Sweden, 2022) 69–73, 74
  urban riots 73
ritual garb *see* religious costume
rivers of blood 64
Robbins, Thomas 92
Robertson, Pat 30
Robison, John 28
Roden, George 111, 117
Roden, Lois 108, 109, 110, 111, 112

Roof, Dyllan 50
Roy, Eleanor Ainge 137
Russian Federation 136

S

Satanism, in movies 151–152, 153–154, 154–155, 161–162, 172, 176
sausages 75
scholarship funds 52
secession 47
Second World War 60
sects in the movies 9–10, 149–178
  choice of films 150
  "deviant" forms of Western society/Christianity 176
  experts and researchers 150, 176–178
  females in sects 177
  oversimplification 175–176
  preconceptions about cults 178
  racist/orientalist stereotypes 176
  supernatural elements 177
Films
  The City of the Dead/Horror Hotel (Moxey, 1960) 153, 177
  The Da Vinci Code (Howard, 2006) 165–166
  The Devil Rides Out/The Devil's Bride (Fisher, 1968) 153–154
  Faults (Stearns, 2014) 170–171
  Holy Smoke (Campion, 1999) 162–163, 176
  Il nido del ragno/The Spider Labyrinth (Giagni, 1988) 160–161
  Il profumo della signora in nero/The Perfume of the Lady in Black (Barilli, 1974) 155–156
  Il treno/Beyond the Door III (Kwitny, 1989) 161, 176
  Indiana Jones and the Temple of Doom (Spielberg, 1984) 159–160
  Les Rivières pourpres II: Les Anges de l'apocalypse/The Crimson Rivers 2: Angels of the Apocalypse (Dahan, 2004) 163–165
  Like Minds/Murderous Intent (Read, 2006) 166–167
  Midsommar (Aster, 2019) 174–175, 176, 178
  Night of the Demon/Curse of the Demon (Tourneur, 1957) 152–153, 177
  The Ninth Gate (Polanski, 1999) 161–162
  Regression (Amenábar, 2015) 171–173, 178
  The Sacrament (West, 2013) 169–170
  The Seventh Victim (Robson, 1943) 9–10, 150–152
  Sound of My Voice (Batmanglij, 2011) 167–169
  Split Image (Kotcheff, 1982) 157–159
  Suspiria (Guadagnino, 2018) 173–174, 177
  Ticket to Heaven (Thomas, 1981) 156–157
  Tutti i colori del buio/All the Colors of the Dark (Martino, 1972) 154–155
secularists 23
segregation 46–47
seven angels of Revelation 108–109
Seventh-day Adventist Church 106, 107, 108–109
Sheikh, Mona 3, 19–20, 21, 25
Shrout, Winston 34
"Skull and Bones" society, Yale University 167n24
Slaughterhouse-Five (Vonnegut, 1969) 60
slavery and the Lost Cause Movement 44, 45, 47, 52
Smith, Al 29
social media 65
social surveys 20–21
social transformations 44
Solar Temple 7, 88
soldiers 19
Sovereign Citizens Movement 4, 27, 32–35, 39
Spain 6, 62–64
Spanish Inquisition 63
St. Paul's Episcopal Church, Richmond, Virginia 48, 51
Stang, Ivan 132
Star Trek (TV and film) 133

Index

Star Wars (films) 133
statues 47–48, 49
Stone, Alan 120
Stone Mountain, Georgia 49, 51
Stoner, Carroll 86
Stover, Romley 34
strainers 136–137, 138, 140
Stranger in a Strange Land (Heinlein, 1961) 132
suicide by cop 100
suicide cults 6–7, 87–88, 90–91, 92
Sweden
  areas of exteriority 67, 68, 73
  Easter/Qur'an Riots (2022) 69–73, 74
  economic and social background 67–68
  elections (2022) 74–76
  Qur'an burnings 6, 59–60, 64, 66, 68, 69–70, 76
Sweden Democrats 74–75
Switzerland 88
symbolic crusades *see* Lost Cause Movement

T

Tabor, James D. 119
Talk Like a Pirate Day 138
Tan Yihui 190
Tarrant, Brenton 4, 66
Taylor, Alan 44, 45
tear gas 102–103
Teed, Cyrus R. 110–111
Temple of the Jedi Order *see* Jediism
textbooks 49
Thornberg, Anders 70, 71
Thornley, Kerry 132
Tiananmen Square, Beijing 189–190
Tidö Agreement 75
Torah scrolls 61
tourist attractions 49, 51
transnational conspiracy theories 4, 27–39
  Anders Breivik 35–37, 39
  modern networks 29–31
  QAnon movement 37–38
  reality and illusion 31

Sovereign Citizens Movement 32–35, 39
traditional networks 28–29
Trump, Donald 4, 27, 37, 38
Turkey 76

U

United Kingdom 133, 134, 137, 140
United Nations 29–30
United States of America
  anti-Catholic conspiracy theories 29
  conspiracy theories 4
  new religious movements 6–8, 136
  QAnon movement 4, 27, 37–38, 54
  terrorists 18, 23
  see also Branch Davidians; Heavens Gate; Lost Cause Movement; Peoples Temple; Sovereign Citizens Movement
universities 52
urban riots 73

V

Van der Haven, Alexander 131, 142
Venema, Derk 138–139, 141
Vonnegut, Kurt, *Slaughterhouse-Five* (1969) 60

W

Waco, Texas 7, 99, 100–103, 118–121
Watkins, Tanya 137
Weber, Max 103–104
Webster, Nesta 29
Wessler, Seth Freed 49
White Genocide Manifesto 4
Whitfield, Stephen J. 62
Wilde, Mienke de 8, 129, 138, 140
Wirathu, Ashin 19, 21–22, 23
witches 173–174
Wolff, Tim 135
women
  additional wives of David Koresh 114–115
  Branch Davidian community 102, 103
  in the Confederacy 48
  depiction in movies 177

World Trade Center bombers *see* Abouhalima, Mahmud
worldviews 87
Wright, Stuart A. 100

X

Xie Jiao see People's Republic of China 10–11

Y

Yellow Turban rebellion 182
Young Muslims of Sweden 71
YouTube 65

Z

Zell, Tim 132
Zhang Jue 182
Zimmerman, George 50